The Church Is Flat

The Relational Ecclesiology of the Emerging Church Movement

By Tony Jones, Ph.D.

D1530615

The Church Is Flat: The Relational Ecclesiology of the Emerging Church Movement by Tony Jones

Published by The JoPa Group
P.O. Box 24361, Minneapolis, MN 55435.

Published in the United States of America.

ISBN-10: 0-61-552431-1

ISBN-13: 978-0-61-552431-3

Thank you for buying from the_book_parlor on Amazon Marketplace.

Shipping Address:	
Martha Lou Hoffmann	
901 N. Monroe Street	
Unit 1416	
Arlington, VA 22201-2360	

Order Date:	Jan 1, 2015
Shipping Service:	Standard
Buyer Name:	Martha Lou Hoffmann
Seller Name:	the_book_parlor

Quantity	Product Details
1	**The Church Is Flat: The Relational Ecclesiology of the Emerging Church Movement [Paperback] [2011] Jones, Tony**
	SKU: LO-1IXM-BXKE
	ASIN: 0615524311
	Listing ID: 0522OWVKASW
	Order Item ID: 69213587089442
	Condition: New
	Comments: Multiple copies available. We ship out within 24 hours of sale. Your purchase supports a non profit. cl 05/22/14

Thank you!

The Book Parlor
1425 W. Broadway
Spokane, WA 99201
www.TheBookParlor.com

Returning your item:
Go to "Your Account" on Amazon.com, click "Your Orders" and then click the "seller profile" link for this order to get information about the return and refund policies that apply.
Visit http://www.amazon.com/returns to print a return shipping label. Please have your order ID ready.

Thanks for buying on Amazon Marketplace. To provide feedback for the seller please visit www.amazon.com/feedback. To contact the seller, go to Your Orders in Your Account. Click the seller's name under the appropriate product. Then, in the "Further Information" section, click "Contact the Seller."

Dedicated to my favorite teachers:

Barney Hall
Bud Jensen
Ginny Jensen
Edward Bradley
Kenda Dean
Rick Osmer

Table of Contents

Preface

I come to this study of the emerging church movement not as a disinterested researcher, but as a member of the movement—indeed, as a founder of the movement. In the summer of 1998, I was invited by Doug Pagitt, a former colleague in youth ministry, to help plan an event for that fall. The event was the "National Re:Evaluation Forum" sponsored by Leadership Network, then Doug's employer. At that gathering, a couple hundred evangelical pastors heard from such speakers as Rodney Clapp, Carol Davis, Stanley Grenz, George Hunsberger, Jimmy Long, Sally Morgenthaler, Christine and Tom Sine, Len Sweet, Thom Wolf, and the as-yet-unknown Mark Driscoll. Original music and artwork were on display. And many in attendance felt that some kind of renaissance within evangelicalism was just around the corner. A newsletter from Leadership Network recapped the event by stating that six themes had emerged that would "represent a framework for discussing the church of the future, the church on the New Edge": Community, Experience, Mysticism, Story, Leadership, and Missional.[1]

I, too, felt that something noteworthy had been inaugurated at that event, even though I felt less affinity for the conservative theology of many participants. The conferees were remarkably young, and the event buzzed with the vibrancy of youth.[2] I co-led the cohort of youth pastors in attendance; the fifty of us met in a room after each plenary session to discuss the implications of what we'd heard on the ministry in which we were engaged. Many of the largest evangelical churches in the country had sent their youth ministry personnel to the conference, and it became clear that, though they were known for hosting large youth ministry training events themselves, they were feeling as overwhelmed by the cultural changes afoot as those of us from smaller churches. The term most in vogue at the forum was "postmodern," the rubric under which these changes were described. Stanley Grenz gave a memorable talk in which he equated the original *Star Trek* television series to the modern mind, and *Star Trek: The Next Generation* to the postmodern mind.

---

[1] "Themes of the Emerging Church," in YoungLeader.org. Dallas: Leadership Network, 1998. Accessed January 27, 2011.

[2] Leadership Network required any church leader who registered for the event to bring someone from their church who was under thirty.

From there, the team of us who had organized the national forum set out to organize regional gatherings for 1999. We ran six, including one in Minneapolis, for which I served as the host, and interest regarding this new movement began to build around Christian circles. By the next year, the "emerging church" label was being used with some frequency.

The evolution of the emerging church movement from then to now I documented in my 2008 book, *The New Christians: Dispatches from the Emergent Frontier*.[3] Therein I argued that the primary characteristic that epitomizes the movement and makes it distinctive is *epistemic humility*, a phrase that will be repeated in this book. An early theme in the movement was that the churches and seminaries from which we were emerging had had grown too certain about their stands on doctrinal issues, polity, and social issues. As an antidote to that certainty, we were drawn to the works of Ludwig Wittgenstein, Stanley Fish, Richard Rorty, and Jacques Derrida. And theologians who advocated a missional posture toward American culture were also popular among us, including Darrell Guder, Stanley Hauerwas, and David Bosch.

But my book, and others that came out in the first decade of the 2000s, neglected to study what has really come to set emerging church congregations apart: ecclesiology. I have come to believe that the ways these congregations practice Christianity and the forms of church leadership and government that they have embraced are, while not necessarily unique, at least rare enough in the American context to warrant study and critique. The conversation about church practices has been robust in the past two decades, in both mainline and evangelical Protestantism. Leadership Network, for example, often gathered evangelical mega-church leaders in the 1980s and 1990s to discuss "best practices" for growing large churches. The contemporaneous conversation in the mainline was a more academic one, focusing on the nature of practice as a remedy for the cultural accommodations made by denominational churches. It is with this backdrop that I turned my attention to the practices of the emerging church movement, as exemplified by the eight congregations that I visited for this study.

---

[3] Tony Jones, *The New Christians: Dispatches from the Emergent Frontier* (San Francisco, CA: Jossey-Bass, 2008).

Choosing which congregations to visit was no mean feat. I considered a couple dozen congregations that could have easily qualified, ultimately settling on the eight about which you will read below. I had the good fortune of a grant from the Lilly Endowment to pay for both the travel and for the transcription of my interviews.

The trips themselves were a joy. Because of my collaboration in the genesis of the movement, I knew the leaders at each of the eight churches. But I made a point to limit my time with them, because I was really most interested in what the parishioners had to say about these places. While each of the pastors is aware of the broader movement—indeed, each has spoken about the movement at conferences, and several of them have written books on the subject—congregants are far less aware. As I recounted in *The New Christians*, I sat next to a man at Jacob's Well in Kansas City who had no idea that there were other churches anywhere that were like his church.[4] And that can be said of each of these congregations. While some members surely ended up at these churches because they Googled "Brian McLaren" or "Doug Pagitt," just as many found these churches because they were invited by friends, or because of any number of the myriad reasons that people choose churches. What these churches don't do is wear their emerging church identities on their sleeves: "emerging" is not in their names or on their marquees, and it seldom appears on their websites. Thus the people who sit in the pews often have only a passing knowledge of the movement of which their church is a part.

I hope this means that their answers to my questions reveal something more than the previous books, for which only the leaders of these and similar churches were interviewed. In fact, I found the honesty expressed in all of the interviews—both individually and in focus groups—to be very heartening. While many spoke of the spiritual injuries they had received at prior congregations, they were, on the whole, very happy with the emerging churches they now attend.

It came as no surprise to me that, as the research and writing of the project progressed, it became clear that some of the congregations more fully embodied the "emerging church" ethos than others. The leadership of two in particular—Ron Johnson of Pathways in

---

[4] Jones, *The New Christians: Dispatches from the Emergent Frontier*, 178.

Denver and Dan Kimball at Vintage Faith in Santa Cruz—have recently taken pains to distance themselves and their churches from the identifier, "emerging," for that term has come to connote more liberal theological predilections than they are comfortable with. Meanwhile, I moved back to Minnesota from Princeton and became a covenant participant in and leader of Solomon's Porch. So as the writing progressed, I simply had more experience with that church than any other, and that fact is reflected in the pages below. And the less frequent mentions of Pathways and Vintage Faith is a result of their own increasing distance from the movement.

Further, all but two of the churches I studied have undergone leadership changes since my research visit—only Solomon's Porch and Journey have the same leadership intact. Even as I put the finishing touches on this book, Jacob's Well has announced that Tim Keel, their founding pastor who left in 2009 to teach at Laidlaw College in New Zealand, will be returning in the summer of 2011 to become their lead teaching pastor; and Karen Ward is leaving Church of the Apostles, which she founded, to begin a new church in Portland, Oregon. That there have been so many leadership changes in these churches does not seem out of the norm for churches in general, especially when one considers that the type of person who successfully plants a church may not be particularly suited to the long-term maintenance of that church. Regardless, these changes have made the congregations in this study something like moving targets.

Of course, any research study is only a snapshot, a moment-in-time, frozen and analyzed. This project is no different. Since I undertook my research visits, the emerging church movement has continued to evolve, as any young movement inevitably does. As a response to the perceived liberalism of some of the movement's leading lights, myself included, other leading voices in American evangelicalism have attempted to differentiate the terms "emerging" and "emergent," and others have embraced the term "missional" as a less controversial moniker. Other changes have taken place within the movement, including the passing of the leadership of Emergent Village, the leading organization in the movement, to a group of volunteers. To the consternation of some, several years of dormancy from that organization ensued, and promises of its resuscitation continue to be unfulfilled. That has left a vacuum within the movement, as Emergent Village had served as a clearinghouse of ideas and resources and a readymade contact point for media.

Another significant change that has taken place since I made my research visits is the rise of the term "missional" as a favored moniker among evangelicals (like Kimball and Johnson) for whom "emerging" seems too liberal. This version of missional church is almost entirely unconnected from the work in the 1990s by Darrell Guder, George Hunsberger, and others connected with the Gospel & Our Culture Network. In fact, their book *Missional Church: A Vision for the Sending of the Church in North America* was more influential among early emergents than it seems to have been among the new "missional tribe."[5] Readers of this book in the second decade of the twenty-first century may wonder why the "missional church movement" does not get more play herein. The answer to that question is twofold: first, "missional" was a word used to describe the emerging movement for most of the 2000s, and it has only been differentiated recently; and second, it is not at all clear that the "missional church" has a particular identity of its own.

Finally, I want to make mention of my great affection for one church in particular.[6] I have spent the past five years living in the Minneapolis area, an A.B.D. Ph.D. student, among other things. When I returned to Minnesota from Princeton, I knew that I could not return to the church of my youth and of my former employment. There was really only one church that I could imagine attending, and that was Solomon's Porch. I had gone to Solomon's Porch as often as I could in the early 2000s, before my New Jersey sojourn, but my employment as a youth minister mostly precluded my involvement in the Sunday evening services at the Porch. However, I was not so encumbered in 2005, and happily began worshipping at Solomon's Porch whenever possible. As time has passed, my friendship with Doug Pagitt has blossomed, and we have even begun a business together. I have become one of a group of people who occasionally lead the sermon discussion time. And I happily call Solomon's Porch home.

---

[5] Darrell L. Guder and Lois Barrett, *Missional Church: A Vision for the Sending of the Church in North America* (Grand Rapids, Mich.: W.B. Eerdmans Pub., 1998).

[6] My section on Solomon's Porch in *The New Christians* comes under the heading, "MyChurch: A Paean to Solomon's Porch." Jones, *The New Christians: Dispatches from the Emergent Frontier*.

I do hope that has not blinded me to the flaws of this congregation. Not unlike a Presbyterian researcher who undertakes a study of a Presbyterian church, I am aware that a special level of prudence is demanded of me when I reflect on and write about Solomon's Porch. The reader, of course, will be the final judge as to whether I have succeeded at this.

After all of my travels, however, to the eight churches reported on below and numerous others that are part of the emerging church movement, I do want to note that in my opinion, Solomon's Porch is unique. I don't mean this in the way that one could say that any church in unique because it has its own set of people, its own history, and its own location. I mean that the particular cast of individuals who have inhabited Solomon's Porch over the past decade have grown a church that is simply not replicable. Doug Pagitt is a singular leader; I have met none like him. And beyond Doug, there is a band that writes all original songs, award-winning original art that hangs on the walls, and a weekly sermon discussion that betrays an astoundingly high level of theological and biblical acumen across the congregation. I say all of this because, if I am spoiled, I am also cognizant that it is extremely rare to have this collection of talent and leadership at a church. I have watched dozens of erstwhile church planters come to visit Solomon's Porch; I've seen scores of seminary students taking notes during our worship gathering for their papers; I've even witnessed the assistants to every Episcopal bishop in the country all descend on our church to eyewitness a worship gathering. I imagine that they all must conclude just how difficult it is to muster the collection of talent and innovation that Solomon's Porch exhibits. Indeed, one can surmise that only by dint of divine providence does this, or any successful church, come into existence.

I write this to say that Solomon's Porch is on the vanguard of the emerging church movement; it takes many of the practices of the movement to the extreme, like the movement's commitment to the creation of art, and the movement's desire to catalyze conversation. I simply ask the reader to bear this fact in mind in reading what follows.

In the end, I hope that this project provokes conversation: within the emerging church movement about how it can be more theologically robust, and beyond the movement about how the practices of the emerging congregations might infect the American church more broadly.

Acknowledgements

First and last, thanks are due to Kenda Creasy Dean. At a Princeton Youth Forum some years ago, Kenda said to me, "I'm a Methodist, and Methodists don't talk like this. But if I weren't a Methodist, I might say to you, 'God is telling me that you should come to Princeton to get a Ph.D.'" Be it prophecy or self-fulfilling prophecy, I arrived on campus less than two years later, and Kenda has shepherded my journey from then till now. Doctoral candidates are known for telling stories of absentee advisors who disappear for months at a time during coursework, exams, and most panic-inducing, during the book. Kenda has never once gone missing. For almost a decade now, she has been a coach and a cheerleader, believing that I would finish even when I and others doubted. And when it came to writing, Kenda knew what it took for me to write in a Princeton-worthy fashion, but she was also adamant that I maintain my own voice throughout. That anyone will ever call me "Doctor," I owe almost entirely to Kenda.

Others, of course, have also been a part of this journey. At Princeton, I learned in abundance from Rick Osmer and Wentzel van Huyssteen, and I thank them and Gordon Mikoski for sitting on my committee. Among my fellow students, Andy Root, Jessicah Duckworth, and Blair Bertrand were especially wonderful colleagues.

Back at home, my parents, Doug and Sarah Jones, were unflagging in their support. My three children have known me their whole lives as A.B.D., and they ask me weekly about when I'll *finally* finish. They are the reason I get out of bed in the morning.

Doug Pagitt is chief among my many friends who continue to encourage me in this endeavor, and Doug has often taken on extra amounts of work so that I could cloister myself off and write.

Finally, my beloved wife, Courtney Perry, came into my life at a time when I had basically given up on finishing this doctorate. But her love breathed newfound energy into my life. I truly believe that I would not have finished without her encouragement.

To these named, and to many others unnamed, thank you for believing in me, especially for those on Twitter and Facebook who kept me honest about my progress.

My thanks to the Lilly Endowment, which funded the Faithful Practices Project at Princeton Theological Seminary and thereby funded my research of the eight congregations in this study. And thanks to the Louisville Institute, also funded by the Lilly Endowment, for awarding me a generous grant to finish the writing of this book.

Note to Readers

This book is a lightly emended version of my dissertation, "The Relational Ecclesiology of the Emerging Church Movement in Practical Theological Perspective," submitted to and accepted by Princeton Theological Seminary in 2011. I decided that rather than pursuing the traditional route of partnering with an academic publishing house and spending a year or more on revisions, then another year on editing, design, and printing, it would be more beneficial to get this book out immediately, while the research and the ideas are still relatively fresh. The advent of electronic publishing and e-readers has made this possible.

But that means that it reads like a dissertation, which is not always the most readable form of prose (nor is it my favorite to write). If you'll forgive me for the sometime stilted prose, I'll forgive you for skipping the sections that don't interest you. Although I do build an argument from beginning to end, you are not compelled to read it in that manner.

Chapter One: The Emerging Church Movement and the Project of Practical Theology

Introduction

This book undertakes a study of the "emerging church" movement (ECM), begun in the 1990s, and particularly the ecclesiology thereof. Just a decade old, the emerging church movement is a topic of much discussion in the mainstream and Christian media and in popular social media like the "blogosphere," but it has, as yet, eluded serious academic study. One reason for this may be that scholars are unsure whether the movement will have a long-term impact on American Protestantism. But, regardless of its lifespan, the ECM has affected the Protestant landscape in North America.[1]

I will argue that the ECM is practicing a new form of congregationalism—a "relational ecclesiology," significant because this burgeoning ecclesiology is not only reflective of the social-media-saturated world in which we now live, but also because it resonates strongly with the ecclesiology proposed by Jürgen Moltmann in the late-twentieth century. While earlier sects, both Protestant and Catholic, have practiced similar polities to what is found in today's emerging church congregations, the recent and rapid advent of technological devices (mobile phones, computers, handheld devices) and the "new media" (websites, blogs, Facebook, Twitter), and the significant generational differences begat by globalization have enabled wholly new forms of intra-church and inter-church relationality. Ready access to theological and biblical resources have at once both allowed church members to investigate their theological questions and also partially mitigated the need for seminary-trained pastors.

In Chapter One, I will present a literature review on the emerging church movement and propose that it qualifies as a "new social movement." I will then set out my understanding of practical theology, relying upon Richard R. Osmer's argument that a consensus has formed in practical theology around four moments of theological

---

[1] The ECM has also influenced other English-speaking countries, including Australia, New Zealand, South Africa and the United Kingdom. It has an growing profile in other countries as well, but that is beyond the scope of this study.

reasoning. I will also apply the transversal rationality approach to interdisciplinarity as developed by Wentzel van Huyssteen to the movement as a whole, showing that emerging church congregations and congregational leaders work in an ad hoc fashion, applying just the kind of transversal reasoning which van Huyssteen advocates for our postfoundational age.

To better understand the ECM, I undertook a mixed-methods, phenomenological study of eight ECM congregations, which will be presented in Chapter Two. I visited these congregations in 2005 and 2006. While there, I observed their worship, conducted one-on-one interviews with the pastors and lay leaders, and facilitated focus group sessions, following an open-ended line of questioning.[2] Using a phenomenological method, I primarily listened for ways that they described their experiences in the congregations, paying special attention to recurring words and phrases and resulting in qualitative data. At each church, I conducted two focus groups (usually 75 minutes long), two one-on-one interviews (45 minutes), and an interview with the pastor. I attended the church's primary worship service and any other activities of the community available to me during the visit, and I thoroughly read the church's literature, both printed and online. Finally, I conducted a church census survey during all of the Sunday worship services at all eight congregations in May, 2006, resulting in 2,020 returned surveys which reveal a plethora of quantitative data about these congregations.[3]

Chapter Three presents the core practices of the ECM, drawn from my own research of the movement. The practices that I observed across the eight congregations fall under the taxonomies of "concrete practices" and "practices of virtue." The former are clear, specific rituals—those which can be quantified, for instance, with a place and time of their occurrence. The latter are not as obvious; lying just beneath the surface of the concrete practices, they are the practices that take place on a less formal basis, but they are just as important to the character of the ECM congregations. The practices which fall into both of these categories form a backdrop of what I have come to call *relational ecclesiology*, for they exemplify the

---

[2] These research tools can be found in Appendices A, and B.

[3] See Appendix C.

characteristics of communal Christian life that these congregations hold most dear.

In their quest for a post-evangelical faith and church, many ECM leaders have intuited their way into a relational ecclesiology; that is, the practices described in chapter three are, in my opinion, theologically underdeveloped. These practices have been operationalized in the congregational setting more quickly than they have been subjected to the scrutiny of (practical) theological reflection. But I will argue that vast theological resources await them in the post-Barthian panentheistic trinitarianism of Jürgen Moltmann. Chapter Four will rely upon Moltmann's work to establish a robust ecclesiology that is relational, eschatological, and deeply pneumatological, particularly significant among emergents who are living amidst the rise of global Pentecostalism. By entering into dialogue with Moltmann, emerging church congregations, and the movement writ large, will be better able to defend their particular form of church, will be more self-critical, and will be better able to develop new practices that jibe with their understanding of the gospel. I hope to begin this very dialogue in chapter four by using Moltmann's ecclesiology in critique of the ECM and using the nascent ecclesiology of the ECM in critique of Moltmann.

Finally, Chapter Five will both critically examine the ECM as it currently stands and propose a way forward. For a truly innovative relational ecclesiology to develop, the emerging church movement will have to get about the hard work of theological reflection on the practices that are developing.

The "Emerging Church Movement"—A Working Definition

The ECM is notoriously difficult to define, both because it is a young movement that is still rapidly evolving and because its adherents regularly defy the definitions put upon them by observers and scholars. Indeed, one of the aspects of church life in late-20th century America that served as an impetus for the ECM was the simple categorizations of churches (i.e., "evangelical," "mainline," "seeker-sensitive," etc.), which some in the ECM saw as a natural consequence of churches' co-option of secular marketing techniques; others simply felt that the extant categories did not adequately describe them, that they did not fit anywhere.

That being said, several scholars have proffered definitions of the ECM. For instance, sociologists Shayne Lee and Phillip Luke Sinitiere have written, "Unlike church models concerned with fine-tuning conventional evangelical approaches by employing more effective methods, emerging churches actively reimagine how people do church and how they perceive and understand the kingdom of God and Christian theology."[4]

The most oft-quoted definition of the ECM comes from *Emerging Churches* by Eddie Gibbs and Ryan Bolger. Gibbs and Bolger sort their interviews with scores of leaders in emergent churches into nine categories, which they consider the core characteristics of the emergent movement: identifying with Jesus, transforming secular space, living as community, welcoming the stranger, serving with generosity, participating as producers, creating as created beings, leading as a body, and merging ancient and contemporary spiritualities. Based on their interviews, they conclude, "Emerging Churches are communities that practice the way of Jesus within postmodern cultures."[5] Scot McKnight, who authors the highly influential blog, *The Jesus Creed*, finds Gibbs and Bolger's definition too broad, and he specifies it further: "Emerging churches are missional communities emerging in postmodern culture and consisting of followers of Jesus seeking to be faithful to the orthodox Christian faith in their place and time."[6]

But those who have attempted to define the ECM offer numerous caveats: the phenomenon resists definition; the adherents do not necessarily agree on polity, worship style, or theology; even the rubric by which the movement is known ("emergent," "emerging," "missional") is debated. The main reason that the ECM resists definition is its lack of a central, organizing structure. While Emergent Village is the most well-known of ECM groups, it does not operate like a traditional denomination or para-church ministry. Instead, Emergent Village and other ECM groups act more as clearinghouses of resources for those who self-identify with the movement. While they

---

[4] Shayne Lee and Phillip Luke Sinitiere, *Holy Mavericks: Evangelical Innovators and the Spiritual Marketplace* (New York: New York University Press, 2009), 86.

[5] Eddie Gibbs and Ryan K. Bolger, *Emerging Churches: Creating Christian Community in Postmodern Cultures* (Grand Rapids, Mich.: Baker Academic, 2005), 44.

[6] Scot McKnight, "Blogossary," in JesusCreed.org. New York: Beliefnet, 2006. Accessed October 26, 2009.

publish books and host occasional conferences, they do not offer adherents any form of official recognition, do not have a paid staff, and
do not provide the benefits common to denominations and para-
church ministries (health insurance, pension, or job placement).

Further, even McKnight's definition above begs certain questions, like what is "orthodox Christian faith," who gets to decide
what is and is not orthodox, and who determines whether a congregation is truly "missional"? The best definition of the ECM for the
purposes of this project comes from the *Encyclopedia of Religion in
America*, for it is more sociological in its approach, and it avoids
Christian and theological euphemisms, and terms that require further
unpacking: "The emerging church movement is a loosely aligned
conversation among Christians who seek to re-imagine the priorities,
values and theology expressed by the local church as it seeks to live
out its faith in postmodern society. It is an attempt to replot Christian
faith on a new cultural and intellectual terrain."[7]

The article goes on to state that the shared assumptions of those
in the ECM include an "awareness that an old Christendom is being
replaced by an emerging postmodern world," a "disillusionment with
how the Christian faith has been accommodated for the Baby
Boomer generation," an "eagerness to explore new ways of articulating and living out their faith," and a "central emphasis on Jesus."[8]
What this definition neglects is any mention of the core practices of
the ECM, so it does not adequately explore how the movement is
particularly unique on the scene of American religion at the turn of
the new millennium. This is an oversight that this book hopes to
correct.

Literature Review

The extant literature on the ECM is surprisingly thin. Although
the movement is relatively young, it has received significant attention in popular media and news media. It has not, however, received
much attention from scholars. The first three citations below are the
only book-length treatments of the movement by those unaffiliated

---

[7] Warren Bird, "Emerging Church Movement," in *Encyclopedia of Religion in
America*, ed. C.H. Lippy and P.W. Williams (Washington, D.C.: CQ Press | A
Division of SAGE Publications, 2010), 682.

[8] Bird, "Emerging Church Movement," 682-83.

with it. The subsequent citations are books that contain only a chapter or two on the ECM and books by ECM proponents or adversaries. However, not one of them deals with what this book addresses: a theological treatment of the relational nature of the movement. Each of them, in turn, hopes to report on or criticize the movement, but each of them misses the key component of the practices that animate these congregations.

The most often referred to book thus far published on the ECM is *Emerging Churches: Creating Christian Community in Postmodern Cultures* by Eddie Gibbs and Ryan K. Bolger. Gibbs and Bolger, professors at Fuller Theological Seminary, interviewed approximately 50 ECM leaders from Western countries (Canada, United States, United Kingdom, Europe, Australia, and New Zealand). The book is organized around their own definition of the emerging church.[9] Thus, they have nine core chapters, each of which is basically a collection of quotes from the leaders they interviewed. While *Emerging Churches* is a valuable resource for those attempting to understand the leadership of the ECM, it presents a perspective obviously slanted toward those very leaders. In other words, by interviewing the leaders who started the faith communities that make up the ECM, *Emerging Churches* provides an uncritical view of the movement. Their purpose was to describe the emerging church movement, but their results are biased because they rely solely on the impressions of those leaders who started the movement and thus have a vested interest in its public perception. By interviewing parishioners and reporting on their experiences in emerging churches, I hope to avoid this particular bias.

The second book that purportedly deals with the emerging church movement at length is Ray Anderson's *An Emergent Theology for Emerging Churches*.[10] Anderson's book is based around the

---

[9] "Emerging Churches are communities who practice the way of Jesus within postmodern cultures. This definition encompasses the [following] nine practices. Emerging churches (1) identify with the life of Jesus, (2) transform the secular realm, and (3) live highly communal lives. Because of these three activities, they (4) welcome the stranger, (5) serve with generosity, (6) participate as producers, (7) create as created beings, (8) lead as a body, and (9) take part in spiritual activities." Gibbs and Bolger, *Emerging Churches: Creating Christian Community in Postmodern Cultures*, 44-45.

[10] Ray Sherman Anderson, *An Emergent Theology for Emerging Churches* (Downers Grove, Ill.: IVP Press, 2006).

early church debate between Jerusalem and Antioch. He concludes that Antiochian Christianity was more culturally relevant for the time, and he encourages the emerging church movement to follow that example. However, his book is very thin on any description—or even understanding—of the ECM. In fact, not unlike the definition proffered by Gibbs and Bolger, it seems that Anderson's encouragement to be more missionally engaged in culture could apply to any church at any time. In other words, there is nothing particularly "emerging" about his emergent theology. Below, I will attempt to make concrete ecclesial proposals based on the actual developing practices in the ECM.

The third full-length treatment of the ECM is Phyllis Tickle's 2008 book, *The Great Emergence: How Christianity Is Changing and Why*.[11] Tickle, a freelance academic, places the "emergence" of Christianity at the turn of the twenty-first century in the context of other epochal shifts in the faith, including the "Great Schism" of the eleventh century and the "Great Reformation" of the sixteenth century. Tickle divides the modern Protestant church into four quadrants—liturgical, social justice, renewal (Pentecostal and charismatic), and conservative (alternatively called "doctrinal evangelicals")—and she writes of the blurring of lines between these formerly discrete categories. Ultimately, Tickle concludes that the majority of Christians will swirl toward a moderate center, and she considers the ECM a forerunner of the coming emergence. Tickle's proposals are valuable, and they definitely have implications for American Christianity far beyond the emerging church movement, but they are not based on research into the movement itself, but only on her anecdotal experience as an advocate of the movement.

The following are among the more serious chapter-length treatments of the emerging church movement. In *Holy Mavericks: Evangelical Innovators and the Spiritual Marketplace*, sociologist Shane Lee and historian Phillip Luke Sinitiere set out to chart the generation of evangelical leaders staking a claim to Billy Graham's role as "America's Pastor," by studying Paula White, T. D. Jakes, Rick Warren, Joel Osteen, and Brian McLaren.[12] Lee and Sinitiere

---

[11] Phyllis Tickle, *The Great Emergence: How Christianity Is Changing and Why* (Grand Rapids, Mich.: Baker Books, 2008).

[12] Lee and Sinitiere, *Holy Mavericks: Evangelical Innovators and the Spiritual Marketplace*.

recognize the relational character of the ECM when they write, "By offering a relational and organic model of spiritual community that emphasizes friendship, fosters dialogue, and makes no claim to having a monopoly on truth, McLaren and the emerging church construct an archetype for a new kind of evangelicalism that addresses the alienation, isolation, and arrant individualism of a postcapitalist, post industrial world."[13]

Tom Sine, a Christian "futurist" and adjunct professor at Fuller Theological Seminary, penned *The New Conspirators: Creating the Future One Mustard Seed at a Time*, in which he develops a taxonomy of young evangelicalism that includes four categories: emerging, missional, mosaic, and monastic.[14] Among the characteristics that define the "emerging stream" are narrative theology and preaching, cultural ministry models, experimentalism, experiential worship, communal leadership models, and a commitment to social justice. In the end, Sine does not pass judgment on any of the four categories, but simply lists them as distinct but interrelated movements.

Rising from the Ashes: Rethinking Church is a lightly edited collection of interviews by freelance writer Becky Garrison.[15] Meant as a primer for mainliners who want to better understand the ECM, Garrison's questions center around practices like "Hospitality to the Stranger" and "Transforming Space." Garrison does not provide even a conclusion, giving the last word to Anglican priest, Ian Mobsby, "so we need to reframe church—away from power abuse and cult and back to their [sic] true identity as radical places of transformative Christian spirituality worked out."[16]

In *Churchmorph: How Metatrends are Reshaping Christian Communities*, Eddie Gibbs's follow-up to *Emerging Churches*, he writes, "Emerging churches represent a spirit of wide-ranging intel-

---

[13] Lee and Sinitiere, *Holy Mavericks: Evangelical Innovators and the Spiritual Marketplace*, 105.

[14] Tom Sine, *The New Conspirators: Creating the Future One Mustard Seed at a Time* (Downers Grove, Ill.: IVP Books, 2008).

[15] Becky Garrison, *Rising from the Ashes: Rethinking Church* (New York: Seabury Books, 2007).

[16] Garrison, *Rising from the Ashes: Rethinking Church*, 164.

lectual curiosity, producing an eclectic spirituality that draws from a variety of church traditions in regard to its forms of worship and expressions of mission."[17] Arguing that both the "emerging" church and the "missional" church have weaknesses, he proposes, "The missional church movement's theological grounding and cultural insights need to be linked with the emerging church's missional engagement in specific contexts for their mutual enrichment."[18]

Recently, several books have been published that forward conservative critiques of the ECM. The first was *Becoming Conversant with the Emerging Church: Understanding a Movement and Its Implications* by D.A. Carson, a New Testament professor at Trinity Evangelical Divinity School.[19] Focusing primarily on books by Brian McLaren[20] and Steve Chalke[21], Carson argues that the ECM's embrace of postmodernist epistemology fatally weakens the movement and therefore *de facto* precludes it from proclaiming orthodox Christianity. Both McLaren and Chalke, by embracing the feminist critique of the penal substitutionary theory of the atonement, have abandoned the gospel, according to Carson. He concludes that, while providing an accurate critique of evangelical consumerism, the ECM is ultimately dangerous.

In *Truth and the New Kind of Christian*, Biola University philosophy professor R. Scott Smith takes a similar tack, arguing that the ECM leads the charge of, "Christians [who] are increasingly accepting of ethical relativism," and thus Christians "are losing our

---

[17] Eddie Gibbs, *Churchmorph: How Megatrends Are Reshaping Christian Communities* (Grand Rapids, Mich.: Baker Academic, 2009), 39-40.

[18] Gibbs, *Churchmorph: How Megatrends Are Reshaping Christian Communities*, 36.

[19] D. A. Carson, *Becoming Conversant with the Emerging Church: Understanding a Movement and Its Implications* (Grand Rapids, Mich.: Zondervan, 2005).

[20] Brian D. McLaren, A Generous Orthodoxy: Why I Am a Missional, Evangelical, Post/Protestant, Liberal/Conservative, Mystical/Poetic, Biblical, Charismatic/Contemplative, Fundamentalist/Calvinist, Anabaptist/Anglican, Methodist, Catholic, Green, Incarnational, Depressed-yet-Hopeful, Emergent, Unfinished Christian (Grand Rapids, MI: Zondervan/Youth Specialties, 2004).

[21] Steve Chalke and Alan Mann, *The Lost Message of Jesus* (Grand Rapids, Mich.: Zondervan, 2003).

understanding of Christian ethical and religious truths as being *objectively* true."[22]   Smith sets forth the "correspondence theory" of truth, arguing that words point to real objects in the world, and Christian truth statements point to real, objective truths that can be empirically tested.   Smith's primary targets are Brian McLaren[23] and Tony Jones.[24]

Kevin DeYoung is a Reformed pastor in Lansing, Michigan, and Ted Kluck is a freelance sportswriter who attends DeYoung's church.   Together they wrote, *Why We're Not Emergent: By Two Guys Who Should Be.*[25]   Therein, they too argue that Christian orthodoxy rests on a foundationalist epistemology and an inerrantist biblical hermeneutic.   They write, "Let us rest confidently in the certain truth that God is knowable and can make Himself and His ways known to us."[26]   Since the emerging church movement does not espouse this epistemology, they conclude that the movement is heterodox.

And another pastor, Bob DeWaay, wrote *The Emergent Church: Undefining Christianity.*[27]   DeWaay proposes that the true center of the ECM is an eschatology based on the works of theologian Jürgen Moltmann and philosopher Ken Wilber, both of whom DeWaay considers thoroughly Hegelian.   Instead of the positive view of history displayed in these authors, DeWaay argues, there is empirical evidence that the cosmos is, in fact, degrading in advance of Jesus' sec-

---

[22] R. Scott Smith, *Truth and the New Kind of Christian : The Emerging Effects of Postmodernism in the Church* (Wheaton, Ill.: Crossway Books, 2005), 13.

[23] Brian D. McLaren, *A New Kind of Christian: A Tale of Two Friends on a Spiritual Journey* (San Francisco: Jossey-Bass, 2001).

[24] Tony Jones, *Postmodern Youth Ministry: Exploring Cultural Shift, Creating Holistic Connections, Cultivating Authentic Community* (Grand Rapids, Mich.: Youth Specialties/Zondervan, 2001).

[25] Kevin DeYoung and Ted Kluck, *Why We're Not Emergent: By Two Guys Who Should Be* (Chicago: Moody Publishers, 2008).

[26] DeYoung and Kluck, *Why We're Not Emergent: By Two Guys Who Should Be,* 51.

[27] Bob DeWaay, *The Emergent Church: Undefining Christianity* (St. Louis Park, MN: Bethany Press International, 2009).

ond coming and Satan's thousand-year millennial reign. He concludes that, "The teaching of Emergent offers spiritual experiences as a replacement for truth. Having no real scriptural base, these young people are seduced and deluded."[28]

Those critical of the emerging church movement, however, have a fatal flaw in their work, and it is a flaw shared by the several who have written in support of the movement. None has as yet investigated the ECM by asking the persons who attend these churches what draws them to their respective faith communities; none has looked closely at the practices these churches have developed, nor have they asked what sustains these congregations over time. The books mentioned above are filled with assumptions about why someone would join an emerging church, but not one puts forward any research as to why their assumptions are true. This study will amend that shortcoming by reporting on what exactly it is that makes an ECM congregation a compelling faith community for so many people.

The Emerging Church Movement as a New Social Movement

One of the noteworthy elements of the emergent church movement is its similarity to other "New Social Movements" (NSM). Coined in relation to the various movements across the West in the 1960s, sociologists use this rubric to describe a change in the way that social movements are understood in contemporary Western societies.

Until the mid-1960s, social theorists and sociologists were beholden to the Marxist conception of social movements as always ultimately about a struggle for economic gain by the proletariat. "In the industrial era, following a Marxist logic, social movements were believed to be centered in the working class. Working class movements were seen as instrumentally based actions concerned with matters of economic redistribution."[29] However, beginning in the mid-1960s, sociologists began to notice that social movements were not following the previously assumed patterns; instead of escaping

---

[28] DeWaay, *The Emergent Church: Undefining Christianity*, 5.

[29] Nelson A. Pichardo, "New Social Movements: A Critical Review," *Annual Review of Sociology*, no. 23 (1997): 312.

economic domination, "social movements [were becoming] instru-
mentalities to abolish, or at least weaken, structures of political and
social domination."[30]

Indeed, sociologist Verta Taylor has called the entirety of
American culture a "social movement society," in which social
movements are *de rigueur* and individuals increasingly find their
identity, meaning, and community in social movements.[31]   Thus, as a
new social movement, the ECM functions in a less radical way than
a traditional social movement, and more as a source of cultural reform and a place of belonging.

Be it the "hippie movement," the environmental movement, the
peace movement, or the GLBT rights movement, late-twentieth
century movements were neither determined by social class nor were
they primarily interested in economic redistribution.   In fact, the emergence of the post-industrial middle class is in large part determina-
tive of NSMs, for the middle class filled the gap between the
proletariat and the bourgeoisie, mitigating the need for more radical
social movements and redefining social movements as mechanisms
for cultural reform rather than mechanisms for the redistribution of
wealth.

New social movement theory has also come under significant
criticism, primarily for the tendency of sociologists to overdetemine
the power of the theory.   Steven M. Buechler and F. Kurt Clyke,
proponents of NSM theory, admit that the theorists tend to "on-
tologize," granting the theory "more explanatory power than it empirically warranted."[32]   Nelson Pichardo, a leading critic of NSM
theory, argues that NSM theory exclusively describes left-wing
movements and has failed to account for the abundance of right-
wing movements since the 1960s.[33]   Pichardo agrees that the evi-

---

[30] Aldon D. Morris and Carol McClurg Mueller, *Frontiers in Social Movement Theory* (New Haven, Conn.: Yale University Press, 1992).

[31] Verta Taylor, "Mobilizing for Change in a Social Movement Society," *Contemporary Sociology* 29 (2000).

[32] Steven M. Buechler and F. Kurt Cylke, *Social Movements: Perspectives and Issues* (Mountain View, Calif.: Mayfield Pub., 1997).

[33] Pichardo, "New Social Movements: A Critical Review," 413-14.

dence does not support the thesis that NSMs are different-in-kind than previous understandings of social movements.[34]

But while critics challenge the thoroughness of the theory, most agree that NSMs are real, and that they are different-in-kind from previous social movements. What is particularly noteworthy for this study are the parallels between NSMs broadly considered and the emergent church movement. First, NSMs are a product of the "new middle class" in the post-industrial West. And, due to the wide diversity of the middle class, "NSMs do not bear a strong relation to the structural role of the participants. There is a tendency of the social base of new social movements to transcend class structure. The background of participants find their most frequent structural roots in rather diffuse social statuses such as youth, gender, sexual orientation, or professions that do not correspond with structural explanations."[35] Indeed, attendees of ECM congregations are not the working class masses of Marxist revolutions; instead, they are actually more wealthy and better educated than most Americans.[36]

Just as the ecological movement in the United States is not determined by economic class[37], neither is the emerging church movement—though there is a certain sense of "oppression" by the conventional church that emergents are attempting to free themselves from. Individuals are drawn to the ECM out of frustration with conventional models of church and conservative theologies, as well as for other reasons, and this sense of frustration is more often than not what defines the movement. What this bodes for the future of the ECM is an open question. While the experience of disenfranchisement from conventional ecclesial life has been the rallying

---

[34] Pichardo, "New Social Movements: A Critical Review," 419-25.

[35] Enrique Laraña, Hank Johnston, and Joseph R. Gusfield, *New Social Movements: From Ideology to Identity* (Philadelphia: Temple University Press, 1994), 6. This is also tied to the common argument that NSMs are indicative of the move "away from the instrumental issues of industrialism to the quality of life issues of postmaterialism." Pichardo, "New Social Movements: A Critical Review," 412.

[36] See Appendix C.

[37] Laraña, Johnston, and Gusfield, *New Social Movements: From Ideology to Identity*, 6.

center around which the ECM has gathered in the past, as ECM congregations have become more established and more content with their ecclesial experience, there has been less reason to convene the gatherings that were constitutive of the movement in its first decade. This issue will be taken up again in chapter five.

Second, whereas in the Marxist matrix social movements were bounded by ideological concerns, NSMs "exhibit a pluralism of ideas and values, and they tend to have pragmatic orientations and search for institutional reforms that enlarge the system of members' participation in decision-making. These movements have an important political meaning in Western societies: They imply a 'democratization dynamic' of everyday life and the expansion of civil versus political dimensions of society."[38] This is seen in the emerging church movement as the value of ordination is questioned and the role of a "clergy class" is undermined. ECM churches are also known for having congregants on both the "left" and the "right" of issues such as biblical interpretation, gender and sexuality issues, and American politics. Across the movement as a whole, leaders have even bragged that "complementarian" conservative Baptists and gay and lesbian mainliners will often share a pew or lunch together at ECM conferences.[39]

Third,

> NSMs often involve the emergence of new or formerly weak dimensions of identity. The grievances and mobilizing factors tend to focus on cultural and symbolic issues that are linked with issues of identity rather than on economic grievances that characterized the work-class movement. They are associated with a set of beliefs, symbols,

---

[38] Laraña, Johnston, and Gusfield, *New Social Movements: From Ideology to Identity*, 7.

[39] Indeed, some of the first strife in the movement happened when church consultant Leonard Sweet told a reporter that emergent politics was equivalent to "Jim Wallis' evangelical updating of the Social Gospel movement, or liberalism's liberation theology of the '70's and '80's." This was the first time that a former proponent of the movement spoke out, on the record, about disappointment with the emerging church. Peter J. Walker with Tyler Clark, "Missing the Point? The Absolute Truth Behind Postmodernism, Emergent, and the Emerging Church," *Relevant* July/August 2006, no. 21 (2006): 73.

values, and meanings related to sentiments of belonging to a differentiated social group; with the members' image of themselves; and with new, socially constructed attributions about the meaning of everyday life.[40]

Indeed, the fact that new social movements are predicated on a shift from economic concerns to personal, symbolic concerns is one of the strongest factors suggesting a correlation between NSMs and religious identity. Whereas Marxist understandings of social movements left little to no room for religious identity, the shift to the personal in NSMs allows for just that; further, it correlates with the rise of religion in the consciousness of sociologists and social theorists in the last several decades. Regarding "new or formerly weak dimensions of identity," the rise of the emerging church movement is contemporaneous with the dénouement of denominational identity as a significant indicator of identity across the American church landscape. As GenXers and Millenials graduated from college and looked for churches, the denominational affiliations that so often characterized their parents' and grandparents' church participation were no longer relevant, leaving an opening for new church identity to emerge.

Fourth, Johnston, Larana, and Gustfield note that the "relation between the individual and the collective is blurred."[41] Instead of being exclusively focused on group identity and group action, NSMs stress that the behavior of individuals is important to the success of the movement. For instance, the green movement is noteworthy for its members' commitments to shopping for organic produce, being "locavores," and composting their domestic food waste, all personal actions. This move is noted in the common NSM phrase, "the personal is political"—a phrase that originated in the feminist movement in the early 1970s.[42] The ECM seems to fit this characteristic,

---

[40] Laraña, Johnston, and Gusfield, *New Social Movements: From Ideology to Identity*, 7.

[41] Laraña, Johnston, and Gusfield, *New Social Movements: From Ideology to Identity*, 7.

[42] Carol Hanisch in *Notes from the Second Year: Women's Liberation; Major Writings of the Radical Feminists*, ed. Shulie Firestone and Anne Koedt (New York: Radical Feminism, 1970).

being that emergent churches highly emphasize the personal choices of their congregants. Among the eight congregations surveyed herein, these activities have occurred: a day for the women of the congregation to discuss the use of anti-depressants, growing an organic garden on the church property, debating the importance of childhood vaccinations, and encouraging members to purchase produce from community-supported agriculture (CSA) farms. However, it is difficult to say whether, in the emerging church, "the *movement* becomes the focus for the individual's definition of himself or herself, and action within the movement is a complex mix of the collective and individual confirmations of identity."[43] That is because, as noted in the preface, many congregants at ECM churches are actually unaware that their congregation is part of a larger movement.

Fifth, and closely related to the previous two characteristics, is that new social movements—for instance, gay rights, abortion rights, pro-life, and New Age—tend to focus on the most intimate aspects of human life: sexuality, habits of consumption, and careers.[44] Again, this shift from the purely economic to the intimately personal has fostered many of the very characteristics that the ECM most highly vaunts, including "authenticity" in worship, "integrity" in leadership, and intimate ecclesial communities. While these characteristics do have economic implications—as do the previously listed NSMs—economics are not primary to the motivations behind the emerging church movement.

Sixth, new social movements seek change in large part because of the "credibility crisis of the conventional channels for participation in Western democracies."[45] This is a reflection of the deep cynicism regarding democracy, particularly seen among GenXers, though not necessarily shared by Millenials.[46] Seen in popular cul-

---

[43] Laraña, Johnston, and Gusfield, *New Social Movements: From Ideology to Identity*, 8. Italics added

[44] Laraña, Johnston, and Gusfield, *New Social Movements: From Ideology to Identity*, 8.

[45] Laraña, Johnston, and Gusfield, *New Social Movements: From Ideology to Identity*, 8.

[46] See Christian Smith and Patricia Snell, *Souls in Transition: The Religious and Spiritual Lives of Emerging Adults* (Oxford: Oxford University Press, 2009).

ture venues like *Saturday Night Live* and the blogosphere, and also in the much more serious venue of anti-globalization protests at the G8 Summit, World Bank, and International Monetary Fund meetings (Berlin, 1988; Madrid, 1994; London, 1999; Seattle, 1999; Genoa, 2001) and the Republican National Convention (St. Paul, Minnesota, 2008), these protests have arisen among the younger generations due to the seeming intractability of Western democracies to purge themselves of corporate special interests. Similarly, participants in the ECM, and especially the leaders, consistently express disillusionment and disenfranchisement with conventional forms of Protestantism, though participants in the emerging church movement do not seem ready to foment revolution, or even to protest, as do these other NSMs. In fact, we will return to this question in the conclusion, as to whether the emerging church has already been co-opted by American Christendom.

Table 1: Characteristics of New Social Movements and the Emerging Church Movement

New Social Movement	Emerging Church Movement
Transcend traditional class lines	Do not come from one class
Exhibit a pluralism of ideologies	Drawn from many theological streams
Involve the emergence of new forms of personal identity	Predicated on personal religious convictions
The personal is political — personal behavior matters	Emphasis on personal activities of congregants
Focus on intimate matters of life	Emphasis on authenticity and intimacy in worship and leadership
Response to crisis of credibility in traditional institutions	Response to crisis in conventional forms of church

At Solomon's Porch a parishioner who is also a religion and philosophy professor at a local community college addressed the congregation for nearly ten minutes about the intricacies of the 2008 Farm Bill and ultimately urged the congregation to communicate with their legislators that they oppose subsidies for corporate farming.   While this would not necessarily be unusual in a mainline/liberal church, this ECM church would be characterized by most observers as "evangelical." At Tribe of Los Angeles, another ECM church, a group of church members travels every year to the Burning Man Festival, an annual gathering in the desert of northern Nevada that promotes decommodification, radical self-reliance, radical self-expression, community, and civic responsibility. Even the annual Emergent Gathering (2001-2007) was billed as an "anti-conference," with no paid speakers, no worship bands, no agenda, and no menu; everyone who arrived was expected to contribute to the content, worship, and food preparation of the event.

So far we can see that the emerging church movement qualifies as a new social movement in multiple ways, especially when it comes to the contradistinction between the movement itself and the institutions that developed previously. Another noteworthy element is the relational position of many ECM congregations *vis-à-vis* the denominations out of which they emerged—denominations that originated in similar circumstances in an earlier age. This leads to the seventh characteristics of new social movements:

> in contrast to cadre-led and centralized bureaucracies of traditional mass parties, new social movement organizations tend to be segmented, diffuse, and decentralized...the tendency is toward considerable autonomy of local sections, where collective forms of debate and decision making often limit linkages with regional and national

organizations. This has been called the "self-referential element'" of the new movements, and it constitutes another sharp distinction with the hierarchical, centralized organization [of the previous social movement models].[47]

The ECM takes some pride in its anti-bureaucratic stance, with leaders often railing against the modernistic excesses of large, mainline denominations.[48] Critics, however, have argued that the emphasis on local autonomy has blunted the reforming impact of the ECM on the American church at large. To date, it does seem clear that the ECM will err on the side of autonomy as opposed to bureaucratizing in the form of twentieth century denominations, though this is another item that will be addressed in the conclusion.

Finally,

> Contemporary social movements are using advanced forms of technology and mass communication as a mobilizing tool and conduit to alternative forms of media…The new technological revolution that began in the 1970s has facilitated the development of a number of independent, non-profit public interest media sites on the World Wide Web (WWW) that advocate social and economic justice. This new outlet for the underrepresented in mainstream media allows for alternatives to the bias in corporate media controlled by profit, and gives ordinary citizens access to information, resources and opportunities for communication. It also assists groups and individuals worldwide to forge links across a wide range of issues.[49]

In the broader world of NSMs, "Networked agencies are characterized by direct action strategies and Internet communications, loose coalitions, relatively flat organizational structures, and more

---

[47] Laraña, Johnston, and Gusfield, *New Social Movements: From Ideology to Identity*, 8-9.

[48] Jones, *The New Christians: Dispatches from the Emergent Frontier*, 180-92.

[49] Victoria Carty, "Protest, Cyberactivism, and New Social Movements: The Reemergence of the Peace Movement Post 9/11," in *American Sociological Association* (Marriott Hotel, Loews Philadelphia Hotel, Philadelphia, PA: 2005), 1-2.

informal modes of belonging focused on shared concern about diverse issues and identity politics. Traditional hierarchical and bureaucratic organizations persist, but social movements may be emerging as the most popular avenue for informal political mobilization, protest and expression,"[50] and this change in organization is clearly evident in the ECM.

Much of the early innovation in the ECM was distributed on Internet venues like theooze.com and emergentvillage.com, and these and other sites also became clearinghouses for announcing local "meet-ups," national and regional conferences, and published books.[51] The ECM also arguably boasts the most robust presence in the "blogosphere" of any stream within American Christianity. Quite simply, the effect of the Internet (as well as mobile phones, instant messaging, and other forms of "new media") cannot be underestimated when tracing the growth of the ECM between 1997 and 2008.

Whereas in some ways the ECM has affinities with earlier American revival and renewal movements in the church, the early and ready adoption of new technologies by the ECM is closer to the use of radio by evangelicals like Billy Graham and Charles Fuller in the 1940s and 1950s. And yet, there are differences here, too. Radio is a medium that allows only for one voice, speaking monologically. The social media in which the ECM trucks is a more egalitarian and dialogical forum for communication. While not everyone can get airtime on a radio station, anyone with internet access can start a blog or post to Facebook. In this way, the adoption of social media by the ECM shaped the movement, enhancing the tendencies that were already latent in the GenXers who founded it. They were reacting against top-heavy and bureaucratic forms of church, be they mainline denominations or evangelical mega-churches. The advent of social media in an unprecedented way allowed for the early leaders of the ECM to refer to the movement as a "conversation" as opposed to a new denominational identity—even as opposed to a

---

[50] Pippa Norris, *Democratic Phoenix : Reinventing Political Activism* (Cambridge, UK ; New York, NY: Cambridge University Press, 2002), 190.

[51] Richard W. Flory and Donald E. Miller, *Finding Faith: The Spiritual Quest of the Post-Boomer Generation* (New Brunswick, N.J.: Rutgers University Press, 2008), 29-31.

"movement"—and to embody that conversational ethos in the media by which they communicated. More recent NSMs like the online groundswell for the presidential campaign of Barack Obama in 2008 or the revolts around the Iranian presidential election of 2009 and 2010 are similar examples of the proliferation of social media.

Clearly, there is much in common between the emerging church movement and the standard definition of a new social movement. In the past, under a Marxist rubric, it would have been unthinkable that a religious reformation would qualify as a social movement, but in the NSM schema, the ECM easily qualifies. This is significant for a number of reasons. First, it establishes the emerging church movement's significance. While some critics may want to dismiss the ECM because it does not fit the criteria of former movements, nor does it boast the massive numbers of adherents necessary to justify classification as a movement, new social movements operate by different methods and are judged by different criteria—criteria that the emerging church movement clearly fits. Thus the ECM qualifies as worthy of study as a "movement." Second, as a new social movement, the ECM is open to the scrutiny of sociologists and social theorists under this rubric.

But most significantly, classifying the emerging church movement as a new social movement gives us insight from the sociological field of study into the ECM. It shows clearly that the ECM is a reflection of its time, a movement in the ecclesial realm that has corollaries in many other areas of twenty-first century Western existence. And, as we will revisit in chapter five, the evolution of other new social movements since the 1960s serves as a harbinger for the challenges and promise facing the emerging church movement in coming decades.

A Consensus Equilibrium Approach to Practical Theology

Recently, Richard R. Osmer has developed what he has come to call a "consensus equilibrium" model of practical theology, an attempt to "identify four core intellectual operations that distinguish practical theology as an academic discipline from other forms of theology."[52] Osmer is not trying to forge a new way for practical theologians, but, having surveyed the field, is attempting to articulate an approach to theological discernment that gathers the varieties of practical theology around the globe. As a result, he has elaborated a scheme of four distinguishable but deeply interconnected "moments," or "moves" within the discipline of practical theology.[53] And prior to these four moves he posits four theoretical (or meta-theological) pre-determinations that guide the theological enterprise.[54] The four moves and four pre-judgments are depicted below.

---

[52] Richard R. Osmer, "Johannes Van Der Ven's Contribution to the New Consensus in Practical Theology," in *Essays in Honor of Johannes Van Der Ven* (Leiden: Brill, forthcoming), np. Osmer has also worked out an earlier version of this scheme in, Richard Robert Osmer and Friedrich Schweitzer, *Religious Education between Modernization and Globalization: New Perspectives on the United States and Germany*, Studies in Practical Theology (Grand Rapids, Mich.: W.B. Eerdmans, 2003). And he dealt with it at length in the epilogue to Richard Robert Osmer, *The Teaching Ministry of Congregations* (Louisville, Ky.: Westminster John Knox Press, 2005), 308-17.

[53] Osmer, *The Teaching Ministry of Congregations*, 304-06.

[54] Osmer, *The Teaching Ministry of Congregations*, 306-08.

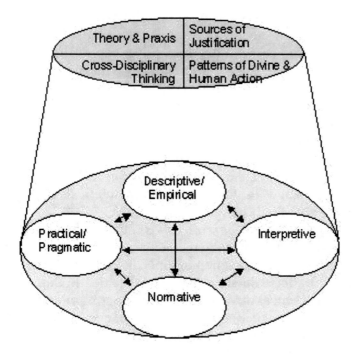

Osmer's four moments proceed thusly: During the *descriptive/empirical* task, the practical theologian attempts to answer the question, What is happening? Putting forth as clear and thorough a description as possible, the theologian explicates a particular Christian practice in a particular social/ecclesial context. This is often accomplished by empirical research, previously borrowed from other disciplines, but now often carried out by practical theologians themselves—in this way, theologians are able to avoid the reductionistic views of religion often imported from the social sciences.

In the *interpretive task*, the theologian "seeks to place empirical research in a more comprehensive explanatory framework."[55] In answering the "Why?" question, the theologian will often turn to social

---

[55] Osmer, "Johannes Van Der Ven's Contribution to the New Consensus in Practical Theology," np.

theorists, psychologists, and anthropologists for aid, but there are also interpretive sensibilities that are uniquely within the province of the theologian. The result is a "thick description" of the data that has been empirically collected.

The relationship between the descriptive-empirical and the interpretive moments deserves extra attention. Whereas various disciplines have long considered this a uni-directional move (from description to interpretation), this naïveté has rightly been undermined by the hermeneutical turn of the twentieth century. The empirical description of the first moment is inevitably colored by the interpretive lens (or *horizon*) that the theologian brings to the theological enterprise. Thus the descriptive-empirical and the interpretive moments stand in their own hermeneutical circle, each amending and potentially correcting the other.

When engaged in the *normative task*, the practical theologian may look most like a systematic theologian, for during this moment she is engaged in the construction of biblical, theological, and ethical norms that will affect Christian (ecclesial) praxis. In this constructive mode, the practical theologian holds the norms of scripture, tradition, and Christian experience in tension and conversation with the aforementioned social theories and other non-theological disciplines. That is, while the practical theologian is likely to be in conversation with the work of biblical scholars, systematic/dogmatic theologians, and Christian ethicists as a part of the normative move, practical theology does not morph into systematic theology, for the normative claims that practical theologians make are always closely tied to the social and ecclesial problematics that initiated the particular theological project. In that way, the norming claims of practical theology are more fluid, local, and provisional—in short, more hermeneutically driven—than other forms of theological reflection.

During the *pragmatic task*, the practical theologian develops "rules of art" for the reformation of Christian praxis in fields such as Christian education, homiletics, and pastoral care.[56] These are creative and fitting responses, borne out of theological discernment, to particular problematics that face the church. The pragmatic moment

---

[56] Osmer defines the Schleiermacherian phrase "rules of art" as, "open-ended guidelines that can assist those who are leading or participating in a particular form of Christian praxis," Osmer, "Johannes Van Der Ven's Contribution to the New Consensus in Practical Theology."

attempts to answer the question, "How to?"—or even, "So what?" The goal is that the church will be better as a result of the specific practical theological reflection—that the practical theologian will offer tools which the church practitioner can artfully apply to the practice of ministry. It is important to note that the pragmatic move in practical theology is not mere application of theological norms—always a danger in practical theology—but is in a real sense *praxis*, that is, theory-guided action.

The remainder of this project is organized assuming the four moments of Osmer's model, but attention must first be given to the meta-theological lenses that precede the four moments, for in them lie the prejudgments that will guide the hermeneutics of the four moments. Four philosophical/theological commitments greatly shape the work of the practical theologian: First, the practical theologian needs to make some claim about how he understands the *theory-praxis relationship*, whether that be neo-Marxist critical theory, neo-Aristotelianism, or another way to approach this relationship. This issue is particularly significant in the study of the emerging church movement because various positions compete in the sensibilities of the ECM leaders. This project will follow Hans Georg Gadamer's emphasis on prejudgment in the Heidiggerian hermeneutic circle, for it provides the best rubric to understand the intuitive theological choices that ECM leaders make in developing practices for their congregations. It also accords with their commitment to epistemic humility and valuing the interpretations of others. For Gadamer, theory and praxis form an ongoing circle, each affecting the other, and together opening up ever-widening vistas of interpretation. [57] Second, scripture, tradition, reason, and experience are all commonly referred to as *sources of justification* in theology, but the question remains as to how these four relate: is one held above the rest (e.g., is scripture the "norming norm"?)? Is there a hierarchy? Do the four stand in mutually critical correlation? This question is exceedingly important to reflect upon during the interpretive and normative moves. In this book, scripture is considered the secondary revelation of God to human beings—Jesus Christ being the primary revelation—but since scripture is always reliant upon human interpretation, it does not automatically trump other

---

[57] Hans Georg Gadamer, *Truth and Method*, 2nd, rev. ed. (New York: Crossroad, 1989).

sources of justification. In other words, other sources maintain the ability to stand in critique of any particular interpretation.

Third, closely related to sources of justification is the theologian's theory of *divine and human action*,[58] which tries to get at the importance, for example, of revelation, how human beings can speak substantively about God, and the position and role of Christ in the theological scheme. Some practical theologians find it problematic to talk about God, choosing to speak only of human beings' experience of God; others talk more freely about the work of God in the world. I find that practical theology's strength is reflecting on the nexus of divine and human action, and looking for the agency of God in both the lives of human beings and in social movements is a most interesting project for the practical theologian. Indeed, I hold that the activity of the divine can only be known when it comes in contact with the activity of human beings. Fourth, several models of *interdisciplinary reflection* are available to the practical theologian, including mutually critical correlation (of David Tracy and Don Browning and many contextual theologians), tranformationalism (of James Loder, Deborah van Deusen Hunsinger and many Barthians), the ad hoc method (of Hans Frei and the post-liberals), and transversal rationality (of Wentzel van Huyssteen). The position that the theologian takes regarding other disciplines has far-reaching impact; in this book, for instance, we will primarily be in dialogue with philosophy (specifically, hermeneutical phenomenology) and Jürgen Moltmann's systematic theology, but also with missiology, social theory, and biblical studies. I will take the position of transverality, as explicated in the next section.

One of the possible shortcomings of Osmer's model is the thoroughgoing nature of these four prolegomena. That is, the practical theologian could get eternally preoccupied with defining, delimiting, and claiming where she stands regarding each of these commitments. Secondly, Osmer insists on his entire scheme functioning as a hermeneutical circle—one can enter the circle at any point, moving from any "moment" to any other, and that each moment is in a perichoretic relationship with the others. While this lends itself to understanding practical theology as developing "rules of art," it can also be daunting. In other words, one must take care not to be over-

---

[58] Also referred to as "theological rationale." Osmer, *The Teaching Ministry of Congregations*, 308.

whelmed by the circular and mutually critical nature of the four moments and remember that this is simply a metaphor for practical theological reflection. I will attempt to avoid this danger by moving from theory to practice to theory to practice over the course of the forthcoming four chapters. In the end, Osmer's model is not just valuable as a schema for a book, but also challenges the practical theologian to deal with the many and diverse theses in the last century of practical theology, from the empirical theologies of European theologians to the Marxist theory of American theologians.

The Promise of Transversal Rationality for the ECM

As mentioned above, interdisciplinarity is a common mode of operation for the practical theologian. This is the mode in which the theologian has a dialogue or conversation with the sociologist or psychologist or with her or his writings. Another way to think about this is that the theologian facilitates a dialogue between the two fields. Mario Midali writes,

> What characterizes this model is the interaction, that is, the reciprocity relationship, the mutual confrontation that exists among the disciplines which, by this process, come out modified and enriched. *Dialogue* is the axis of this relationship; the dialogue's intent is not directed exactly to promote a harmonious and free-of-conflicts working together, but rather to second the awareness that a group

work is being done, that it should be analyzed and critically evaluated together with its results.[59]

Although interdisciplinary thinking undeniably has limits, Osmer points out many successful examples of interdisciplinarity in Christian education, with fields such as cultural anthropology (John Westerhoff, Ellis Nelson, and Chuck Foster), cognitive developmental theory (James Fowler), and critical social theory (Thomas Groome), each assisting the practical theologian in her own reflection. "True interdisciplinary thinking," Osmer writes, "operates in a manner that respects the integrity of different fields and coordinates their use in a methodologically explicit fashion."[60] That last point is significant. Interdisciplinarity succeeds only when all parties put their cards on the table and nothing—no presuppositions, normative claims, or hidden agendas—is undeclared.[61]

The mode of interdisciplinary reflection most suited to this particular project is based upon the work of philosophers Calvin Schrag and J. Wentzel van Huyssteen. "Transversal rationality" has developed contemporaneously with the field of practical theology, though it has yet to be robustly applied within practical theology, and it is

---

[59] Mario Midali, *Practical Theology: Historical Development of Its Foundational and Scientific Character* (Roma: LAS, 2000), 239. Midali goes on to warn of the possible dangers of interdisciplinary thinking. Among them is the common struggle of group work: one discipline (or both) often feels the needs to "guard its territory," per se, thus impeding the interdisciplinary progress. An additional problem is that of language: an expert in any given field has a "linguistic tool kit" that allows her to function in her discipline. It is extraordinarily difficult for a theologian to enter another discipline and master the language of that discipline to a working degree. And, of course, the deeper one enters into disciplines and sub-disciplines, the more precise the language required. Finally, Midali warns, the objective demands of interdisciplinary dialogue require, 1) the clarification of all ideological presuppositions, 2) the articulation of the normative claims of the social sciences (even if the sociologist or psychologist claims that his science is morally neutral), 3) study of the distinct ways that theology and the social sciences frame the problems they are attempting to solve, 4) evaluation of each discipline's methods and procedures, and 5) a vigorous debate on the various results achieved by the interdisciplinary work.

[60] Osmer, "Johannes Van Der Ven's Contribution to the New Consensus in Practical Theology," np.

[61] See Appendix D for an essay on other modes of interdisciplinary reflection.

particularly resonant with this project because it "takes seriously the challenge of postmodern thinking to all totalizing, modernist attempts to secure true knowledge though foundationalist strategies" by acknowledging that "knowledge is constructed on the basis of social practices, language, and values that are local and contextual."[62] Being that the emerging church movement originated in an environment with just these postmodern tendencies, transversal rationality makes a fitting approach to a study of the movement.

Schrag has proposed a way to recover the resources of rationality in the face of the postmodern challenge.[63] Postmodern theorists have taken aim at rationality, at least as it has been understood since the Enlightenment; some of the most radical postmodernists have attempted to dispose of rationality altogether. Rationality, it has been claimed, does not truly exist; or if it does exist, it is unattainable. Claims of true knowledge, some postmodernists have claimed, are used to oppress and subjugate others. Schrag, however, argues that the problem of the modern era was that we *overdetermined* the capabilities of rationality.[64] He cautions us not to throw out the baby with the bathwater. Rationality still has a lot to offer—indeed, Schrag proposes that it is rationality itself that allows us to communicate across disciplines.

Van Huyssteen warns against the totalizing features of postmodernist theories, which ultimately acquiesce to multiple rationalities with no way to judge between them. Instead, he suggest that we should look for postfoundational models of rationality:

> Over against the objectivism of foundationalism and the extreme relativism of most forms of nonfoundationalism, a postfoundationalist notion of rationality helps us to acknowledge contextuality, the shaping of a role of tradition and of interpreted experience, while at the same time enabling us to reach out beyond our own groups, communities,

---

[62] Osmer, *The Teaching Ministry of Congregations*, 308.

[63] Calvin O. Schrag, *The Resources of Rationality: A Response to the Postmodern Challenge*, Studies in Continental Thought (Bloomington: Indiana University Press, 1992).

[64] Schrag, *The Resources of Rationality: A Response to the Postmodern Challenge*, 7.

and cultures, in plausible forms of inter-subjective, cross-cultural, and cross-disciplinary conversations.[65]

In other words, a postfoundationalist framework preserves the ability to adjudicate between the many rationalities that confront us in a postmodernist context by refusing to forsake the various elements that human beings draw upon when making decisions between competing paradigms of understanding. And, most significantly for those of us who derive our rationalities from communities of faith, "a postfoundationalist approach to rationality does...allow theology to remain tied to specific communities of faith without being trapped by these communities."[66] Further, van Huyssteen's postfoundationalist approach opens the possibility for understanding divine revelation beyond the fideistic and naturalistic approaches of modernism, freeing the theologian to speak openly of divine disclosure without chilling out dialogue partners from other fields of study.[67]

As a practical theologian, Richard Osmer prefers van Huyssteen's postfoundational approach over a nonfoundational, radically postmodern approach because it acknowledges the resources of rationality that are shared by human beings, it is not bound by rules but operates by rules of art, and it maintains the ability to "move across cultures, domains, and disciplines in terms of transversal reason."[68]

This happens by what Schrag and van Huyssteen call "transversal rationality." As opposed to rationality that functions foundationally, as was claimed during modernity, Schrag proposes that rationality works "transversally"[69] in three dynamic moves: praxial

---

[65] J. Wentzel van Huyssteen, *Alone in the World? Human Uniqueness in Science and Theology* (Grand Rapids, Mich.: Wm. B. Eerdmanns Pub. Co., 2006), 10.

[66] van Huyssteen, *Alone in the World? Human Uniqueness in Science and Theology*, 12.

[67] van Huyssteen, *Alone in the World? Human Uniqueness in Science and Theology*, 17.

[68] Osmer, *The Teaching Ministry of Congregations*, 311.

[69] "The use of the concept/metaphor of tranversality in all of these approaches exhibits interrelated senses of lying across, extending over, intersecting, meeting and converging without achieving coincidence," Schrag, *The Resources of Rationality: A Response to the Postmodern Challenge*, 149.

critique ("the performance of critical discernment"[70]), articulation (the rational moment of discourse, dialogue, and argument), and disclosure (the rational step back to gain referential perspective and maintain openness[71]). Schrag argues that rationality works in such a way that it is a point of connection between diverse disciplines, making interdisciplinary communication possible.

Building on Schrag's thesis, as well as the work of philosophers such as Joseph Rouse, Nicholas Rescher, and Larry Laudan, J. Wentzel van Huyssteen proposes a post-foundational model of relationship between theology and the sciences. Like Schrag, van Huyssteen thinks that the resources of rationality were overdetermined and totalized during the modern period, however he finds the theories of radical postmodernists just as unhelpful. Relying on the work of more moderate postmodernists, van Huyssteen shows how rationality really works in more contextual and pragmatic ways than previously assumed. Whether in scientific or theological research programs, rationality is local, experiential, and communally determined. These "epistemological overlaps" are the dialogue points between theologians and scientists.

As opposed to the correlational and transformational families, little work has been done in relating the transversal/post-foundational model to practical theology. This is sure to change as the promise of this model of interdisciplinary reasoning becomes more prominent. In one of the few examples of how this model might look, Schrag describes the staff of a psychiatric hospital gathering to discuss the treatment of a patient: "There are the administrators, the doctors, the nurses, the assistants to the doctors and nurses, the patients and the families of the patients. All of these groups play some role in the program and process of psychiatric healing. The exercise of decision making, with its multiple rationales, is transversal to the different groups and various social roles that make up the institutional process."[72] With this in mind, hope-

---

[70] J. Wentzel van Huyssteen, *The Shaping of Rationality: Toward Interdisciplinarity in Theology and Science* (Grand Rapids, Mich.: W.B. Eerdmans, 1999), 137.

[71] Schrag, *The Resources of Rationality: A Response to the Postmodern Challenge*, 141.

[72] Schrag, *The Resources of Rationality: A Response to the Postmodern Challenge*, 152.

fully the promise of this method for the practical theologian becomes more apparent.

Having surveyed the various options of interdisciplinarity, it is my proposal that the transversal rationality of van Huyssteen offers the best options for the pastor-theologians of the emerging church movement and the postmodern context in which they do ministry. Since the naissance of the ECM, the pastors who have founded communities of faith have been unabashed about their postmodernist proclivities. And, if anything, postmodernism is characterized by a pastiche of overlapping and even contradictory rationalities. Jean-François Lyotard famously wrote that the postmodern condition is an "incredulity toward metanarratives," [73] and the pastors and parishioners of ECM churches, described in chapter two, struggle between the exclusivistic fideism of conservative evangelicalism and the liberal relativism of mainline Protestantism. The former allows only one story—one rationality—an odious option for ECM practitioners. But the latter seems to have too easily forsaken what it truly unique about Christianity, at least to those in the ECM.

Stephen Conner, commenting on the postmodern condition, writes,

> Jean-François Lyotard's formula for the emergence of postmodernism, the "suspicion of metanarratives," those universal guiding principles and mythologies which once seemed to control, delimit, and interpret all the diverse forms of discursive activity in the world has compelled wide agreement. The postmodern condition, we are told repeatedly, manifests itself in the multiplication of centres of power and activity and the dissolution of every kind of totalizing narrative which claims to govern the whole complex field of social activity and representation. The waning of the cultural authority of the West and its political and intellectual traditions, along with the opening up of the world political scene to cultural and ethnic differences, is another symptom of the modulation of hierarchy into heterarchy, or differences organized into a unified pattern of

---

[73] Jean François Lyotard, *The Postmodern Condition: A Report on Knowledge*, Theory and History of Literature; V. 10 (Minneapolis: University of Minnesota Press, 1984), xxiv.

domination and subordination, as opposed to differences existing alongside each other but without any principle of commonality or order.[74]

Michel Foucault calls the radical incommensurability experienced in the world today "heterotopia."[75] Following Foucault, Connor writes, "We can see the defining characteristic of the postmodern as lying not in a revolution in culture, but in an important readjustment of power relations within and across cultural and critical-academic institutions."[76] The result has been an "explosion of culture," replete with dialectical tensions: the academy is in a "crisis of self-definition,"[77] yet is rapidly expanding;[78] academic disciplines are growing in size and birthing sub-disciplines and sub-sub-disciplines,[79] yet the boundaries between academic fields are blurred or altogether erased;[80] and the breakdown of differentiation between disciplines has fostered more holistic and cross-departmental study,

---

[74] Steven Connor, *Postmodernist Culture: An Introduction to Theories of the Contemporary* (Oxford: Basil Blackwell, 1989), 8.

[75] Connor, *Postmodernist Culture: An Introduction to Theories of the Contemporary*, 8.

[76] Connor, *Postmodernist Culture: An Introduction to Theories of the Contemporary*, 11.

[77] Connor, *Postmodernist Culture: An Introduction to Theories of the Contemporary*, 17.

[78] Connor, *Postmodernist Culture: An Introduction to Theories of the Contemporary*, 13.

[79] Conner provides this example: "Elderly academics might smite their brows at the appearance of yet another newsletter devoted simply to listing every new article on sea-imagery in Shakespeare, but the fiction that such publications were only second-order phenomena, which had little to do with real critical judgment, could not last long in the face of the growing apprehension that the subject had come to consist in this self-referential activity of listing and mapping, generating gaps in order that they might be closed, but always leaving the possibility of more work, a different approach, another application," Connor, *Postmodernist Culture: An Introduction to Theories of the Contemporary*, 13.

[80] Connor, *Postmodernist Culture: An Introduction to Theories of the Contemporary*, 16.

yet the entire academic enterprise is becoming more operational-ized.[81] Ultimately, this has led to a period of increasing *sublimity*:

> What is particular to postmodern theory...is the desire to project and to produce that which cannot be pinned down or mastered by representation or conceptual thought, the desire to which has been identified by Jean-François Lyotard as the pull towards the sublime...Here, will and surrender, mastery and renunciation spiral together in an indissoluble helix which is itself another version of the set towards the sublime. Such a theory asserts its legitimacy through the forms of its discrediting, unmakes and decentres itself only to produce suppler forms of authoritative discourse. Postmodern theory yields the vision of a cultural "heterotopia" which has no edges, hierarchies or center, but is nevertheless always framed by the theory that wills it into being, a theory that, in its authoritative disavowal of authority, prevents it everywhere, in a pervading inclusiveness, or "perclusion."[82]

It is in this very heterotopic setting that ECM pastors have set out to establish new faith communities, often unhinged from existing denominations. And, among the detritus of the formerly dominant Constantinian Christianity, these pastors are drawing from the multiple and overlapping rationalities of their congregants' lives. Tim Keel, of Jacob's Well in Kansas City, writes of his love of *Wired* Magazine. Doug Pagitt, of Solomon's Porch in Minneapolis, leads a home group study of quantum physics. Brad Cecil, of Axxess in Arlington, Texas, trains his staff in the philosophy of Richard Rorty. Nanette Sawyer of Wicker Park-Grace in Chicago curates art exhibits in her church. Each of these has artfully looked for transversal connections between the theological and ecclesial rationalities in which they were trained in seminary and various rationalities in their own heterotopic churches.

---

[81] Connor, *Postmodernist Culture: An Introduction to Theories of the Contemporary*, 15.

[82] Connor, *Postmodernist Culture: An Introduction to Theories of the Contemporary*, 17.

The ECM is, no doubt, one of the first ecclesial responses to the advent of postmodernist culture. What remains to be seen, when investigating eight ECM churches and their core practices, is whether the ECM's response to the sublimity of the postmodern condition is theologically and ecclesially tenable.

Chapter Two: An Inside Look at Eight Emerging Churches

The Changes in American Protestantism Leading to the Emerging Church Movement

The first seeds of what would become the emerging church movement were sown in American Protestantism in the mid-1990s. By that time, American evangelicalism was deep in the throes of the "seeker sensitive" church. Pioneered by celebrity pastors Bill Hybels of Willow Creek Community Church in South Barrington, Illinois and Rick Warren of Saddleback Community Church in Orange County, California, seeker sensitive churches tended to be "megachurches" that were focused on reaching suburban Baby Boomers.[1] The *modus operandi* of the seeker movement was to make church relevant to the experiences of suburban Baby Boomers, and to lure back to church the "seekers" of that generation who had left the church during their college years.[2] Evangelical churches undertook this task by employing the same marketing strategies and even ar-

---

[1] "The conventional definition of a megachurch is based on Protestant congregations that share several distinctive characteristics: 2,000 or more persons in attendance at weekly worship; a charismatic senior minister; a seven-day-a-week congregational community; and multiple social and outreach activities. In 1970 there about ten such churches in the United States this figure grew to 250 by 1990, and by 2005 there were more than 1,200." Paul L. Knox, *Metroburbia, USA* (New Brunswick, NJ: Rutgers University Press, 2008).

[2] "A seeker church is one that tailors its programs and services to attract those who are not church members." Kimon Howland Sargeant, *Seeker Churches: Promoting Traditional Religion in a Nontraditional Way* (New Brunswick, N.J.: Rutgers University Press, 2000), 2.

chitectural patterns of suburban shopping malls.[3] Everything in the seeker church was meant to be inoffensive, to offer a "wide front door" in an attempt to make church palatable to the Baby Boomers, many of whom had been turned off to church and religion during the 1960s and 1970s.

Although it achieved great success among Baby Boomers, seeker sensitive churches had more difficulty attracting GenXers.[4] By the mid-1990s, the evangelical foundation Leadership Network was convening consultations of seeker church leaders to address the problem of missing GenXers.[5] While the Baby Boomers generally came back to church with the birth of children and the purchase of homes in the suburbs, GenXers were not following the same pattern.

Sociologists Richard Flory and Donald E. Miller have looked extensively at the uniquenesses of religious practice among the post-Baby Boomer generations. In their first book, *GenX Religion*, they conclude that, in contrast to the religion of Baby Boomers, the religion of GenXers is

> experiential;
>
> entrepreneurial;
>
> communal;
>
> race-, ethnic-, and gender-inclusive;

---

[3] "The seeker church practice of emulating 'the shopping mall' does not delineate one fixed program for attracting seekers and achieving growth but instead represents a particular ideology of outreach that justifies an innovative, seeker strategy...the ideology of the shopping mall church expresses two related notions about the moral order. First, it expresses the idea that religion has become a privatized, consumer good... Second, the ideology of the shopping mall church not only *describes* the preferences of religious consumers but also *prescribes* how churches should respond to these preferences— churches should aim to have the best product available that conforms with the expectations fostered by today's religious environment." Sargeant, *Seeker Churches: Promoting Traditional Religion in a Nontraditional Way*, 131.

[4] "GenXers are the 80 million Americans who were born between 1961 and 1981." Richard W. Flory and Donald E. Miller, *Gen X Religion* (New York: Routledge, 2000), 3.

[5] Jones, *The New Christians: Dispatches from the Emergent Frontier*, 41.

and insistent on "authenticity in how one approaches one's religious beliefs."[6]

In their second book, *Finding Faith*, Flory and Miller delve even more deeply into "the spiritual quest of the post-boomer generation," noting four overriding influences in the burgeoning spirituality of the post-boomer generations. First, most GenXers were reared by Baby Boomers, a generation deeply impressed by the societal upheavals of the 1960s. The Boomers, influenced by the Civil Rights Movement, the Vietnam War, and the Sexual Revolution, parented in such a way as to undermine their children's sense of traditional lines of authority. This, in turn, has led to a weakening of the ties between GenXers and the denominations that have controlled American Protestantism until very recently. Second, "the world has become a global village." The cultural heterogeneity that is fostered by revolutions in communication, media, travel, and the like have "democratized" access to information.[7]

Moreover, post-Boomers tend to exhibit a growing distrust of large-scale institutions, brought on not only by the ethical failures in corporate America, but also by the headline-grabbing moral failures in institutional Christianity. Finally, the advent of postmodern patterns of thought have undermined religions' claims of universal truth and absolute moral certitude and placed them instead on the shifting sands of "whatever."[8]

Flory and Miller develop a four-part taxonomy of responses to the spiritual and ecclesial practices of the GenXers.[9] The "Innovators...represent a constantly evolving, or *innovating*, approach to religious and spiritual beliefs and practices."[10] The "Appropriators"

---

[6] Flory and Miller, *Gen X Religion*, 234-41.

[7] Flory and Miller, *Finding Faith: The Spiritual Quest of the Post-Boomer Generation*, 7-8.

[8] Flory and Miller, *Finding Faith: The Spiritual Quest of the Post-Boomer Generation*, 9-10.

[9] Flory and Miller, *Finding Faith: The Spiritual Quest of the Post-Boomer Generation*.

[10] Flory and Miller, *Finding Faith: The Spiritual Quest of the Post-Boomer Generation*, 14.

seek to make church relevant to young adult generations by appropriating cultural trends, including music, clothing, and technology. The "Resisters" attempt to undermine the influence of postmodern trends by focusing on rational belief and the written texts of Christianity. And the "Reclaimers" are those whose response to the postmodern situation is to reclaim traditional and ancient forms of Christianity including liturgy.[11] It is into the first category that Flory and Miller place the emerging church, though, as we will see below, the influence of "reclaiming" is also very influential within the movement.

After describing some of the same churches, authors, and networks that will be described below, Flory and Miller describe the ethos of the Innovators as a group of Christians who are "disillusioned or dissatisfied with the form of Christianity they have received," and thus, "seeking a more holistic approach to faith that combines both the cognitive and a greater sense experience of the divine," they are "almost completely uninterested in rational, propositional expressions of their faith."[12] Noting that the Innovators are "solidly middle class," Flory and Miller argue that the critical faculties learned in college and graduate studies enable the Innovators to reflect critically on the patterns and institutions of Christian life inherited by their generation.[13] In this way, the Innovators offer the most radical break from Baby Boomer and Seeker Church Protestantism:

> These groups, whether newer "emerging" churches or more established ones, frame their approach in contrast to what they see as an overly institutionalized and inwardly focused church, seeking instead one that is focused on building

---

[11] Flory and Miller, *Finding Faith: The Spiritual Quest of the Post-Boomer Generation*, 14-15.

[12] Flory and Miller, *Finding Faith: The Spiritual Quest of the Post-Boomer Generation*, 36.

[13] Flory and Miller note that, contrary to James Davidson Hunter and other sociologists, advanced education among Innovators has not led "to a secularization of their beliefs, but to a more involved, critically engaged faith." Flory and Miller, *Finding Faith: The Spiritual Quest of the Post-Boomer Generation*, 37-38. Cf. James Davison Hunter, *Evangelicalism: The Coming Generation* (Chicago: University of Chicago Press, 1987).

community, both within the religious group and with the surrounding community, and engaged in various ways with the larger culture. These churches are innovating in terms of their responses to the larger culture, introducing forms of ritual and symbol into their worship services and creating new forms of religious life that emphasize community and belonging, as well as service both within the church and to the larger community.[14]

From their observations, Flory and Miller identify the signature characteristics of Innovator churches: "First, there is a prevalence of visual representations and expressions of the sacred; second, most of these congregations tend to be small in size and high in commitment; third, there is a general disinterest in established forms of religion; and fourth, there is both an inward experience and an outward expression of the spiritual."[15]

They go on to conclude that the Innovators occupy a precarious position in American Protestantism, for they seem to face the possibilities of either becoming co-opted by institutionalized Christianity or fading from influence. To occupy a middle ground between these two, it seems, is unlikely, a conclusion with which I will concur in chapter five. The emerging church movement, just as Flory and Miller note, will have a hard time standing on its own without ultimately coming under the patronage of mainline denominations.

The characteristics of the Innovators—and the other post-Baby Boomer categories—mark a clear difference from the seminal studies of Baby Boomer spirituality. In *After Heaven*, Robert Wuthnow writes that, whereas their parents reacted to the uncertainties of world wars by "clinging to safe, respectable houses of worship in which a domesticated God could be counted on to provide reassurance," the Baby Boomers, "having learned that they could move around, think through their options, and select a faith that truly captured what they believed to be the truth, took the choice seriously, bargaining with their souls, seeking new spiritual guides, and rediscovering that God dwells not only in homes but also in the byways

---

[14] Flory and Miller, *Finding Faith: The Spiritual Quest of the Post-Boomer Generation*, 39.

[15] Flory and Miller, *Finding Faith: The Spiritual Quest of the Post-Boomer Generation*, 39-40.

trod by pilgrims and sojourners."[16] Christian Smith writes that evangelicals in the late twentieth century "operate with a very strong sense of boundaries that distinguish themselves from non-Christians and from nonevangelical Christians."[17] These are just two ways that the spirituality of the generation preceding the emerging church movement is both distinct from but also anticipatory of that which is developing within the ECM: GenX Christians, too, consider their religious life to be full of options, oftentimes even beyond the confines of Christianity; and they see the role of their religion to be more intimately involved with culture than separate from it.

Whereas the religion of Baby Boomers is surely different than their parents' and grandparents' religion, seen, for instance, in the growth of evangelical suburban mega-churches and the demise of urban mainline churches, the differences between Baby Boomers and GenXers may be even more prominent. Richard Osmer has argued that, of late, "generational discontinuity has become more pronounced; that is, the values, beliefs, and life experiences of youth are often quite different from those of their parents and grandparents."[18] In times of cultural upheaval like the current advent of postmodernism and globalization, Osmer writes, the cultural rift between children and parents widens. Youth look specifically for patterns of life that will differentiate them from their parents and grandparents, and parents and grandparents often retrench in older cultural habits as a guard against the new and unknown. While Osmer's observations seem accurate when discussing GenXers and their parents, Millenials—now in their twenties—do not seem to exhibit the same level of generational discontinuity with their parents.[19]

The birth of the emerging church movement in the 1990s can be seen in this context. As pastors and laypersons in their twenties, they began reconsidering the forms of church in which they were

---

[16] Robert Wuthnow, *After Heaven: Spirituality in America since the 1950s* (Berkeley: University of California Press, 1998), 57.

[17] Christian Smith, *American Evangelicalism: Embattled and Thriving* (Chicago, Ill.: University of Chicago Press, 1998), 124.

[18] Osmer, *The Teaching Ministry of Congregations*, 180.

[19] Smith and Snell, *Souls in Transition: The Religious and Spiritual Lives of Emerging Adults.*

raised in the 1970s and 1980s—"In contrast to seeker-sensitive or purpose-driven church models that ask a tactical question, 'How can we present the gospel more effectively in our contemporary culture?' emerging churches ask an existential question, 'What should the people of God look like in this culture?'"[20] As a result, some GenXers who were raised in suburban mega-churches are regentrifying abandoned urban churches; and some who were raised in mainline denominational settings are joining local, autonomous congregations. This is, of course, concurrent with many other shifts that have broadened the generational rift between GenXers and their parents, including the technology/computing revolution and the well-documented change in saving and spending habits.

Christian Smith, however, disagrees with Osmer on this point. In *Soul Searching* and *Souls in Transition*, Smith ultimately concludes that the religion of teens in America is essentially conventional.[21] Instead of rebelling against their parents' religious practices, adolescents generally practice (or do not practice) religion in a very similar pattern to their parents.[22] It is my contention that both Osmer and Smith are correct. Based on the National Study of Youth and Religion, Smith's conclusions are based upon the majority of responses among teens and emerging adults. However, the ECM has been instigated primarily by individuals who fit into the "creative class." That is, if Smith's conclusions represent the religious lives of the two standard deviations in the middle of the Bell Curve of American religion, the ECM leaders and congregants are drawn primarily from the "innovators" and "early adopters"—those most likely to create and embrace ecclesial innovations.[23]

---

[20] Lee and Sinitiere, *Holy Mavericks: Evangelical Innovators and the Spiritual Marketplace*, 86.

[21] Christian Smith, *Soul Searching: The Religious and Spiritual Lives of American Teenagers* (Oxford: Oxford Press, 2005). Smith and Snell, *Souls in Transition: The Religious and Spiritual Lives of Emerging Adults*. See also Kenda Creasy Dean, *Almost Christian : What the Faith of Our Teenagers Is Telling the American Church* (Oxford ; New York: Oxford University Press, 2010).

[22] Smith, *Soul Searching: The Religious and Spiritual Lives of American Teenagers*, 68.

[23] Everett M. Rogers, *Diffusion of Innovations*, 5th ed. (New York ; London: Free Press, 2003), 272ff.

This is also in line with what Richard Florida has dubbed the "rise of the Creative Class."[24] "The Creative Class," Florida writes, "consists of people who add economic value through their creativity. It thus includes many knowledge workers, symbolic analysts and professional and technical workers... The distinguishing characteristic of the Creative Class is that its members engage in work whose function is to 'create meaningful new forms.'"[25] As opposed to the traditional Marxian metric of a class by whether they control the means of production or how much property they own, Florida argues that the property of the Creative Class is intangible, "because it is literally in their heads."[26] The Creative Class contributes to the economy by creating *meaning*.

In the early days of the ECM, leaders verbally associated themselves with Florida's thesis, considering their tribe to be the Creative Class among younger American Protestants. Florida defines the "highest form of creative work as producing new forms or designs that are readily transferable and widely useful,"[27] and this is exactly what the church leaders described below have attempted to do when experimenting with new ecclesial forms, be it leadership, preaching, or the Lord's Supper. When seen thusly, one can concur with Smith's position on the religious conventionality of most younger Americans, but also affirm that, among the most innovative and creative members of the younger generations, a sense of generational discontinuity has fostered their development of the ECM.

The other major difference between Smith's conclusions and mine is sample. In both of Smith's studies, he undertook a broad,

---

[24] Richard L. Florida, *The Rise of the Creative Class: And How It's Transforming Work, Leisure, Community and Everyday Life* (New York, NY: Basic Books, 2002). In his more recent book, Florida argues that his thesis holds in spite of the economic collapse. Richard L. Florida, *The Great Reset : How New Ways of Living and Working Drive Post-Crash Prosperity* (New York: Harper, 2010).

[25] Florida, *The Rise of the Creative Class: And How It's Transforming Work, Leisure, Community and Everyday Life*, 68.

[26] Florida, *The Rise of the Creative Class: And How It's Transforming Work, Leisure, Community and Everyday Life*, 68.

[27] Florida, *The Rise of the Creative Class: And How It's Transforming Work, Leisure, Community and Everyday Life*, 69.

random sample of teenage and emerging adult Americans, and thereby arrived at his thesis of religious conventionality among these populations. My survey, on the other hand, is much more narrowly focused. Only those who have self-selected these unconventional ecclesial communities are included. Therefore, the people that I interviewed are much more likely to articulate the kind of generational discontinuity that Osmer describes than the religious conventionality that Smith found.

Developments in the 1990s—Three Phases of the Emerging Church Movement

With a strong foothold in the suburbs, evangelical mega-churches were thriving in the 1990s. But a contingent of the most influential mega-church pastors had noticed a trend that, in their opinion, GenXers were not following the Baby Boomer pattern of dropping out of church in college, only to rejoin church when they married, settled in the suburbs, and had children. Whether this was actually a trend among Baby Boomers is disputed, but it was at least the assumption of these suburban mega-church pastors. GenXers raised in the church were indeed dropping out of their parents' churches in college, if not before,[28] but they were not coming back to church in their twenties. Reasons for their exodus from the church vary, but one recent study suggests that when the evangelical church wed itself to conservative politics, it attracted Baby Boomers but left GenXers and Millennials feeling disaffected.[29] Still other GenXers didn't need to drop out of church, because they hadn't been reared in the church to begin with—it was common among the aforementioned group of pastors to refer to the GenXers as the "first unchurched generation" in America.

Some mega-church pastors turned to evangelical college ministries like Campus Crusade for Christ and InterVarsity Christian

---

[28] In fact, studies show that most Americans drop out of church during their junior and senior years in high school. Cf. Carol E. Lytch, *Choosing Church: What Makes a Difference for Teens*, 1st ed. (Louisville, Ky.: Westminster John Knox Press, 2004).

[29] Robert D. Putnam, David E. Campbell, and Shaylyn Romney Garrett, *American Grace: How Religion Divides and Unites Us* (New York, NY: Simon & Schuster, 2010).

Fellowship for help in understanding the younger generations,[30] while others turned to a prominent evangelical foundation in Dallas, Leadership Network. In 1997, Leadership Network hired Doug Pagitt away from Wooddale Church, a nationally prominent evangelical church in Minnesota, to form a "Young Leaders Network." This new group was meant to answer the "postmodern problem," namely, that relativism, increasing in American culture, was inhibiting the matriculation of GenXers into church (particularly into suburban mega-churches). For two years, Pagitt toured the country, acting as a talent scout, looking for what he considered the most innovative GenX pastors. What he formed became the nucleus of the leadership of the ECM. Pagitt and company also organized multiple conferences that brought national recognition to the group, and they published many of their ideas in the popular newsletters of Leadership Network.[31] While his background was in evangelicalism, Pagitt also looked within the mainline, and early events of the Young Leaders Network boasted the rising stars of evangelicalism alongside young United Methodist and American Baptist clergy. These were the primary achievements of the *first phase* of the emerging church movement in the United States.[32]

But tensions arose early between the Young Leaders Network and the parent organization, Leadership Network. While the latter did work with mainline Protestant denominational churches, its staff was composed of committed evangelicals. Meanwhile, the group of twenty or so who coordinated the Young Leaders Network was ex-

---

[30] One of the first books in this category was by InterVarsity staff member Jimmy Long, *Generating Hope: A Strategy for Reaching the Postmodern Generation* (Downers Grove, Ill.: InterVarsity Press, 1997).

[31] Jones, *The New Christians: Dispatches from the Emergent Frontier*, 41-48.

[32] The ECM, as defined herein, is the American version of a movement within Western, Protestant Christianity that has iterations in many other Western countries. For interviews with both American and British leaders, see Gibbs and Bolger, *Emerging Churches: Creating Christian Community in Postmodern Cultures*. Also see Garrison, *Rising from the Ashes: Rethinking Church*. And for a British perspective on the "emerging" forms of worship, see Jonny Baker, Doug Gay, and Jenny Brown, *Alternative Worship: Resources from and for the Emerging Church* (Grand Rapids: Baker Books, 2004). While substantive, the emerging movements within continental Europe, Australia, New Zealand and elsewhere have yet to be thoroughly studied.

ploring the works of post-liberal theologians (e.g., Rodney Clapp, Stanley Hauerwas, George Lindbeck, Nancey Murphy, and Hans Frei) as well as some of the most radical, deconstructivist postmodern philosophers (e.g., Jacques Derrida, Richard Rorty, John D. Caputo, and Jean Baudrillard), and this didn't sit well with some of Leadership Network's constituency. Among the Baby Boomers gathered by Leadership Network, there was an agreed upon convention that conversations were meant to tackle issues of practice in the church, but divisive issues of theology were avoided. Politeness was the rule. At public events, the content of the addresses by the Young Leaders was not only increasingly odious to Leadership Network, but the tone of the young leaders was often abrasive, purposefully meant to "deconstruct" what they saw as the ills of the modern, evangelical church. This, too, discomfited many in Leadership Network who had cultivated a more gentlemanly approach to ecclesial affairs.[33]

By the time that Pagitt left Leadership Network to plant a church (Solomon's Porch) in Minneapolis, the parting of the ways had begun. Several attempts were made to salvage the relationship between Leadership Network and the young leaders, then known as "Terra Nova," but none succeeded. Brian McLaren's bestselling book, *A New Kind of Christian*, was released under an imprint of Leadership Network in 2001, and that was the last official partnership between Leadership Network and the founding members of the ECM.[34]

The release and success of McLaren's book, concurrent with the severing of the ties with Leadership Network, represent the beginning of the next chapter of the emerging church movement. A fictional dialogue between a burned-out evangelical pastor and a postmodern charismatic Episcopal layman, *A New Kind of Christian* has sold over 100,000 copies,[35] garnered a cover story in *The Chris-*

---

[33] I mean that quite literally. Leadership Network was heavily dominated by men, reflective of its evangelical origins. It also cultivated an atmosphere in which civility was at a premium, and the members of the Young Leaders Network often did not abide by this.

[34] McLaren, *A New Kind of Christian: A Tale of Two Friends on a Spiritual Journey.*

[35] Bird, "Emerging Church Movement."

tian Century,[36] and provoked a less-than-charitable review in *Christianity Today* that claimed, "The old kind of Christian is the best hope for church renewal."[37] McLaren's name quickly became synonymous with the newest appellation for the group, "Emergent Village," a name chosen in 2001 after the official break from Leadership Network. Contemporaneously, the leaders of Emergent Village were approached by Mark Oestreicher, publisher at Youth Specialties, and offered a publishing partnership. Oestreicher's offer was based on the fact that the members of the Young Leaders Network had a rising profile within evangelicalism, and they seemed to be the natural outgrowth of the pioneering youth ministry of the 1970s that provoked Mike Yaconelli and Wayne Rice to found Youth Specialties. The offer was accepted, Emergent Village incorporated as a 501(c)(3) non-profit corporation, and the movement entered its *second phase.*

Lasting from approximately 2001 until 2008, the second phase of the ECM was noteworthy for its rise in prominence within evangelicalism. In partnership with Youth Specialties, Emergent Village released a dozen books during this period and hosted national conventions in 2003, 2004, and 2005 that were attended by thousands of pastors. Brian McLaren was given a regular column in *Leadership*, a Christianity Today International periodical, and his books were analyzed in a series of articles in the parent publication. Another article, this time highlighting Doug Pagitt and Solomon's Porch, appeared on the cover of the *New York Times* in 2004, [38] and Tim Keel and Jacob's Well appeared on the *Christian Century*'s cover in 2006.[39] International speaking engagements followed for many of the leaders of Emergent Village, as well as those tangen-

---

[36] Jason Byassee, "New Kind of Christian: An Emergent Voice," *Christian Century*, November 30 2004.

[37] Mark Galli, "The Long View: The Virtue of Unoriginality," *Christianity Today*, April 1 2002.

[38] John Leland, "Hip New Churches Sway to a Different Drummer," *New York Times*, February 18 2004.

[39] Jason Byassee, "Emerging Model: A Visit to Jacob's Well," *Christian Century*, September 19 2006.

tially connected to the movement. Emergent Village formalized its structure, adding a half-time, paid national coordinator in 2006.[40]

But the second phase of the emerging church movement also included the beginnings of a rift in the movement. Bloggers began to debate the terms "emerging" versus "emergent" as personal and ecclesial qualifiers, the former becoming the preferred appellation of those who mixed traditional, evangelical theology with innovative methodology, and the latter signifying allegiance to Emergent Village and a more progressive theology. Prominent Reformed pastor Mark Driscoll left Emergent Village and began speaking out against the group, and the publications of Christianity Today International took a generally negative view of the books and ideas coming out from Emergent Village leaders.

But just as evangelicals were moving away from the ECM, many mainline Protestants were discovering it. Groups such as Presbymergent, Anglimergent, and Luthermergent developed, respectively, within the Presbyterian Church (USA), the Episcopal Church, and the Evangelical Lutheran Church in America denominations. These mainline iterations of the emerging church had already been introduced to missional theology by some in their midst, and they found new affinities with the emerging church movement. Some in the mainline were attracted to emerging church leaders because of their ability to attract younger members, while others appreciated the post-evangelical and post-liberal theology and the social justice engagement of the movement. Brian McLaren, though dis-invited from some evangelical speaking engagements,[41] became a regular on the mainline circuit, speaking at numerous presbytery, synod, and diocesan assemblies.

As of this writing, the emerging church movement is entering what can be considered its *third phase*. The position of national coordinator was eliminated by Emergent Village,[42] and the entire board of directors voluntarily resigned, passing the leadership of the orga-

---

[40] I was the national coordinator of Emergent Village from 2006-2008.

[41] "Mclaren Talk Canceled by Kentucky Baptists," *Christian Century*, March 22 2005.

[42] Brandon O'Brian, "Emergent's Divergence: Leaders Hope Decentralizing Power Will Revitalize the Movement," *Christianity Today*, January, 2009 2008.

nization to a new, younger crop of leaders (notably, a group largely without book contracts and public speaking careers). McLaren has signed a major, two-book deal with secular publisher, HarperOne, the first book of which is entitled, *A New Kind of Christianity: Ten Questions that Are Transforming the Faith.*[43]   And Doug Pagitt has announced his plans to run for the Minnesota state legislature. Some critics see this as the dénouement of the ECM, while others see it as a continuing threat to evangelicalism. Meanwhile, advocates tend to believe that emergent thinking has woven itself into the very fabric of American Protestantism, making it less noticeable, but just as powerful, as a movement. For instance, at the close of 2009, high profile blogger Andrew Jones announced that, after twenty years, the ECM was no longer radical, writing,

> 2009 marks the year when the emerging church suddenly and decisively ceased to be a radical and controversial movement in global Christianity. In many places around

---

[43] Brian McLaren, *A New Kind of Christianity: Ten Questions That Are Transforming the Faith* (San Francisco: HarperOne, 2010). The ten questions are:

1. Narrative – What is the shape of the biblical narrative?

2. Authority – How is the Bible authoritative?

3. God – Is God violent? How do we deal with violent Bible passages?

4. Jesus – Why is he important?

5. Gospel – What is the Gospel? Do Jesus and Paul have the same one?

6. Church – What do we do about the church?

7. Sexuality – How do we deal with sexual issues – including, but not limited to, homosexuality?

8. Eschatology – Can we find a better vision for the future?

9. Pluralism – How should followers of Jesus relate to people of other religions?

10. What-do-we-do-now? How do we continue these conversations without killing each other?

the world, the movement has already been either adopted, adapted, or made redundant through the traditional church catching up or duplicating [emerging church] efforts. In some countries there have been strategic partnerships during 2009 or a significant rethinking process that has led to a new level of maturity, a sense of completion, or an re-evaluation of original vision and current practises [sic].

In 2009, the emerging church either grew up, stopped being offensive, switched gear from experimental to normal, became the new mainstream, or a bit of each.[44]

Being an evangelical, however, Jones may be blind to the current radicality of the ECM among mainline groups, mentioned above as indicative of the third phase of the movement. Further, every year sees new books published from within conservative evangelicalism, meant to attack and discredit the ECM.[45] So it seems that the ECM is still a hotly debated topic on both sides of American Protestantism. And even in Catholicism there is growing interest, led by Fr. Richard Rohr, a Jesuit priest who founded the Center for Action and Contemplation and was, in 2010, on a speaking tour called, "The Emerging Church," in which he linked the movement with the non-dualistic thinking in Catholic mysticism. The ECM's relevance to church life in America has certainly evolved over the past decade, as any movement must, but it is arguably still one of the most potent reform movements within the modern church.

Empirical Research Method

In order to proffer an inside look at the emerging church movement, I will now take a closer look at eight congregations that have been closely linked to the movement. Studying these churches—both the people who populate them and the practices that animate the congregations—will provide insight into the movement,

---

[44] Andrew Jones, "Emerging Church Movement (1989 - 2009)?," in TallSkinnyKiwi.com. 2009. Accessed January 5, 2010.

[45] For example, John S. Bohannon, *Preaching and the Emerging Church: An Examination of Four Founding Leaders: Mark Driscoll, Dan Kimball, Brian Mclaren, and Doug Pagitt* (Clarksville, Virginia: CreateSpace 2010).

insight that will ultimately lead us to conclusions about where the movement can go from here, and what role the movement plays in the broader landscape of American Protestantism. While the conclusions I will draw from the data from these eight churches is not necessarily generalizable across all of American Protestantism—or even across the emerging church movement—it is reflective of the movement in many respects.

The eight congregations were chosen based on an array of criteria: their reputation as representative of the emerging church movement, the presence of the founding pastor,[46] the personal identification of the pastor and the congregation with the ECM, and the willingness of the congregation's leadership to be involved in the study. These congregations also demonstrate many of the characteristics of Flory and Miller's categories of "Innovators" and "expressive communalism."

I made contact with the churches' leadership in the autumn of 2004 by email and began visiting the churches during that semester. Between October, 2004 and May, 2006, I visited, in this order, Cedar Ridge Community Church in Spencerville, Maryland, Solomon's Porch in Minneapolis, Minnesota, House of Mercy in St. Paul, Minnesota, Journey in Dallas, Texas, Pathways Church in Denver, Colorado, Church of the Apostles in Seattle, Washington, Jacob's Well in Kansas City, Missouri, and Vintage Faith Church in Santa Cruz, California.

This research draws on the principles and methods of phenomenological research, which accords with both the Gadamerian hermeneutic and the transversal methodology discussed in chapter one. Phenomenology, broadly conceived, is the branch of philosophy concerned with the intuitive experience of phenomena as it is consciously perceived by human beings. From the first-person point-of-view, human beings structure their experiences of objects in reality by imputing the phenomena they experience with meaning. Thus, phenomenology is the study of how, why, and in what way human beings, as subjects, experience the world. The point of phenomenological research is to identify specific phenomena as they are experienced, interpreted, and articulated by the individual actor—to look

---

[46] This changed at Journey Church in Dallas. Between the time I made initial contact and arrived for the site visit, the founding pastor, Scott Gornto, resigned and was replaced by Danielle Shroyer.

for transversal connections.[47]   This is an exclusively qualitative mode of research, and, regardless of the sample size, results are not necessarily generalizable. Thus, all conclusions based on the research are made provisionally.

On the other hand, phenomenological research recognizes the subjectivity—and, therefore, inevitable bias—of both the researcher and the subject of the research. A phenomenological method allows me, as a proponent of the emerging church movement, to also act as a researcher of the movement, assuming that I can recognize and account for my own biases and attempt to bracket my predispositions insofar as I am consciously able. In fact, phenomenological research actually thrives on a sympathetic researcher, for the success of focus group and individual interviews is somewhat reliant upon the researcher developing a rapport with the interviewees. Since the goal of phenomenological research is the unmasking of conventional interpretations of experience in order to uncover a depth of information, empathetic interviewing is particularly useful.[48]   Thus, phenomenological research is a particularly useful tool for the practical theologian who wants to embed research in her project. That is because practical theological projects are often concerned with the spiritual lives and practices of persons and communities with whom the theologian is sympathetic. With phenomenological method, these sympathies do not preclude useful and honest research conclusions.[49]

---

[47] "The empirical phenomenological approach involves a return to experience in order to obtain comprehensive descriptions that provide the basis for a reflective structural analysis that portrays the essences of the experience." Clark E. Moustakas, *Phenomenological Research Methods* (Thousand Oaks, Calif.: Sage, 1994), 13.

[48] Indeed, I have found this to be the case. My standing as an advocate of these churches have put the parishioners at ease, especially since they are aware of the vocal critics of the emerging church movement in print and in blogs. Much of their initial defensiveness is overcome within the first moments of the interview.

[49] Phenomenological research methods are particularly helpful at bringing the experiences and interpretations of individuals to the foreground, thus challenging normative, institutional, and "official" articulations of reality. So, done well, phenomenological research can give a voice to the voiceless. This aspect also makes phenomenological methodology appropriate for investigation of a group that stands decidedly outside of the traditional ecclesial institutions.

My initial research question was not all that different from many who study the faithful in America: Who are you and why do you go to this church? From there, I asked a question that pushed closer to the heart of my research: What are the core practices that set this church apart (from the other faith communities in your area)? And from there I pressed toward my true research question: *What are the core characteristics—theological and practical—of these emerging churches?*

My line of questioning in focus groups and individual interviews generally followed this pattern:

Who are you? (What do you do? How do you want to define yourself?)

What brought you to this church? (How did you find out about it? What got you in the door the first time?)

What kept you at this church? (Why didn't you keep looking after you visited here?)

By the time I had gotten through those questions, the interviewees were usually talking very openly and candidly about the characteristics of their church. Often, they were compelled to visit and to stay by some of the same factors, which inevitably generated a robust discussion in a focus group. Having heard their answers, I reflected back some of what I've heard, using key words that I'd jotted down, and then I would ask: "Some attributes of this church have emerged over the last hour, characteristics that you all seem to agree on. So, with that in mind, *what are the things that this church does that inculcate these attributes in the community?*" This final question, of course, got them talking about the core practices of the church without necessarily using the somewhat esoteric language of "practice" (although I did, at times, use that word).[50]

The following are descriptions of my research at the eight congregations, in the order in which I visited them. I have given a bit of the history of each church, as well as some subjective reportage about the look and feel of their worship services and physical locations.

---

[50] My working definition of "practice" is developed below.

Cedar Ridge Community Church, Spencerville, Maryland[51]

Located just outside the Washington, D.C. Beltway, one passes the Idara Jaferia Islamic Community Center, the Kali (Hindu) Temple, a large shopping mall and several strip malls, and a hodge-podge of residences and small farms on the way to Cedar Ridge Community Church. Beautiful Community Korean Church is on the way, as is St. Paul United Methodist, the marquee of which reads, "Spiritually Empty? Stop In For Fill Up." A maze of new road construction and improvement surrounds the church as farms continue to give way to subdivisions and townhomes.

Cedar Ridge, however, maintains the farm aesthetic. "The Barn" is just that—an old barn refurbished to house classrooms and offices. It is clearly visible from the road, as is the farm's original brick silo, built in 1890. The church sits on 63 acres of rolling grass and backs onto a protected reservoir. The church has recently begun a community farming project on part of the land.

The worship building, on the other hand, is utterly non-distinct. From the outside it is a pre-manufactured, aluminum-sided brown building.[52] Just inside the doors is a smallish common area with bagels, coffee, and a welcome desk. Small classrooms ring the sanctuary. Inside the sanctuary, heavy, metal cushioned chairs are arranged in a U around a thrust stage. On the thrust stands a simple Advent wreath made of wrought iron and a simple table with a plain, two-and-a-half foot high cross on top of it. Behind, on the main stage, is an array of band equipment, bookended by lighted Christmas trees. The primary colors in the room are maroon and gold, with a non-descript industrial carpeting on the floor. Around the exterior walls are prayer/communion stations, each with lighted candles, and back in the middle, unlighted votive candles ring the thrust.

---

[51] Research visit on December 12, 2004.

[52] This surprised me, since Pastor Brian McLaren is known for his love of the visual arts and his advocacy for their use in churches. He explained to me that at the time that the worship space was being built, the leadership of the congregation—himself included—was most influenced by Willow Creek Community Church and the seeker-sensitive movement that emanated from that church. That movement, McLaren told me, encouraged church architecture that was more in keeping with the design of shopping malls than traditional church buildings.

The high, industrial ceiling is a cross between a cathedral and a gymnasium. Windows around the top of the sanctuary walls are shaded shut.

The worship services, held at 9:00 a.m. and 11:00 a.m., are relatively simple in format. The first half of the service consists of music, led by an 11-piece band, and a welcome and prayer, and the second half is a sermon by Brian McLaren[53] and communion, served at stations around the sanctuary.

Cedar Ridge was founded by McLaren and his wife, Grace, in the early 1980s. "We were kind of a place for charismatics and non-charismatics to come together," he told me, "And I think we were trying to hit some kind of a balance of depth and vitality. So that's how it started. Just eleven people, a house church, and from there it grew." When I asked McLaren if there were any particular theological impetuses that inspired them to start a new church, he responded,

> So, we were interested in charismatic-informed worship and social justice. And there just wasn't any place you could put that together. Add to that the fact that I was teaching [English] at a university, and so many of the churches that were in our area were so intellectually narrow and rigid, I could never invite a friend, any of my colleagues or students from the university who were not already sub-culturally indoctrinated to attend any of these churches. Since I first became a Christian I have been really interested in evangelism, so I think we wanted to have a place where we could invite our friends who were not already inside. But that became a bigger issue for us a few years later. Really at the beginning it was: how can we integrate social justice with vibrant worship and biblical-rootedness?

In focus groups of parishioners, McLaren gets a lot of the attention, and many of the members of Cedar Ridge seem to have come for the first time as a result of reading a book by him or finding him online. And while his empathetic preaching gets some notice, the focus group participants also repeatedly mention the ethos of worship at the church. In a group of young adults, one person mentions

---

[53] Brian McLaren, the founding pastor of CRCC, resigned in 2006 to pursue a full-time writing and speaking career.

that communion seems "chaotic," and the rest of the group concurs. When asked to elaborate, she says that every week during communion, people engage in various activities: go to a communion station to be served or go to a communion table and serve themselves, meet with a prayer counselor, stay in their chairs, visit the offering "towers." Another focus group member adds that one of the regular communion servers has pink hair, and several others in the group laugh at the thought of their former churches allowing someone with pink hair to serve communion.

Of the eight churches in this study, Cedar Ridge comes off as the most traditional, at least on the surface. The average age of adults in the congregation on the day of my survey was 41.5, nearly a decade older than the average age of worshipers in all eight churches.[54] Not coincidentally, it is the oldest of the eight congregations, it has the oldest senior pastor of the eight congregations, and it is structured in a relatively traditional way. But, as seen in McLaren's comments above, the church was founded in order to break away from the traditional, evangelical modes of thought while still leaving room for evangelism and charismatic worship. So, while Cedar Ridge can be seen as on the vanguard of the ECM, it also has the vestiges of the more conventional evangelicalism from which it grew.

Solomon's Porch, Minneapolis, Minnesota[55]

Solomon's Porch was founded in January, 2000, by Doug Pagitt, who jokingly stated, "We wanted to see how that whole Y2K thing turned out before starting a church." Pagitt was a teenage convert to evangelical Christianity and attended an evangelical college and seminary before working as a youth pastor at a prominent Twin Cities mega-church. In 1997 he moved to Texas to work for Leadership Network and was the convener of the Young Leaders Network that would eventually evolve into Emergent Village. Yet all the while, Pagitt and his wife, Shelley, had planned to move back to Minnesota to plant a church in South Minneapolis.

The church started in a loft space in the trendy Linden Hills neighborhood of South Minneapolis, surrounded by boutique stores

---

[54] See Appendix C.

[55] Research visit on January 23, 2005.

and upscale restaurants. Many of the initial congregants came from the Pagitts' own circle of friends, including not a few from Pagitt's youth group at his former church. Solomon's Porch quickly grew in size and influence, garnering local and national media attention.[56] Outgrowing that space, Solomon's Porch moved to another loft—this one above a sheet metal plant—in a very different locale: the downtrodden Phillips Neighborhood just south of downtown Minneapolis.

By 2005, Solomon's Porch had moved two more times, landing in its current space, the former Hobart United Methodist Church, in 2004. When Solomon's Porch moved into the abandoned Methodist Church, they removed all of the pews and brought in couches and other living room furniture which sits in a concentric circle around the "stool that spins," from which Pagitt and other members speak. The walls are covered with art created by members of Solomon's Porch, and the wall that used to be behind the altar is being filled with portraits ("Porchtraits") of church members, in lieu of the traditional picture directory distributed by many churches.

Worship, scheduled for 5:00 pm, usually starts closer to 5:15. The music is both composed and performed by members of the church. After a song, there's a call-and-response invocation, also written and led by someone in the church, and after some more music, Doug stands to welcome everyone, making a special point to welcome visitors. A member of the community is then interviewed about her life, and she tells about her struggles with sexual abuse at the hands of a former boyfriend. For the sermon, Doug sits on the aforementioned stool and, for about forty minutes, guides the congregation through two chapters of the Gospel of Matthew, often referring to the "Tuesday Night Bible Discussion Group," which helped him prepare the sermon. At the end, he hurriedly leads a short discussion on the Bible passage as the children are ushered back to their parents by volunteer childcare workers. The communion that follows is almost anarchic, as the approximately 150 people stand and serve one another from loaves of bread and bottles of grape juice and wine placed throughout the room. The worship gathering ends with community announcements, emceed in a hu-

---

[56] Leland, "Hip New Churches Sway to a Different Drummer." Kim Lawton, "The Emerging Church, Part One," in *Religion and Ethics Newsweekly* (USA: PBS, 2005).

morous fashion by another member of the community, and a sung benediction.

During Pagitt's public welcome to worship, he mentions that the Sunday evening worship gathering is merely one of the things that Solomon's Porch does during the week, and this came up repeatedly in focus groups and interviews. Interviewees said that Solomon's Porch is an active community—that weekly church suppers, yoga classes, book study groups, and music and art collaborations are just as much a part of the fabric of the community as the worship service. Art was frequently mentioned, and it's hard to miss in the sanctuary. And the community is obviously proud of the homemade music; "I don't think I ever feel closer to God than when Ben is singing," said one focus group member. Another mentioned that the songs are not as "singable" as traditional church fare, and others agreed; but they also agreed with the person who said, "But it's okay to just sit and listen here—there's no pressure to sing."

Although Pagitt is clearly a strong leader—and well known in the emerging church movement because of the books he's written and his public speaking—he demurs when asked about his influence on the practices of the congregation. At Solomon's Porch, there exists a fairly radical commitment to eliminating the categories of "clergy" and "laypersons," and that is seen, for instance, in the weekly communion, which is not presided over by an ordained person, but is introduced by a different member of the community each week. Pagitt, however, does preside over other traditional pastoral duties, like the dedications and baptisms of babies and the commissioning of Solomon's Porch members who are leaving the community to minister elsewhere. On the other hand, he will "ordain" anyone in the congregation to perform weddings. The lay leadership of the congregation is patterned after natural food co-ops, with an elected group called the "Leadership Co-op," and other teams responsible for the children's ministry, communion, and cleaning of the church building.

Solomon's Porch is on the vanguard of the emerging church movement. By jettisoning so many aspects of conventional Christianity—pews, ordination, and language like, "church," "service," and "sanctuary"—Solomon's Porch is among the most radical instantiations of the movement. Pagitt's accusation that monological sermons are not sermons at all—he refers to traditional preaching as "speaching"—in favor of his own, "implicatory dialogue," has been assailed by both liberal and conservative Protestants. [57] But Solomon's Porch is also looked to as an innovative and model congregation, often hosting groups of denominational officials and seminary classes at Sunday worship, and Pagitt is a frequent speaker on the circuit of pastors' conferences. Of the eight congregations studied herein, Solomon's Porch has taken the most steps away from traditional ecclesial systems and expressions.

House of Mercy, St. Paul, Minnesota[58]

"Long Black Veil," a 1959 country ballad made popular by Lefty Frizzell is being played by the House of Mercy Band as people enter—the band is made up of a guitar player, a mandolin player (singing harmony), bass, resophonic slide guitar, and a drummer playing brushes.

House of Mercy meets at 5:30 p.m. on Sunday evenings in the sanctuary of First Baptist Church of St. Paul, an American Baptist Church (USA) congregation.[59] The sanctuary is a large, high ceilinged room, vintage early-20th century. An imposing organ is framed by dark stained wood. On the communion table are three pottery cups, a matching pitcher, and a basket of bread.

To begin the service, the band sings a "House of Mercy" song—taken from their own hymnbook, full of old-timey hymns by Johnny Cash, the Carter Family, and the Louvin Brother, as well as some that they've written—and the three co-pastors walk up onto the platform, standing behind the communion table.[60] They open with a reading from James Alison, a Catholic theologian who is going to spend the upcoming month of March as a theologian-in-residence with the church; they then read—a bit stiffly—some announcements directly from the bulletin.

---

[57] Doug Pagitt, *Preaching Re-Imagined: The Role of the Sermon in Communities of Faith* (Grand Rapids, Mich.: Zondervan, 2005).

[58] Research visit on February 20, 2005.

[59] House of Mercy has since moved to an Evangelical Lutheran Church in America church building in another part of St. Paul, and the congregation has switched its affiliation from ABC (USA) to ELCA.

[60] One of the three, Mark Stenberg, left House of Mercy to found another emerging church congregation, Mercy Seat, in North Minneapolis in 2006.

The congregation numbers about 250, which fills about half of the sanctuary. The congregation is all white, and a diverse mix of ages, married and single, with and without kids. Dress is very casual, including jeans and hooded sweatshirts, and some of the younger men leave their winter caps on.

The band is introduced one by one, and people applaud as the guest musicians are introduced. The band leader asks everyone to stand, and the band leads the congregation in "Keep on the Sunny Side of Life." The guest bass player, "one of the best bass players in the state of Minnesota," is introduced and sings a solo, the lyrics of which are, "blessing Judas, in spite of what he done...bless the lonely, bless the meek..." The congregation applauds at the end.

The other noteworthy aspect of House of Mercy worship is the sermon. Two of the three co-pastors have published books dealing with preaching and biblical hermeneutics, and all three of them preach—sometimes in tandem—in a wry, ironic, literary style. Otherwise, the service includes an invocation prayer, a responsive psalm reading and prayers for the community, and communion served by the pastors at the front of the sanctuary.

The intellectual, literary character of the congregation and its leadership is also seen in its small group offerings, which include a study of Torah scholar Avivah Gottlieb Zornberg's commentary on Exodus,[61] and "Dan's Backyard BBQ Bible Study," billed on the House of Mercy website as follows:

> Learn the methods used by contemporary scholars in their study of the Bible e.g., the Historical Critical method, Narrative method, Structuralism, Post-Structuralism, and Post-post-structuralism. We will cover the Gospels, a little Hebrew Bible (that's what some scholars call the Old Testament (see you're already learning)), some Paul, and whatever other stuff we feel like. Learn to read the Bible for yourself and see if the preacher you heard last week is full of it.[62]

---

[61] Avivah Gottlieb Zornberg, *The Particulars of Rapture: Reflections on Exodus* (New York; London: Doubleday, 2001).

[62] http://www.houseofmercy.org/content/category/10/61/50/. Accessed March 30, 2009.

When I sat down at a blues bar to ask the three co-pastors why they started a church, Mark Stenberg answered succinctly: "We were really kind of sad that people were hearing the good news as bad news, basically, in a nutshell." That sentiment is reiterated on their website,

> It all began in Russell's kitchen in St. Paul, Minnesota on a bitter cold Saturday morning in February of 1996. Debbie, Mark, and Russell—frustrated by contemporary Christian popular culture and saddened that so many of their old friends apparently wanted nothing to do with the Jesus story—asked each other: "What if we started our own church, what would it look like?"…
>
> The three of them agreed that their new church would have to be
>
> .   Christian and not religiously generic;
>
> .   intellectually honest and rigorous;
>
> .   beyond the bounds of popular free church forms of worship and open to "liturgical eclecticism";
>
> .   evangelical in the broad sense of being grounded in the good news of God's grace and not the bad news of shame and religious manipulation;
>
> .   a stimulus for social justice, consciousness-raising, and acts of mercy.[63]

"We were serving churches that we didn't want to invite our friends to," Stenberg continued. So they banded together and started a church that is reflective of their own ironic-hipster ethos, and their particular theological perspective. "We're all three closeted, left-wing Barthians," Stenberg volunteered, "Kierkegaard, Barth, Luther—that's our tribe." And about the music—the "blood hymns," as they call them—he said, "We dare people to be smart enough to

---

[63] http://www.houseofmercy.org/content/category/4/15/33/. Accessed January 20, 2010.

be ironic about it." By that, I took him to mean that while the congregation sings the old time songs in their hymnbook with gusto, they also realize that the theology in those songs is from a different era and their assent is not required.

Outside of the church building, House of Mercy also cultivates the same ethos: ironic urban hipster infused with postliberal biblical criticism. In other words, they take theology seriously, but they don't take themselves too seriously. For instance, they have instigated a Lenten "art crawl" through the Frogtown neighborhood in St. Paul and sponsored shows at the Turf Club Bar. In 2010, Rathbun began curating a lectionary blog called "The Hardest Question," in which he attempts to ask the most difficult literary or theological problem posed by the text each week; in a kind of wandering midrash, rife with pop culture references, he challenges preachers to attack the text's hardest question head-on in their sermons. And Debbie Blue's writings on "sensual orthodoxy" have been highlighted at the Calvin Festival of Faith and Writing.[64]

House of Mercy has a very urban—and urbane—vibe, with a paradoxical mix of liberal Kierkegaardian theology, preaching that is inspired by Jewish midrash, and bluegrass hymnody. Theirs is a unique worshipping community, and of the eight that I studied, may be the least possible to replicate because it seems that very few pastors could pull off this mix, and very few congregations would agree to it. American Protestantism, as Max Weber observed, is remarkable for its earnestness, not its irony.

Journey, Dallas, Texas[65]

In 1999, an unremarkable Baptist church in Dallas looked to ECM pioneer Chris Seay, the founding pastor of University Baptist Church-Waco, for help in reaching out to GenXers. Seay recommended that Gaston Oaks Baptist Church hire Scott Gornto, a Texan who had recently graduated from Fuller Theological Seminary in Pasadena, California. Gaston Oaks did just that, and Gornto started the Journey Gathering, a group for young adults. That group became Journey Church in 2001 as a part of the "church-within-a-church"

---

[64] Debbie Blue, *Sensual Orthodoxy* (St. Paul: Cathedral Hill Press, 2004).

[65] Research visit on January 15, 2006.

movement of the ECM, but as the new church grew, its relationship with Gaston Oaks Baptist became more strained. Gaston Oaks assumed that Journey would eventually funnel young adults into their congregation, but the members of Journey considered theirs a church unto itself. Gornto left the ministry in late 2004 to pursue a full-time counseling career, and Journey's "Pastor Search Posse" began a nine-month search for a new pastor. They ultimately chose Danielle Grubb Shroyer, a Texan who had earned her M.Div. from Princeton Theological Seminary and was working as a chaplain in New Jersey. Shroyer was known to the community because years earlier, while a student at Baylor University, she had served as an intern for Gornto.

Meeting in a couple converted Sunday school rooms on the second floor of Gaston Oaks Baptist, the worship setting at Journey is dark, with the windows shrouded in black, candles around the room, and seven television screens scattered about.[66] About fifty people wander in for the 6:00 p.m. worship service on Sunday night; they are a young crowd, mostly in their twenties, and the only children in attendance are Danielle's young daughter and son.

The worship service opens with the playing of an audio recording from *God Said Ha!*, the one-woman Broadway play of renowned atheist and comedienne Julia Sweeney. The highly irreverent clip would clearly be shocking to any visitor with a churchgoing background. A young man then mounts the small stage, welcomes everyone to Journey, explains that it's "Bad Blazer Night," and leads the congregation in a collect which is projected on the screens. After the band leads fours songs, a young woman stands behind the lectern and presents a dramatic reading from Ezra while trance music plays through the sound system and abstract art is projected on the screens.

Danielle opens her sermon talking about how important stories are in her family, and about how they sat around the Christmas table and told stories for hours. She reflects on being "people of the Book" in her church as she was growing up, and she quotes from Miroslav Volf's book, *The End of Memory*.[67]

---

[66] In 2007, Journey moved out of Gaston Oaks Baptist and into the ground floor of an office building.

[67] Miroslav Volf, *The End of Memory: Remembering Rightly in a Violent World* (Grand Rapids, Mich.: W.B. Eerdmans Pub. Co., 2006).

When she asks the congregation for their reflections on story and memory, a dozen hands go up. A man talks about his dad reading *Where the Wild Things Are* and bouncing him on his knee. Another man remembers reading *The Catcher in the Rye* in high school, and then about how much he hates that book now because it reminds him of how stupid he was. A woman shares about seeing *Schindler's List* and *Dances with Wolves* and being confronted with others' pain for the first time. Another woman shares about reading *Sadako and the Thousand Paper Cranes*. She was deeply moved by the story and went on to fold 1,000 paper cranes in response.

A half dozen more people share before Danielle asks people to share their memories of Journey. A man shares about the pranks of the "Man Group," which leads to several others speaking about their memories of that group. The discussion gets somewhat boisterous before Danielle shifts the discussion, asking people to talk about their favorite stories from the Bible. A woman shares that she liked the Mosaic plagues as a kid, and a man talks about Mephibosheth, whom he calls the "gimpy kid" in the Old Testament.

Danielle shares her own favorites, and then talks about the overall story of the text—it's telling us to "remember, remember, remember." She says,

> We want scripture to be central to our life of faith because the story is formative for us...At Journey we center our lives on the *grand* narrative of scripture, and I love that we put "grand" in front of it. We don't want to be the type of community who lets the Bible do the remembering for us. We want to do the remembering. We don't want to slip into amnesia, to forget where we come from.

The offering is introduced by a young woman who also gives announcements in a fun, friendly, lighthearted way: there's a book club, and an opportunity to lead worship at a community for developmentally challenged persons. She then invites everyone to dinner. About half of the congregation gathers at a Mexican restaurant thirty minutes later.

In focus groups and interviews, those who attend Journey mentioned some common themes. Most prevalent was that Journey feels like an outpost of honesty and authenticity among the large and conservative congregations in Dallas. Evangelical mega-churches like Prestonwood Baptist, Watermark, Irving Bible Church, and Pantego

Bible Church loom large in the imaginations of those at Journey, and many consider Journey a refuge from the mega-church.

That environment has bred an unusually high level of commitment among the three or four dozen people who make up the core of Journey, of whom Shroyer says,

> Everyone is really committed. You know, they're just committed to this place. They believe in it. They're not going anywhere...They're invested in this place, and so they really do feel like this is the place that they give their gifts and their talents and their time and I just—you know, every time I see that, I'm just honored, so I just try to make sure I don't do anything to mess it up.

But the mix of the conservative church culture of Dallas and the youth of Journey can also breed cynicism, which came up repeatedly in the focus groups—a cynicism that was unique to Journey among the churches I studied. Many at Journey seem to be sour on the idea of church altogether. They seem to be barely committed to Journey, and they feel little to no connection to the broader church. Not that the leadership of Journey doesn't recognize that danger. In the words of associate pastor Luke Miller,

> I really hope that we don't become so much about nothing that we're not really providing anything helpful or useful for people. I would hope that—one of my hopes is that we would become a place that seeks to look at the world through Christ's eyes and seeks to transform the world in the way that Christ would have us to transform it, and not that we just become about, "We have freedom so we can do whatever we want to now"—that our deconstruction would allow us to see Christ in a new way instead of just sit and deconstruct it.

Outside of the Sunday evening worship, the core members of the Journey community are in almost constant contact with one another via text messages on their mobile phones. Beyond the officially sanctioned events like "Pub(lic) Theology" and post-worship dinner gatherings, the Journeyers meet often and informally, brew beer together, and generally consider one another their best friends.

Of the eight churches in this study, Journey is best seen as a small, Baptist outpost; a group of young adults, highly committed to one another in the shadow of Dallas's tall steeples. While Journey is surely an autonomous church, it also functions somewhat as a parachurch ministry for disaffected young adults. Unlike House of Mercy, however, the members of Journey are keenly aware of their standing in the emerging church movement, and several of them have traveled together to attend Emergent Village events.

Pathways Church, Denver, Colorado[68]

Pathways was founded in 1993 by Ron Johnson, a Denver Seminary graduate with a relatively evangelical theology but an innovative method: his church in urban Denver spun off a new congregation every time they got to 300 in attendance. The theory behind Johnson's method was that churches cease being "communal" when they exceed 300 persons. By the time Johnson resigned in 2009, Pathways had included up to five "communities" at three distinct locations: Washington Park, Uptown, and Highlands.

When I visited in 2006, the first service of the day was held at 8:30 a.m. in the Grant Street Community Center, a former theater. Fifty to sixty people attended, sitting in folding chairs. All were white, with ages ranging from the 20s to the 60s. The service opens with music, the words projected on a screen that stands atop the stage. The band is also on the stage, with two singers, a keyboard, and drums. I was greeted by three different people as I entered the worship space. Johnson stands up to give announcements and is surprised by a brief happy birthday video in his honor. Then he talks a bit about the process of buying a new building:

> Our vision is to see our city reflect the redemption of God. We want to see a local incarnation of that vision in two neighborhoods. We want you to think about which service and which location you're going to attend, because we want that to become your congregation. The "Ridiculous Campaign" raised $500,000 in six weeks because it was bathed in prayer. We need to not get cocky, and we need to bathe this next transition in prayer, too.

He continues, "The Super Bowl is next Sunday. We're going to cancel the evening services so that you can use that opportunity to

---

[68] Research visit on January 29, 2006.

reach out to your family and friends. Please party responsibly, as the scripture says, 'Be drunk not with wine but with the Spirit.'"

Jenee, the "regional worship pastor" at this location, preaches. She stands on the floor behind a music stand. A candelabra stands behind her, and another candle and the communion elements sit on a simple, draped table behind her. She asks everyone to write down the most disappointing thing about their bodies. She reads an extended passage from Corinthians, then talks about the Greek focus on beautiful bodies and beautiful minds, and she connects that to the American obsession with beauty and celebrity.

She then reads from Genesis (both passages are printed in the bulletin) and transitions to her own story, talking about being a dancer for Janet Jackson and battling with eating disorders. It culminated in her collapsing with a heart condition while running laps in college. Her struggles lasted for eight more years, but she now sees that her body obsession was masking what she really wanted, which was "to be seen, without shame and without fear, as Adam and Eve were seen by God before their sin." The repercussions of her struggles remain—she has spiritual and physical problems. She confesses and repents every day about selling out to that idea that she will be happier if her body is just right.

In the course of the sermon, she quotes N.T. Wright and references Melissa Etheridge's bald post-chemotherapy performance at the Grammys (though she wonders if Etheridge is a "believer" or not). "Now, how do we practice this?" she asks. She encourages people to "obliterate the category" of beauty as we know it—thin, tall, and blonde. Instead, she encourages the congregation to reconsider the category of beauty, and she gives examples of other things about people that are beautiful. For instance, one of her friend's hands get agitated as he gets excited. She talks about how beautiful she considers this. She transitions to communion and prays a Trinitarian prayer—the lights dim as she prays.

With piano music in the background, the guitar player/singer, Josh, reads a poem about God and the body. He invites everyone to stand and "continue in worship." He leads a song, and after another song, he says the words of institution as two couples come forward and hold the elements. "At Pathways, we practice an open table. If you are a follower of Jesus, we invite you to come forward and partake of communion. If you are a 'spiritual explorer,' we invite you to sit and ponder your questions." Soft, jazzy recorded music plays in the background as people come forward.

After communion, a video is played in which an elder of the church talks about his vocation—he raises money at the University of Denver. He mentions how great his life is, yet there are still things that he wants, like a wife and children. "God is holding those things out from me because he is still shaping me."

The female singer invites us to "give of our tithes and offerings," and the band plays a song written at Mars Hill Church in Seattle. As people leave, they are warmly greeted again at the door by an older man who smiles, pats them on the back, and encourages them to "Have a great day!"

Johnson confers with Jenee about how she can tighten up her sermon, which went about 10 minutes too long for his liking. Volunteers set up folding chairs, more than doubling the number available for the next service.

Johnson and I attended two more services at that location in the morning and the evening service, at 7:00 p.m., held at the Temple location, a large former synagogue. It's got a massive organ and priceless stained glass windows. Decorative painting is interspersed with paint peeling from the walls. The band is in an orchestra pit area, stage right—it has a jazzier vibe with heavy keyboards, but otherwise the service matches the morning services.

When Johnson and I sit down in a diner at the end of a long Sunday, he is soft spoken. "I'm happy with the way things have unfolded," he says. He goes on to talk about the growth of the church on the neighborhood model, and about his love for the city of Denver. "Seeing God's redemption reflected in the city" is not only the church's vision statement, but it is a concept to which Johnson repeatedly refers. Pathways identifies as an urban congregation, one that is in fact made up of five "neighborhood" congregations.

But Pathways is also church caught in the middle. The five individual congregations do not really have much autonomy in mission or identity, so they do not really function as "congregations" in the traditional sense. And the church is also in the middle theologically: allowing women to preach, in contradistinction to its evangelical roots, but still pietistically asking congregants not to drink too much at Super Bowl parties. Since my visit, Pathways has undergone more transition: Ron Johnson left unhappily to found another church in Denver, the five-congregation model has been abandoned, and the

Highlands campus of the church broke off from the rest over the issue of homosexuality and became the GLBT-inclusive Highlands Church.[69] Of the eight congregations I visited, Pathways has the most evangelical language and practice. The congregation, as time went on, did not in any way affiliate with the emerging church movement, a change since Johnson's heavy involvement in the Young Leaders Network in the late 1990s.

Church of the Apostles, Seattle, Washington[70]

Church of the Apostles, announces their website,

> Is a young, emerging, Episcopal and Lutheran mission congregation. We are a future church with an ancient faith. In the story of Jesus, we have glimpsed God's future and know that "thiscouldchangeeverything." So our purpose is to helpgodchangeeverything, by participating in God's future, within today's culture and our local zipcode, living and serving in intentional, sacramental community in the way of Jesus Christ.[71]

Founded by Karen Ward, an African-American woman and life-long Lutheran who was, for a time, an executive at the Evangelical Lutheran Church in America's Chicago headquarters, Church of the Apostles meets in an abandoned ELCA church building that still smells a bit like the homeless shelter it used to house.[72] Folding chairs and a few couches face the front of the old church sanctuary. A sheet is stretched across the front wall, upon which is projected a looping cartoon depiction of Jesus' life. The band—bass, piano, percussion, xylophone—plays a repetitive jazz riff in a minor key, and Ryan, a pastoral intern, invites people to begin the service with "open space." Light streams through alabaster windows, and people

---

[69] Eric Gorski, "Evangelical Church Opens Doors Fully to Gays," *Aurora Centinal*, December 20, 2009.

[70] Research visit on March 18, 2006.

[71] "Church of the Apostles: Story," http://www.apostleschurch.org/about/story/.

[72] In January, 2011, Karen Ward announced that she would be leaving Church of the Apostles to plant a new church in Portland.

paint, pray, and talk quietly. The crowd is all white, and primarily in their 20s and 30s, with only a couple of children in attendance.

At 5:15, people are invited to stand. Guitar music begins, and the song "40 Days" about Jesus' days in the wilderness is sung. The words are in Lenten purple on the screen. From the back, one of the pastors says, "Welcome to Lent. It's day eighteen of the Lenten journey, and Jesus is tired and hungry." He reads a reflection on the Ten Commandments, as "Decalogue: The Ten Words" is projected in large letters on the screen, and a film reflection is shown purpose-fully out-of-focus on another screen. He asks a series of questions about why God would give a list of rules and laws.

The band leads the congregation in "Kyrie Eleison, Christe Eleison" to a techno-trance beat, broken up by the chant of a cantor. The song goes on for over five minutes.

Rachel, a layperson, stands up to share her story. She tells of how she is motivated by a calling to stand up and advocate for those who need advocacy: the blind, the autistic, etc. But tonight she wants to talk about a failure. She tells about when she was a youth pastor, and two times that she had failed to advocate for those who desperately needed it. At the end of her story, she says, "This is my story," and the congregation responds, in Twelve Step fashion, "Thank you, Rachel."

The song, "Invocation" is led by the band ("Today when we hear your voice, we won't harden our hearts, Heaven and earth meet here, and we will hear your voice"), and the Gospel lesson is introduced with the words, "Please rise for a story from the journey." The bass player gives a contemporary, narrative version of the cleansing of the Temple.

Tim, another seminary intern, stands up under the heading (on the screen), "Reverberations." Tim's sermon is intense and whis-pery, interpreting the cleansing of the Temple to be an example of Jesus' compassion for the oppressed, and for all of us. Then the band leads a mournful version of the hymn, "O Sacred Head, Now Wounded." Tim leads prayers that were written down during "Open Space," and people are asked to share the peace of Christ with one another.

Ward finally makes her first appearance—she had been "VJing"[73] the service at the sound booth—to invite the congregation to give their offerings. The band sings, "God is Good," as the offering is taken and then processed forward along with the Eucharistic elements. Ward prepares the communion table as the band continues to play, and everyone stands as she leads a communion liturgy. The communion is quiet and reflective, with people both taking the elements and returning to the art they had been creating during open space. After the Eucharist, Ward invites Father Travis forward as hip hop music plays. He leads announcements, and announces the Sanctorum service the next night, a "goth mass," using a liturgy and vestments from the Middle Ages. The prayer, "St. Patrick's Breastplate," is the closing benediction, and the band leads, "For My Ashes" as people chat and file out.

Ward refers to the Fremont neighborhood as a "church-free zone" prior to the planting of Church of the Apostles. She says that rather than looking for a city in which to plant a church, she went hunting for a Lutheran bishop who would understand her ecclesial vision, and she found one in Seattle who had been a missionary in Africa and desired that same kind of missional outlook in his diocese. Church of the Apostles started in a coffee shop across the street from its current location, migrated to this ELCA building, and hopes to eventually add a brewpub and restaurant. "It's a beat-up, old brick church building on the corner," Ward said, "And it's perfect for what we're doing. Just the size for a neighborhood church."

Church of the Apostles is the most denominational among the eight congregations in this study—and Ward the most denominationally loyal of the pastors. While bending the official rubrics with the goth mass and the "Dr. Seuss Liturgy," the Book of Common Prayer is still the foundation of both the worship and the dynamic between clergy and laity at Church of the Apostles. In conversation, Ward often refers to her dual denominational affiliations and to the attempts to garner financial support from those systems. And, indeed, I have heard officials from both the Episcopal Church and the Evangelical Lutheran Church in America point with pride to Church of the Apostles as an example of successful new church development in their denominations.

---

[73] VJ means "video jockey;" like a disk jockey, but with video clips rather than musical tracks.

Jacob's Well, Kansas City, Missouri[74]

Jacob's Well meets in an early twentieth century building that they purchased a couple of years ago, after the Roanoke Presbyterian Church congregation disbanded. Located in a hipster neighborhood of 1920s bungalows, cafes, and pizzerias, the people of Jacob's Well have made a point to leave up the old softball tournament trophies and other reminders of the previous congregation's life. They consider themselves a continuation of the Christian presence in the neighborhood.

Worship begins a bit past 10:30 a.m. with a couple songs. There's an announcement about Palm Sunday and a reading from a Henri Nouwen book. After a welcoming time and a communal reading from Zechariah, there's more singing—the second set is louder and more upbeat, and half a dozen people sway with hands raised as they sing. Then there's a short call-and-response reading from the Psalms with light piano music in the background.

The crowd is overwhelmingly white and, though primarily young, there's also a healthy percentage of older folks and children. The sanctuary is full—Jacob's Well is on the verge of moving from two to three services per Sunday.

During the welcome time, I ask the man next to me why he's at Jacob's Well, and he replies,

> My wife and I had made a list of churches to visit to get our girls involved a couple years ago, and there was an article in the Kansas City *Star* about this church. This was the first one that we visited, and we've never gone to another one. We came for the girls, but I come back because of the way that Tim [Keel] gives so much of the history behind the Bible. Like the story of the fisherman that Jesus called. I mean, I had heard that story a thousand times in Catholic church growing up, but I always assumed that they were just a couple of guys out to fish on a Saturday afternoon. I had no idea how much they had to give up to follow Jesus.

[74] Research visit on April 9, 2006.

That's what I mean by Tim giving the history behind the Bible.[75]

About five minutes into his sermon, Keel reads the Palm Sunday passage from Mark, then he asks how people "sensually experienced" the passage—he had asked them to close their eyes and try to "sense" the passage as they heard it. Keel moderates the comments for almost ten minutes, calling on respondents by name. He then passionately takes up the preaching again, reflecting on the idea of pilgrimage and introducing the Stations of the Cross. "The pilgrimage from Jericho to Jerusalem is a journey to freedom. This pilgrimage is what we're on as a community."

Keel goes on to preach a complex message about freedom from tyranny and power, using the image of the man in front of the tanks in Tiananmen Square, a quote from Henri Nouwen, an allusion to *National Lampoon's Vacation*, and the weaving in and out of many passages of scripture. The sermon is over forty-five minutes long.

Keel transitions to communion by inviting everyone to the table, but saying that those who don't want to participate can hang back and meditate. He asks people to drop their palm branches and coats ("What is *covering* you? What is protecting you?" he asks) in the center aisle as they come forward. But instead of coats, everyone is given a purple card, asked to write down what is covering them, and drop the card in the aisle as they come forward. The band plays a couple more songs as people take communion by intinction, and by the end the center aisle is full of purple cards.

At 12:10, Keel gives a benediction and several announcements. Then everyone joins hands, creating a aisle-less body, and sings an upbeat benediction song that they all seem to know without any lyrics on the screen. The band keeps playing and there is a buzz of activity as the service ends.

On Saturday night, Keel had taken me to the church where there was an African dinner underway. Realizing that the neighborhood surrounding the church was attracting more and more African immigrants, the leaders of Jacob's Well also realized that they were not very well connected with those Africans. So they welcomed their

---

[75] Tim Keel resigned as pastor of Jacob's Well in September, 2009. In January, 2011, the church announced that Keel would be returning later that year in the new position of teaching pastor.

African neighbors to a Saturday night potluck supper. And, in an attempt to break down the myth that there is one African culture, the guests were invited to cook the foods particular to their African culture. The same thing went for music. And, against one wall, a large paper map of the African continent was being colored by African children, explaining to the Jacob's Well children which part of Africa they had come from.

"Now we're a church," Keel says, "We're not a church plant anymore. We are really not settled, and we're really trying to discern what God is doing among us. We know it's time to grow up." Keel acknowledges that the building has shaped the congregation's life, but he also says that the building is beginning to inhibit the life of the church. He talks of possibly opening other Jacob's Well campuses at nearby struggling churches, or of buying a warehouse downtown for a larger worship space. Mainly, Keel talks about leadership being a sensitivity to the movement of God's creative Spirit: "Control kills creativity," he says, in critique of traditional church systems. "When you create an environment of trust and safety through values that are in the DNA of the church, then you can trust God's Spirit completely with no fear."[76]

Of the eight congregations, Jacob's Well has seen the most dramatic numeric growth; since its founding in 1998, it has grown to three worship services and over 1,200 in attendance on an average Sunday. The formerly Presbyterian building which they own and in which they meet belies a functionally evangelical worship formula, over ninety percent of which consists of music and preaching. Confessional prayers, announcements, and other liturgical acts are scarce. Even during Keel's two-year absence, Jacob's Well has continued to thrive and to attract a large number of congregants in their 20s and 30s.

Vintage Faith Church, Santa Cruz, California[77]

In the mid-1990s, Dan Kimball and Josh Fox were both members of the youth ministry staff at Santa Cruz Bible Church, a conserva-

---

[76] This is echoed in Keel's book, Tim Keel, *Intuitive Leadership: Embracing a Paradigm of Narrative, Metaphor, and Chaos* (Grand Rapids, Mich.: Baker Books, 2007).

[77] Research visit on April 23, 2006.

tive, evangelical mega-church known for the global radio ministry of its senior pastor, Chip Ingram. Having watched the youth ministry grow, Kimball and Fox morphed their Sunday night gatherings into a young adult service, Graceland. Quickly, Graceland became the archetype of the "church-within-a-church" model, a briefly popular take on church growth in which mega-churches would plant daughter churches within their own buildings. Kimball and Graceland hosted a national conference on this model in October, 2000.[78]

In early 2004, the name change to Vintage Faith Church demarcated the birth of a truly independent congregation, which then rented space from Santa Cruz Bible Church for the next couple years. On Easter 2006, a few weeks before my visit, Vintage Faith relocated to First Presbyterian Church, just blocks from downtown Santa Cruz, built in 1939. First Presbyterian Church was a small, struggling congregation at the time, and Vintage Faith came into their building and initiated a thorough remodel, including video and sound in the sanctuary, a refurbished children's wing, and a state-of-the-art coffee shop and art gallery. Having become Presbyterian in order to keep the building, Vintage Faith absorbed the remnants of the congregation of First Presbyterian in 2008. This recurring theme of dependence on and independence from denominations is a particularly important one for the emerging church movement, and it will be addressed in chapter five.

When I attended, it was the first Sunday that Vintage Faith had met in collaboration with First Presbyterian Church, a point in the journey that led to the eventual merger. At the 9:00 a.m. service, about sixty-five people from First Presbyterian attended, and they were provided with a printed bulletin with the "Order of Worship." The service was a combination of the First Presbyterian pastor leading worship and prayer, the First Presbyterian pianist playing the offertory, Kimball preaching, and Fox leading the singing. Several older members, in their Sunday best, showed up at 10:00 a.m., just as the service was ending—it seems that the move to 9:00 a.m. wasn't communicated to everyone.

At the 11 a.m. service, the sanctuary is full, with around 250 in attendance. "Two Churches with One Vision" is the line used to promote the merger of these churches—the promotion of this vision

---

[78] "Church Champions Update: Ideas, Impact and Innovation," in Dallas: Leadership Network, 2000. Accessed February 11, 2010.

from the platform is much stronger at the second service than it was at the first. There is much buzz in the room, and the First Presbyterian pastor gets a big round of applause when he is introduced by Kimball.

The worship service itself consists of two opening songs, a welcome from Kimball, more songs, a scripture reading and sermon by Kimball. Entitled, "What Is Church?", it is part of a series, "Living Church: The Joy of Missional Community." After some more singing, there is a closing set of announcements. Kimball's preaching is lively and pointed. He makes a point to talk about themes, like sexuality and hell, that are often avoided in the seeker-sensitive environment in which he was shaped. He uses the video screen extensively, utilizing both still images and video clips. And he ends the sermon with specific and practical applications for his listeners.

In the bulletin, much space is committed to the "Two Churches, One Vision" theme, including a page titled, "extreme makeover: church edition," which exhorts members of both congregations to be patient with one another, including in the parking lot. Vintage Faith has brought to the partnership not only youth, but money, and they are presently undertaking an expensive renovation of the Fellowship Hall, transforming it into a café, art gallery, and musical performance space. In conversation, Kimball expresses some inner conflict about the merger, and he wonders aloud if it will work. His writing and speaking take him away from the community a lot, and he also expresses anxiety about how that will affect the merger.

Kimball hopes that Vintage Faith Church will indeed become what the church's vision statement declares, "A Worshiping Community of Missional Theologians." His sermons are pointedly theological, as are the multi-part themes that he chooses. Now, a couple of years removed from the merger, there are only vague remnants of First Presbyterian; the community is thoroughly shaped by what the church's website calls, the "Vintage Vibe."[79] But while he is theological, Kimball is also acutely aware that his theology is more conservative than many ECM leaders, and he has tacked away from Pagitt and McLaren.[80] When asked if he and his church are part of

---

[79] "Vintage Vibe," http://www.vintagechurch.org/about/vibe.

[80] Robert Webber et al., *Listening to the Beliefs of Emerging Churches: Five Perspectives* (Grand Rapids, Mich.: Zondervan, 2007), 151-54.

the emerging church movement, Kimball demurs, but it can hardly be denied that he is. He may protest that the movement has become too liberal for his taste, but he is still widely recognized as one of the leaders of the movement. Plus, Kimball has written two books heavily reliant upon the category, including one titled, *The Emerging Church*.[81]

Initial Observations

While this book is most concerned with the central practices of the eight congregations profiled above, we will do well to make some initial observations and analyses of these churches. Certain characteristics across the congregations are noteworthy. For one, only two of the eight churches are still pastored by their founders: Doug Pagitt at Solomon's Porch and Dan Kimball at Vintage Faith. At least one of the founding pastors has left the other six churches. While it is not unusual for pastors to move on from churches, the departure of a founding pastor almost always leaves a congregation in something of an identity crisis. As of this writing, Cedar Ridge, Journey, and House of Mercy have survived these transitions well, while Pathways and Jacob's Well are still in the midst of the transitions.

It cannot be ignored that the strong personality and leadership styles of these eight founding pastors have played a significant role in the rise of their churches to a place of national prominence. McLaren, Pagitt, Shroyer, Keel, and Kimball have all written books, which is a sign both of their talent and their ambition, and their books have helped to shape the movement of which they are a part. Based on his survey of worshipers from 462 congregations across the United States, Reginald Bruce has concluded, "Congregations with an empowering leadership climate and transformational leaders are more likely to be financially strong, growing, and filled with attenders who are more involved in their religious lives."[82] According

---

[81] Dan Kimball, *The Emerging Church: Vintage Christianity for New Generations* (Grand Rapids, Mich.: Zondervan, 2003). Dan Kimball, *Emerging Worship: Creating New Worship Gatherings for Emerging Generations* (Grand Rapids, MI: Zondervan, 2004).

[82] Reginald A. Bruce, "Leadership in High Performing Congregations: Uncovering the Secrets of Success," in *Society for the Scientific Study of Religion* (Rochester, New York 2005), 1.

to Bruce, transformational leadership is particularly significant in voluntary organizations like churches because worshipers and volunteers are "free to come and go as they please." As opposed to "Laissez Faire" leadership and "Transactional" leadership, Bruce writes that "Transformational" leadership in a church shows a direct correlation with the congregation's vitality as measured by financial health and numeric growth over a five-year period.[83]

It may go without saying, but it seems that a transformational leader is necessary to start a church from scratch and oversee its development over a decade, especially when that church is experimenting with ecclesial forms and is only tangentially connected to or completely disconnected from denominational systems of support, as are the eight churches in this study. When a new church is planted outside of the ecosystem of a traditional denomination, and when the founding pastor makes a promise—be it stated or implicit—that *this* church will be *different*, then the onus is indeed on that pastor to cultivate a community of ecclesial experimentation while simultaneously fulfilling the normal pastoral duties that the parishioners expect. The proof that these eight pastors are transformational leaders is simply that they have fulfilled this promise sufficiently that people have kept filling the pews (and couches) for a decade. The other side of the coin is that it is difficult for a congregation to maintain vitality after a transformational founding leader exits, and whether this is possible for these congregations remains to be seen in all eight of these churches. Both the sustainability of the promise of *difference* and the risk that the churches will suffer when the founder departs will be considered in chapter five.

Another commonality among the eight congregations is the relative importance of physical space. Each of the congregations has moved locations over the past ten years—Solomon's Porch has moved four times—and all but Cedar Ridge either has rented space or is renting space. Several of them have dramatically restructured the space in which they meet, a practice that will be taken up in chapter three. Noting Flory and Miller's assertion that emerging church congregations tend to distrust institutions, it might strike some readers as surprising that so many ECM churches are reliant upon the edifices built by denominational systems in the twentieth

---

[83] Keel's book actually addresses this. Keel, *Intuitive Leadership: Embracing a Paradigm of Narrative, Metaphor, and Chaos.*

century. Further, Flory and Miller's claim that GenXers value race-, ethnic-, and gender-inclusivity seems to be debunked by my site visits, in which very few non-whites were witnessed in any of the congregations. This, of course, could be a weakness in my sample set, but it is also a common complaint against the emerging church movement.[84] Emerging church leaders, like many pastors, are desirous of ethnically diverse churches, but, also like many conventional churches, have struggled to realize this vision.

Flory and Miller are correct in asserting that GenXers question traditional lines of authority and thus at least arrange the pastor-parishioner relationship differently, and at most ECM congregations do away with ordination and clergy altogether. This will be explored in depth in chapter five, as will their claims regarding democratized modes of communication.

Regarding Flory and Miller's four-fold taxonomy—Innovators, Appropriators, Resisters, and Reclaimers—it is clear from the profiles above that, despite their rhetoric, not all ECM churches fit into the first of these categories. While Flory and Miller's taxonomy is primarily sociological, these four approaches cannot be divorced from the congregations' implicit theological commitments, for it is by theology that ECM leaders and congregations make their decisions about how they stand relative to Christian tradition. Pagitt and McLaren and their churches can easily be classified as Innovators, both in belief and practice. Karen Ward at Church of the Apostles, however, fits more neatly into the category of Reclaimer, with her invocation of a medieval "goth mass" and other elements of the Lutheran and Anglican traditions. Kimball's and Johnson's more traditionally evangelical and conservative theology echo Flory and Miller's description of Appropriators—understanding and even embracing the culture in which they live, but maintaining the same theological standards in which they were trained.

Analyzing these eight congregations in light of the description of New Social Movements proffered in chapter one results in a similar conclusion. Traditional movements, based on Marxian rubrics, were motivated by ideological concerns and the struggle for property and wealth between the bourgeoisie and the proletariat. New social movements, on the other hand, transcend traditional class lines, ex-

---

[84] See Soong-Chan Rah, *The Next Evangelicalism : Releasing the Church from Western Cultural Captivity* (Downers Grove, Ill.: IVP Books, 2009), 108ff.

hibit multifarious ideologies, and are directed more toward personal identity than class cohesion. Regarding these characteristics, the eight congregations profiled in this chapter can be seen representing the emerging church movement as a new social movement, albeit in a qualified way. This substantiates my claim that these eight congregations are part of a larger movement and that the impact of the practices of these churches goes well beyond the congregations themselves, and even beyond the emerging church movement.

Most definitely, congregants of ECM churches are supremely concerned with personal identity and formation. As we shall see, many members of these congregations have joined ECM congregations at some personal and emotional cost. Since all of these churches are approximately a decade old, congregants are necessarily attending a different church than that in which they were reared. For many, both the beliefs and practices of these churches run counter to the those of the their parents; several communicated in focus groups and interviews that their parents and siblings "just don't get" the ECM church they now attend, or that they do not consider it a "real church." Both the personal convictions and the personal behaviors of ECM members motivate them to personally identify with a church that is not necessarily understood by others in their immediate social circles.

Similarly, as chapter three will demonstrate, the foci in new social movements on personal authenticity and integrity, matched by a disaffection for traditional institutions, is prevalent in the emerging church movement. The one characteristic of NSMs that does not seem common the ECM, at least insofar as my survey indicated, is the transcending of traditional class lines. These ECM congregations, as noted above, are overwhelmingly white. They are also highly educated, with 73% holding a college degree, as opposed to 31% of Americans overall.[85] From a theological perspective, the glaring weakness of the ECM, both in these eight sample congregations and, anecdotally, across the movement as a whole, is the inability thus far to engage persons who are not white, upper-middle and upper-class Americans. Surely there are people in other cultural cohorts who are just as disaffected with the conventional church, yet they have not found a home in the ECM. While failure on this count

---

[85] Kurt J. Bauman and Nikki Graf, "Educational Attainment: 2000," *Census 2000 Brief* (2003).

does not disqualify the ECM from being a new social movement, it is a serious weakness in the movement, and one that will be addressed from an ecclesiological perspective in chapter five.

Chapter Three: The Core Practices of the Emerging Church Movement

Having profiled and offered an initial analysis of the eight emerging church congregations under consideration, we will now turn our attention to the core practices thereof. It is my contention that, viewed phenomenologically, the way in which congregants of these ECM churches practice their faith and articulate these practices gives the best insight into what animates the ECM. In this chapter, I will proffer what I consider to be the core practices of the movement, at least as represented by these eight sample congregations.

But first, a theory of practice must be considered. The concept of practice has received a great deal of attention in practical theology over the past two decades, and with good reason. Practices offer insight into the core convictions of those who claim the Christian faith. For, whereas many Americans will articulate some commitment to Christian faith when asked, investigating the practices of their faith provides the researcher with understanding as to what is really motivating an individual or community and what they truly value: "Like a river whose current cut a canyon over time, Christian practices carve what Dorothy Bass has called a 'cruciform pattern' in the Christian community, a way of life that gives the church its distinctive identity as a community conformed to the passion of God."[1] Further, a consensus has formed in the field of practical theology that practices are the sites of Christian formation. That is, the practices that communities of faith inculcate in their members have a significant shaping effect on those members: "practices do things—and, the Christian asserts, through these practices, God does things as well."[2] Therefore, there is a two-fold purpose in studying the practices of these congregations—and, before that, explicating our understanding of practice—first, to better understand the congregations and the movement, and second, to prepare to offer constructive suggestions for the development of practices in the movement so as to facilitate the further Christian formations of the

---

[1] Kenda Creasy Dean, *Practicing Passion: Youth and the Quest for a Passionate Church* (Grand Rapids, MI: W.B. Eerdmans Pub., 2004), 152.

[2] Dean, *Practicing Passion: Youth and the Quest for a Passionate Church*, 153, n. 20.

congregations' members. The assertion that we can speak conclusively about what God does in practices is one that I find dubious and will challenge below.

The renaissance in Neo-Aristotelian thinking, led by philosophers such as Alasdair MacIntyre and theologians such as Stanley Hauerwas and William Cavanaugh, has been felt in practical theology as well as other disciplines. Most significantly, the conversation in practical theology has centered on the importance of "practices."[3] But Neo-Aristotelianism is not the only way to approach the concept of practice. In order to provide a framework for investigating the core practices of the eight ECM churches studied herein, we will first look to three theoreticians to help us understand the concept of practice: Alasdair MacIntyre, from within the Neo-Aristotelian camp, and Jeffrey Stout and Pierre Bourdieu, coming from significantly different perspectives.

Alasdair MacIntyre and a Neo-Aristotelian Concept of Practice

For MacIntyre, the problem in modern society is one of fragmentation. That is, there are many competing moral systems and accompanying moral languages; this is a result of the dramatic pluralization of society. However, it is not just that several moral systems are competing, but that none of these systems remains intact; thus persons are not able to defend their moral positions with integrity. Facts, once valorized, have been dethroned, and science has turned out to have only limited powers of prediction. There is, MacIntyre claims, nowhere to stand to make a moral argument. The solution that he proposes is a return to an heroic, virtue-laden society. Following Artistotle, MacIntyre posits that morals, virtues, and individuals find their meaning only in a shared tradition (the *polis*, in Aristotle). His argument rests on several terms which, in the course of defining and explaining them, explicate his system.

For MacIntyre, a practice is

> Any coherent and complex form of socially established cooperative human activity through which the goods internal to that form of activity are realized in the course of trying to achieve those standards of excellence which are appro-

---

[3] Miroslav Volf and Dorothy C. Bass, *Practicing Theology: Beliefs and Practices in Christian Life* (Grand Rapids, Mich.: W.B. Eerdmans, 2002).

> priate to, and partially definitive of, that form of activity,
> with the result that human powers to achieve excellence,
> and human conceptions of the ends and goods involved, are
> systematically extended.[4]

In other words, practices are socially established and carry epistemic weight. Practices form the linchpin of MacIntyre's system, both giving meaning to the tradition and deriving their meaning from the tradition. In fact, MacIntyre argues that, as a result of diverse socially established practices, human beings from different traditions know the world differently because, in some ways, they inhabit different worlds.

Internal goods, as seen in the definition above, is a key concept within MacIntyrian practice. They are the goods that can only be achieved from within a practice, and they, too, give meaning to the practice. To elucidate this concept of internal goods, MacIntyre lists some things that are and are not practices: chess is, checkers is not; architecture is, bricklaying is not. The former two are practices, not only because they are more complex than the latter, but because they have internal goods that the latter do not. Further, internal goods are, like practices, socially established by the tradition over time. And *virtues* are those human capacities and characteristics that aid a person at becoming better at the practice and achieving the internal goods.

Another key concept for MacIntyre is that of *tradition*. He argues that every practice is socially established and thus ensconced within a tradition. For moral reasoning, this means that a person cannot understand the reasoning of one tradition from outside that tradition. So a Christian makes moral arguments that are fully comprehensible to others who are within the Christian tradition, but to those who stand within another religious tradition, the Christian arguments are incomprehensible. Moral reasoning, language, and tropes are internal to a specific tradition. In his later works, MacIntyre moderates somewhat on this point, acknowledging that a person can "stand in someone else's shoes," per se, and gain an understanding, albeit imperfect, of the thinking of someone in another tradition.

---

[4] Alasdair C. MacIntyre, *After Virtue: A Study in Moral Theory*, 2nd ed. (Notre Dame, Ind.: University of Notre Dame Press, 1984), 187.

Finally, in *Whose Justice, Which Rationality?*, MacIntyre writes about the Aristotelian concept of *phronesis*, or practical judgment.[5] The ability to make evaluative judgments and take action, MacIntyre argues, is also moderated by tradition and the community. The tradition, over time and through the weight of authoritative thinkers, has determined what is a virtuous action. This is inculcated in the young persons of the tradition, and they carry it out everyday when they use practical syllogisms. The first step in a practical syllogism is to make an evaluative judgment about what is "good" in a particular situation. The second step is to determine if the present situation fulfills the qualities needed for step one to be applicable. The action then takes place, often entirely at a subconscious level.

Among the most vocal proponents of Neo-Aristotelianism in practical theology are Craig Dykstra and Dorothy Bass who define Christian practices as "things Christian people do together over time to address fundamental human needs in response to and in the light of God's active presence for the life of the world."[6] The Aristotelian tradition, and MacIntyre specifically, is so attractive to mainline Protestants like Dykstra and Bass because it is fundamentally an ethical system, and liberal theology since Immanuel Kant has been drawn away from revelation and toward ethics. Further, MacIntyre allows for the appreciation of the one thing that liberals have had over conservatives in the twentieth century: namely, tradition.

Much attention in the emerging church movement has been given to the Neo-Aristotelian position of Hauerwas and others, for it has provided a "third way" forward between conservatism and liberalism. Especially among the crowd that claims the moniker "missional," this posture is attractive because it emphasizes the church's role as one of prophetic counter-resistance to the capitalism and militarism that they see as rampant in American culture. But Neo-

---

[5] Alasdair C. MacIntyre, *Whose Justice? Which Rationality?* (Notre Dame, Ind.: University of Notre Dame Press, 1988).

[6] Miroslav Volf and Dorothy C. Bass, *Practicing Theology : Beliefs and Practices in Christian Life* (Grand Rapids, Mich.: W.B. Eerdmans, 2002), 18. Bass and Dykstra's influence on the field of practical theology cannot be understated, especially because Dykstra, vice president for religion at the Lilly Endowment, has directed Lilly funding toward the study of Neo-Aristotelian practice theology. Notably, preeminent Protestant theologian and ethicist, Stanley Hauerwas, is also a proponent of this school of thought.

Aristotelianism alone falls short as a posture for the emerging church movement, for it too often encourages the church to be over against culture, and the ECM congregations that I studied are vigorously engaged in culture. They are, for example, among the early adopters of new technology, a characteristic that seems counter to that of Neo-Aristotelianism. The Neo-Aristotelian position is part of the picture for understanding the practices of the emerging church movement, but it is only a part.

Jeffrey Stout and the Pragmatist Concept of Practice

Jeffrey Stout counts himself in the long and illustrious line of American pragmatist philosophers like Charles Sanders Pierce, John Dewey, Ralph Waldo Emerson, and William James. Since those founders of the movement, the pragmatists have questioned the traditionalists like MacIntyre, who adhere to the philosophical understanding that action follows theory, thus implying that the philosopher's job is to get the theory right, and then to pass that on to the student. Since human beings share a deep quest for knowledge, and behavior follows knowledge, the first and primary goal is correct theory, and proper action will result. This theory, favored since Plato, has fallen into disfavor as studies of human behavior have shown that individuals often act against their own best interests, and often in contradiction to the beliefs that they hold most dear.

The pragmatists counter that both human reflection (theory) and action are simply aspects of one complex human response to a problem. That is, a problem presents itself to an individual or a collective, and a complex mix of action and reflection takes place to deal with the problem. Pragmatic philosophy takes as one of its primary goals to tear down the veil between action and reflection, which is in line with the ECM sentiment that action and reflection are inextricably interconnected. Similarly, this sentiment jibes with the Gadamerian hermeneutic that I am following in this book.

Stout disagrees with MacIntyre that Western society is crippled by incommensurability and fragmentation. Instead, he argues, there are a variety of social practices and moral languages in the modern world because modern persons and societies deal with a wide variety of problems. As our society has gotten more complex, we have developed varying solutions to deal with the problems that confront us. What impinges upon moral reasoning in the present day is not a multiplicity of voices, says Stout, but the tendency toward "moral Esperanto": the belief that one moral language can ultimately harmonize all of the competing moral voices of our society. This, too, accords with the emerging church movement insofar as the movement has embraced the postmodern claim that no one rationality or language is sufficient for the articulation of Christian truth.[7] Instead, Stout proposes that we become better "moral bricoleurs" who solve the problems that confront us using the best of the resources that we have available. In fact, Stout claims that this is what human beings have always done, and he criticizes MacIntyre for idealizing a *polis* that only existed in Aristotle's imagination.[8]

Stout claims that liberal democracy, far from being a collection of fragments, is itself a tradition. He argues that democracy fulfills MacIntyre's definition of a tradition in that it has survived over several generations and, most importantly to a pragmatic philosopher, it seems to be working. Three elements characterize Stoutian democratic practice. The first is hermeneutical enrichment; that is, in a democracy, things get better through conversation. As people actually talk through and converse about their ideas, those ideas become sharper and richer. The second characteristic is *ad hoc* immanent critique, which is the ability for anyone to ask anyone else for their compelling reasons for believing the way they do at any time. The result of immanent critique is that individuals and groups are constantly asked to defend and re-articulate their positions, often to disparate audiences who will demand different rationale and justification. Stout's third characteristic of democratic practice is a dialectical relationship between reflection and action; put simply: Is it working? In other words, the true test of democratic practice is to

---

[7] This is seen most explicitly in McLaren, *A Generous Orthodoxy: Why I Am a Missional, Evangelical, Post/Protestant, Liberal/Conservative, Mystical/Poetic, Biblical, Charismatic/Contemplative, Fundamentalist/Calvinist, Anabaptist/Anglican, Methodist, Catholic, Green, Incarnational, Depressed-yet-Hopeful, Emergent, Unfinished Christian.*

[8] Jeffrey Stout, *Democracy and Tradition* (Princeton, N.J.: Princeton University Press, 2004).

put it into practice; the poles of theory and action are in constant dialectical relation.[9]

When it comes to the place of theology in democratic practice, Stout follows theologian James Gustafson in proposing that a "conversable theology must have something distinctive, something recognizably theological to say. It must at least make clear what difference theology makes and how an educated person could believe its distinctive claims."[10] Stout warns theologians against constant worries about methodology, which he compares to the speaker who keeps clearing his throat but never gets around to speaking. He also warns against reliance upon foundationalist philosophies which have rightly been dethroned. Instead, Stout encourages theologians to draw from a variety of normative sources, including sacred texts, tradition, and modern science, and to develop theologies that are fluid and conversable. That is, theological truth claims can be engaged in public debate and can be modified and altered as a result of having to give a defensible answer in the public debate. Finally, Stout argues that theologians have much to learn about self-reflexivity, that is, the ability to criticize oneself. Having developed a conversable theology, Stout writes, theologians will be able to critically retrieve traditional elements of faith, modify them, and innovate new elements.

Stout's influence on the field of practical theology is thus far small, with the notable exception of several public debates with Hauerwas on the proper frame for theological reasoning. Stout has championed Barthian scholar George Hunsinger as modeling the kind of pluralistic religious thinking that he promotes.[11]

Pierre Bourdieu: Strategies, Rules, Force Fields, and Practice

Pierre Bourdieu comes to the practices conversation from a significantly different vantage point than MacIntyre and Stout. A

---

[9] In chapter five, I will propose that emerging church congregations consider Stoutian democracy as central to their polity and that they develop democratic practices.

[10] Jeffrey Stout, *Ethics after Babel: The Languages of Morals and Their Discontents* (Boston: Beacon Press, 1988), 168-69.

[11] Stout, *Democracy and Tradition*, 108-17.

French sociologist, Bourdieu's entire corpus can be seen as an attack on the dualisms common in his field: subject vs. object; subjectivism vs. objectivism; agent vs. structure. He rejects such dualisms because, in each case, he finds truth in both positions. Social reality exists, he argues, both within and outside of the individual body; the sociologist's job is to uncover the hidden points at which the structure has been internalized by the human actor(s).

One of the ways in which Bourdieu overcomes traditional dichotomies is his introduction of the concept of *strategy* in place of the traditional role of *rule*. By doing this, Bourdieu introduces the element of time, with its qualities of movement and irreversibility, into human action. Thus he proposes that human beings do not act as a result of rules, known or unknown, but as a result of strategies that have been internalized. Since these strategies most often take place at a preconscious level, and since they occur at a certain moment in time and place which hides their eventual outcome, they are a complex combination of structure and (preconscious) agency.

This leads to Bourdieu's central concept, that of the *habitus*, which he describes as,

> Systems of durable, transposable dispositions, structured structures predisposed to function as structuring structures, that is, as principles which generate and organize practices and representations that can be objectively adapted to their outcomes without presupposing a conscious aiming at ends or an express mastery of the operations needed in order to attain them. Objectively "regulated" and "regular" without being in any way the product of obedience to rules, they can be collectively orchestrated without being the product of the organizing action of a conductor.[12]

The *habitus* is a theory of action that is both cognitive and bodily prereflective rather than conscious, durable though changeable, reproductive and generative. It is a theory of human action that marries agency and structure; that is, the rational human actor exists, but she acts as a result of deeply structured structures. So, Bourdieu recovers human agency in sociology, but without going so far as vol-

---

[12] Pierre Bourdieu, *The Logic of Practice* (Stanford, Calif.: Stanford University Press, 1990), 53.

untarism.[13] In *The Logic of Practice*, Bourdieu writes that the phrase from the sporting world, "a feel for the game," almost perfectly sums up what he means by *habitus*: a player who knows the game (practice) of soccer so well that she reacts to the plays and the movement of the ball at a prereflective level; she has internalized the game. Yet no one would argue that she is not an autonomous rational actor. [14]

A second element of Bourdieu's work is the concept of a *field* of cultural production. A field is an arena of production of goods, services, knowledge, and status, and Bourdieu uses it in place of the traditional sociological tropes of population, race, etc.[15] Bourdieu refers to it as a "force field," which gives it some spatial feel, but he says it is unlike a soccer pitch, on which the lines are clearly drawn.[16] What he is explicit about, however, is that a field is an arena of struggle. Within a field, there is a finite amount of capital, both economic and cultural, and the struggle within the field is over that capital. As young persons are socialized into the field, they learn their *habitus* at a very early age—that is, whether they are among those entitled to a share of the capital or not. Those who are born into the upper class, for instance, expect conservation of the existing hierarchy. Others, at the middle level of economic and cultural capital, hope for succession, while the lower classes hope for subversion of the entire field. However, what they all agree on is that the field is worth struggling over—this is the *doxa*, or the deep structure of the field. And the way that the *habitus* is transposable is that those who have much capital in one field are likely to have much capital in other fields as well.

Bourdieu thus proposes a research program for sociologists:

---

[13] For an explication of voluntarism, see Ann Swidler, "Culture in Action: Symbols and Strategies," *American Sociological Review* 51 (1986).

[14] Bourdieu, *The Logic of Practice*, 66.

[15] Pierre Bourdieu and Randal Johnson, *The Field of Cultural Production: Essays on Art and Literature*, European Perspectives (New York: Columbia University Press, 1993), 29-73.

[16] Pierre Bourdieu, *The Rules of Art: Genesis and Structure of the Literary Field* (Cambridge: Polity Press, 1996), 232.

$$[(habitus)(\text{capital})] + \text{field} = \text{practice}^{17}$$

While he never fully explicates this equation or explains why *habitus* and capital stand in a closer relation to one another than they do to field, his point is to show the relationship that *habitus*, field, and capital have with one another in determining human action.

Michel de Certeau has further elucidated the line of thinking begun by Bourdieu, reflecting on the "practice of everyday life."[18] According to de Certeau, "strategies" are used by organizations and institutions to structure and organize human experience, and, ultimately, to perpetuate the existence of the institution. "Tactics," however, are utilized by individual human actors to navigate within these strategies. While somewhat bound by the strategies in which they move, human persons—both individually and in groups—have enough agency to make ad hoc decisions within the strategies. Like Bourdieu, de Certeau finds a middle ground that upholds the best of both post-structuralist and rational actor theories.

Applying the theories of MacIntyre, Stout, or Bourdieu, the practical theologian can assert that practices are the sites of Christian formation. Following Bourdieu, a practice is the nexus of structure and agency, and thus there is no better place for practical theology to study a movement like the emerging church movement than by looking at its core practices. In investigating a practice, we must be sophisticated enough to recognize the various elements that have gone into the development of the practice in question, and we must do the empirical and interpretive work to get beneath and behind what the practice seems to be at first glance. MacIntyre and Stout, though they disagree on the moral situation of the present day, each strongly argues that a practice is deeply embedded in a specific tradition. Understanding the MacIntyrian *tradition*, roughly parallel to Bourdieu's *field*, is paramount. Further, we must take seriously Stout's recommendation of a "conversable" theology, although his mish-mash of normative sources remains troubling. In the end, Stout

---

[17] Pierre Bourdieu, *Distinction: A Social Critique of the Judgement of Taste* (Cambridge, Mass.: Harvard University Press, 1984), 101., quoted in , David Swartz, *Culture & Power: The Sociology of Pierre Bourdieu* (Chicago: University of Chicago Press, 1997), 141.

[18] Michel de Certeau, *The Practice of Everyday Life* (Berkeley: University of California Press, 1988).

and MacIntyre are at odds over this very point: the former says that a theologian must be a bricoleur of normative sources, and the latter argues that the tradition has already authoritatively decided what is normative. Bourdieu, however, is more helpful because he reminds us that a practice is much more complex than simply arguing over the sources of normativity. Instead, he posits that practices are the results of complex processes, developed over time, by which people compete for the cultural capital available in their own environment. Practices, when viewed from a Bourdieuian perspective, reflect both conscious and subconscious motivations. Bourdieu succeeds in a way that neither MacIntyre nor Stout does because his concept of *habitus* acknowledges both the conscious, rational actions taken by human actors, and the motivating structures in which those actors are caught but of which they are most often unaware. Thus, Bourdieuian analysis offers the practical theologian a better chance at a thick description of the practices in a congregation or a movement because it takes into account both the conscious decisions of the actors and the overriding and prereflective structures that subtly dictate limits of human agency.

The Limits of "Practice"

In some ways, Bourdieu limits the expanse of this study, for while we investigate the practices that animate these eight congregations, it cannot be ignored that many of the congregants had long-established internalized strategies when they joined the churches in question. What people bring to their practice of Christianity begins, in the case of most American churchgoers, with their family of origin and the church of their childhood. For example, the leaders at Solomon's Porch in Minneapolis are wont to say that when they formed the church in 1999 and 2000, they basically started *ex novo*. However, every member of the initial core team came with extensive church experience and thus, according to Bourdieu, already had an established religious *habitus*.

Further, using practice as the defining hallmark of church, and even Christian, identity has come under some criticism of late. Andrew Root and Blair Bertrand, for instance, write that Neo-Aristotelian practice theory falls short in the face of Kierkegaardian existentialism, for "Kierkegaard contended that human action itself was bankrupt because human action existed next to an abyss, the abyss of infinite freedom, a freedom that forced human action to crash on the rocks of anxiety."[19]   For Root and Bertrand, practices are not only ineffectual at forming a person Christianly and deepening faith, but they even have the potential to be harmful, leading a person to the self-deception that she or he is actually doing something to avoid the abyss of nothingness that is the human condition.

Nicholas M. Healy has penned an even more thoroughgoing critique of practice. First, he notes that "there is no settled definition of what a practice is" among the theologians who have developed what he calls the "new ecclesiology."[20]   Indeed, Healy points out that even Dorothy Bass and Craig Dykstra admit that their definition of practice may entail "almost any socially meaningful action."[21]

Secondly, Healy argues, "Fixing a practice's precise shape and thereby determining the meaning of utterances made as it is performed is difficult to do, too, because of the evident fact that we all live within more than one cultural or sub-cultural setting, as indeed Christians have done throughout their history." Here Healy is taking aim at ecclesiologists like Stanley Hauerwas and William Willimon who, in their popular book, *Resident Aliens*, argue that the Christian church is a discrete community and, much like an Aristotelian *polis*, defined by its practices.[22]   But Healy notes that every practice one finds in a church is also practiced elsewhere. Even the Eucharist, ostensibly the one practice that sets the Christian church apart from other communities of people, is able to be interpreted in myriad ways, as the history of Christianity makes clear. Thus, "practices as concretely performed are not patterns of behavior with sufficiently fixed meanings that they can do the task required of them" by the new ecclesiologists.[23]

---

[19] Andrew Root and Blair Bertrand, "Reflection on Divine and Human Action as the Core of Youth Ministry," in Andrew Root and Kenda Dean, *The Theological Turn in Youth Ministry* (Downers Grove, IL: InterVarsity Press, 2011).

[20] Nicholas M. Healy, "Practices and the New Ecclesiology: Misplaced Concreteness?," *International Journal of Systematic Theology* 5, no. 3 (2003): 289.

[21] Volf and Bass, *Practicing Theology: Beliefs and Practices in Christian Life*, 22.

[22] Stanley Hauerwas and William Willimon, *Resident Aliens: Life in the Christian Colony* (Nashville: Abingdon Press, 1989).

[23] Healy, "Practices and the New Ecclesiology: Misplaced Concreteness?," 295.

Healy then takes to task Reinhard Hütter and Stanley Hauerwas as two exemplars of new ecclesiology. Healy criticizes Hütter for having a vision of the church that is too idealized and therefore too sociologically thin: Hütter does not adequately take into account that many churchgoers, fallible human beings that they are, partake in Christian practices with non-Christian intent—attending church and taking the Eucharist, for example, to please a spouse—thus negating Hütter's claim that the theological intent behind the practices is, in fact, constitutive of the church. Similarly, Healy objects to Hauerwas's ecclesiology for relying "too heavily upon the assumption that the practices of the church are at least for the most part performed according to their abstract and ideal descriptions. Ordinary concrete mis-performance or non-performance and its effect upon character formation and church witness is left out of the picture."[24]

Ultimately, Healy finds both Hütter's and Hauerwas's ecclesiologies too anthropocentric, and he asks for a "more robust account of the doctrine of God—the triune God—as the starting point for theological reflection."[25] In other words, the church is constituted by *who God is* and *what God does* rather than by *who humans are* and *what humans do*.

Jürgen Moltmann has a similar perspective on the Aristotelian conception of practice:

> Man makes himself human. Man is what he makes of himself, says the Aristotelian doctrine of virtue. "Practice makes a master." By doing justice over and over again, we become just men. By practicing humanity we become true men. According to this conception, which at first glance is quite persuasive, man's humanity or inhumanity is up to man.[26]

Moltmann then relies on Luther to critique Aristotelian practice,

> Luther called it blasphemy "that our works create us or we are the creatures of our works. . . . We are our own gods,

---

[24] Healy, "Practices and the New Ecclesiology: Misplaced Concreteness?," 301.

[25] Healy, "Practices and the New Ecclesiology: Misplaced Concreteness?," 301-02.

[26] Jürgen Moltmann et al., *Theology of Play* (New York: Harper & Row, 1972), 45.

creators and producers." For him the basic principle of the Aristotelian doctrine of virtue becomes blasphemy when it is applied to the fundamental relationship of man to the ground of his existence, his relationship to God. He therefore rejected the anthropology of the self made man and opposed it with the Christian anthropology expressed in the brief formula: "Man is justified by faith" (*Hominem justificari fide*). By this he meant that no form of action leads us from an inhuman to a human reality of man, for there is no way to get from doing to being.[27]

Practices have doubtless been a powerful rubric for practical theologians over the past two decades, and in this very book they will be relied upon heavily. What a study of practices can do is elucidate the core identity of a community and even shed light on the core theological convictions of that community. What practices cannot do, however, is tell us anything about God. The practices of a community, instead, tell us how a community responds to the work of God.

In the end, using practice theory to determine what is constitutive of a Christian community falls short. On the one hand, practices are not unique to the emerging church movement, or to any other ecclesial group, making it impossible to use this rubric to differentiate the ECM from other groups of faith communities. And on the other hand, practice theory, at least in its Aristotelian sense, is not theological enough for our purposes because it is too anthropocentric in its perspective. For this reason, I will turn to Jürgen Moltmann in chapter four to provide a more robustly theological framework for understanding and evaluating the emerging church movement.

Using "Practice" to Investigate the ECM

However, investigating the practices of ECM congregations is valuable when undertaken from another angle. Instead of using practices as an ecclesiological indicator, I will use practices phenomenologically—that is, I will look at the practices of the ECM churches in question as primary ways that these communities *make meaning*—the way they cultivate and organize their experiences of the nexus of divine and human action. In other words, our interest is

---

[27] Moltmann et al., *Theology of Play*, 46.

in practices, not as *prescriptive*, but as *descriptive* of ECM congregations: the practices of these ECM congregations tell us what these people believe about God. Practices, both concrete and virtuous in nature, are recognized because they are clear responses to what individuals and communities believe about God. They are not unilateral, however, for the practices, once engaged, also shape the beliefs of the individuals and the communities. Practices are inextricably caught up in the hermeneutical circle. Once we survey these practices, and uncover the relational ecclesiology of Jürgen Moltmann in chapter four, we can propose ecclesial reforms in chapter five that will aid the ECM in fostering congregations that are both sustainable and in keeping with their core convictions about the activity of God.

Communities of Practice and the Promise of Ambiguity

Bourdieu's conception of practice and my phenomenological approach to the practices of eight emerging church congregations are supplemented by Etienne Wenger, who writes about communities of practice. Wenger writes, *"Practice is about meaning as an experience of everyday life."*[28] What humans do, Wenger contends, is negotiate meaning—both organize established meaning and create new meaning—by a constant process of participation in and reification of practices. And those practices, he continues, take place in communities of actors. Theologically speaking, we might add that these communities are constituted by the presence of the Holy Spirit and that the actors are collectively seeking to respond to the activity of God's Spirit in their community and in the world at large.

Participation in communal practices is "the social experience of living in the world in terms of membership in social communities and active involvement in social enterprises."[29] As individual actors participate in the production and organization of meaning, those practices inevitably calcify—"Any community of practice produces abstractions, tools, symbols, stories, terms, and concepts that reify something of that practice into a congealed form."[30] Wenger em-

---

[28] Etienne Wenger, *Communities of Practice: Learning, Meaning, and Identity*, Learning in Doing (Cambridge, U.K.; New York, N.Y.: Cambridge University Press, 1998), 52.

[29] Wenger, *Communities of Practice: Learning, Meaning, and Identity*, 55.

[30] Wenger, *Communities of Practice: Learning, Meaning, and Identity*, 59.

phasizes that participation and reification are not bipolar opposites but instead compose a complementary duality. As a community participates in practices over time, those practices harden; but the community is also in the process of reevaluating the reified practice as new members join, old members leave, and the practice's potency wanes. Consequently, participation increases and new practices emerge. To again add theological nuance to Wegner's argument, the ecclesial community, at its best, is actively seeking God's Spirit, listening for the revelation of the Spirit in the current age, and forging practices that are resonant with that revelation, with the history of the church, and with the contemporary tools at its disposal.

For Wenger, practice is a source of communal coherence, and he posits three key dimensions: the *mutual engagement* of the participants in the community; the negotiation of the practice as a complex *joint enterprise*; and the *shared repertoire* of "routines, words, tools, ways of doing things, stories, gestures, symbols, genres, actions, or concepts that the community has produced or adopted in the course of its existence, and which have become part of its practice."[31] Finally, Wenger notes that ambiguity, far from being an "obstacle to overcome," is actually "an inherent condition to be put to work."[32]

While some Christians speak confidently of their direct revelations from God—what God wants of them and their community—participants in emerging church congregations are not wont to speak of God in this way. Instead, the movement of the Spirit in a community, and in the world, is sensed more ambivalently, and spoken of less confidently. I observed this in the vast majority of my research interviews, and, theologically, this is not a negative. Instead, it is reflective of the epistemic humility characteristic of the movement. Indeed, as Wegner posits, this ambiguity actually serves to make the practices in the ECM the subject of frequent, immanent critique. Therefore, it can be argued that because the practices core to the ECM are considered temporary, *ad hoc* responses to the movement of God's Spirit, always subject to critique and overhaul, they are actually more robust than the practices of more traditional and conventional ecclesial communities. That is because ambiguity, when "situated in the context of a history of mutual engagement"

---

[31] Wenger, *Communities of Practice: Learning, Meaning, and Identity*, 72-83.

[32] Wenger, *Communities of Practice: Learning, Meaning, and Identity*, 84.

opens up "an opportunity for negotiation."[33]   Thus, ECM churches will do well to heed Wenger's admonition: "It is useless to try to excise all ambiguity; it is more productive to look for social arrangements that put history and ambiguity to work."[34]   What happens when a community embraces ambiguity and enters into the accountable back-and-forth of negotiation is that new meanings emerge, and new practices with them. Thereby, the community of practice stays engaged with the hermeneutical circle and the practices in which they engage remain fresh.

Practices of the Emerging Church Movement

The practices detailed below will show eight emerging church movement congregations each negotiating ambiguities: to embrace traditional ecclesial practices, to spurn them, or to redefine them; to engage broader denominational structures or to rebuff them; to accept the traditional doctrinal positions of their theological forbears, or to revise and rewrite them. Each church has done a bit of each, and the negotiations continue—both within the congregations themselves, and across American Protestantism as the church-at-large determines the importance of the ECM.

Ongoing negotiation of Christian practice has been part of the life of Christian faith communities for two millennia. The reason that we no longer baptize in a river like John the Baptist or share the Eucharist during a Seder meal like Jesus is because the church has had to continually renegotiate these rites and their meanings as the surrounding cultural conditions have evolved. In the early church, when the rite of baptism was to his mind being abused, Ignatius of Antioch instituted a safeguard, ordering that baptism only be performed by duly appointed bishops, and the practice of baptism has not stopped evolving since. Communion, prayer, singing, preaching, scripture reading, and more have similarly been negotiated and renegotiated throughout the centuries in the church. Christian practices—both those with biblical precedent, and those without—are unavoidably ambiguous, leading to their constant renegotiation.

---

[33] Wenger, *Communities of Practice: Learning, Meaning, and Identity*, 84.

[34] Wenger, *Communities of Practice: Learning, Meaning, and Identity*, 84.

Negotiation of Christian practice is not unique to the emerging church movement, but the cultural context of the movement has led to new forms of negotiation. For example, the advent of social media has led to a period of debate and conversation about the nature of Christian practice that is very different than when such things were decided by church councils, a pope, or even the annual meeting of an American denomination. The flowering of liberal democracy in the American context, the increasing voice of women in institutions across society, and this new technology have all resulted in more voices being included in ecclesial discussions than ever before. As a result, the ECM has pioneered some new ways of being church, but even these ways are in line with a long history of negotiating the ambiguities of the Christian life.

Within Nicholas Healy's critique of the definitions of practice—or lack thereof—he makes a salient point about the two categories into which the practices described by the new ecclesiologists fall. The first are "clearly structured, requiring specific actions at specific times and places," and the second are "loosely structured, if they have any structure at all, so they can be performed in many different ways."[35] Under the first rubric fall practices like the Lord's Supper, Baptism, and collective recitation of the Lord's Prayer, and under the second fall items like hospitality, fellowship, and fasting. Healy's is a valid criticism of the theories of practice that have been ascendant in the past two decades of practical theology and ecclesiology. But it is also a helpful framework for categorizing the types of practices in which congregations engage, and so I have adopted Healy's taxonomy for my description of ECM practices that follows. The first group of practices are considered "concrete practices," and the second "practices of virtue." *Concrete practices* are those which take place at a specific time and place, are regular, and are relatively easy for participants to describe. *Practices of virtue* are more ethereal in nature, less contingent upon time and location, and thus somewhat less describable. MacIntyre writes, "A virtue is an acquired human quality the possession and exercise of which tends to enable us to achieve those goods which are internal to practices and the lack of which effectively prevents us from achieving any such goods."[36] In invoking the phrase, "practices of virtue," I am relying

---

[35] Healy, "Practices and the New Ecclesiology: Misplaced Concreteness?," 290.

[36] MacIntyre, *After Virtue: A Study in Moral Theory*, 190.

on MacIntyre's definition insofar as it includes those theological qualities, referred to biblically as the "fruits of the spirit," that are instantiated in the actual, lived activities of emerging church congregations. Any form of church life will concentrate on some of these virtues more than others, and the ECM is no exception.

The use of practice theory herein will be less normative than those proposed by Bass, Dykstra, and most others in American practical theology. Instead, it will be more in line with those who use practice as a phenomenological descriptor, even definer, of the church.[37] None of the practices listed below is unique to the ECM, but the particular combination that makes up this list will allow a characterization of the ECM, thus enabling us to set out an initial ecclesiological suggestion for the ECM in chapter five.

Concrete Practices

Communion

The first and most notable concrete practice in the eight ECM congregations that I studied, and in the many that I have visited subsequently, is the practice of the Lord's Supper. Along with baptism, the Lord's Supper has been a defining mark of Christian community for two millennia. Communion, instituted by Christ himself, has long been identified as the marker of a true church, where, in the words of Martin Luther, "The gospel is taught purely and the sacraments administered rightly."[38] Of course, these marks of the church have been negotiated and renegotiated myriad times since their inception. By way of background, it should be considered that among evangelical churches, out of which six of the eight congregations sprung, communion is far less common than in liturgical, mainline churches. It is not uncommon for an evangelical church to celebrate communion only quarterly. However, all but one of the churches I visited served communion during my visit and do so each Sunday; only Vintage Faith Church does not.

---

[37] See, for example, Diana Butler Bass, *The Practicing Congregation: Imagining a New Old Church* (Herndon, Va.: Alban Institute, 2004).

[38] Robert Kolb, Timothy J. Wengert, and Charles P. Arand, *The Book of Concord: The Confessions of the Evangelical Lutheran Church* (Minneapolis: Fortress Press, 2000), 43.

At Journey, congregants come forward to receive communion—an aspect of their practice of communion that is disparate from
the Baptist tradition from whence they came—and they do so in si-
lence. At Cedar Ridge, it was interesting to note how many parishioners did not take communion, but instead stayed seated or went
immediately to the prayer counselors at the back of the sanctuary.
At Church of the Apostles, in keeping with their Lutheran/Episcopal
tradition, communion holds a special and sacred place. Karen Ward,
the self-proclaimed "Abbess" of the church, is also the (Episcopal)
priest and (Lutheran) pastor. While she inconspicuously ran the
video board during the majority of the worship service that I attended, it is notable that she came to the front of the sanctuary and
presided over communion, the one aspect of worship that she pub-
licly directed. Also noteworthy is that she donned a stole, a vest-
mental mark of an ordained clergyperson in both the Lutheran and
Episcopal traditions. Ward's direction of communion deviated little
from "Holy Eucharist: Rite Two" in the *Book of Common Prayer*,
though hers was an abbreviated version, and she led the liturgy with
far less formality than most priests of her tradition do.

As for the congregation at Church of the Apostles, worshipers
came forward to receive communion from their priest, but there was
also "Open Space" around the sanctuary during which individuals
could create art and reflect on their worshipping experience as they
took communion. In fact, though the administration of the Eucharist
stood at the geographical center of the sanctuary, it was not nearly
the focal point that one might expect. As communion began, many
congregants went immediately to the Open Space areas to continue
working on the art pieces that they had begun earlier in the service.
And whereas a conventional church might have an organ or a piano
softly playing during the distribution of communion, the Church of
the Apostles band was playing music that was both too loudly and
too melodically complex to be ignored.

Solomon's Porch may have the most distinctive practice of the
Lord's Supper of all eight churches. The rite is introduced by a different person each week—there is no requirement or expectation that
the introduction be by a clergyperson or even a leader in the congregation. Those introductions vary widely, from a rubric out of the
Book of Common Prayer, to a personal reflection on what communion means, to a perfunctory explanation of how communion is
shared at Solomon's Porch. That lattermost explanation is a com-

mon element in the practice, and it includes mention of the many settings of bread, juice, and wine around the room; the choice of drinking wine or juice and the choice of individual cups or a common cup; and the choice of staying in the main worship room which becomes noisy and active during the sacrament or retreating to a quieter, meditative space adjacent to the sanctuary. The entire congregation then stands and in unison recites a creed:

> We take communion, by serving and eating bread and wine together,
>
> in community with followers of Jesus around the world and throughout all ages.
>
> We enter this mystery proclaiming and having faith of Jesus as the Messiah, whose life, death, burial, resurrection, and ascension
>
> show the love of God for the world,
>
> free us from sin,
>
> and initiate the kingdom of God in our world in new ways,
>
> for the benefit and blessing of all the world.

The participation in the Lord's Supper is a hubbub of activity, with worshippers alternatively serving themselves and each other, and children freely participating as well. After several minutes, the person who introduced communion shouts over the din, "May the life of Jesus be in you," and the congregation responds, "And also in you." Then all join hands and recite the doxology from the biblical book of Jude, "To him who is able to keep you from stumbling and to present you before his glorious presence without fault and with great joy—to the only God our Savior be glory, majesty, power and authority, through Jesus Christ our Lord, before all ages, now and forevermore! Amen."[39]

These statements—the nouveau creed and the doxology from Jude—are the only two elements of worship at Solomon's Porch that

---

[39] Jude 24-25.

are repeated each and every week. All other elements, including how communion is introduced and served, are regularly changed. While it may not be surprising that Ward's Lutheran-Episcopal church plant would practice communion on a weekly basis, it is more surprising for Pagitt's. Pagitt came of age in a conservative, evangelical mega-church, and he was educated at the evangelical Baptist Bethel College and Seminary in St. Paul, Minnesota. Neither place encouraged the weekly practice of the Lord's Supper, nor the recitation of creeds. But when asked, Pagitt makes it clear that from the inception of Solomon's Porch, the "core team" that founded the church decided that communion should be a weekly occurrence. Along with just a few other core practices—dialogical sermons, the use of only original music, seating in the round—weekly communion was frequently mentioned in focus groups and interviews as what gives Solomon's Porch its identity.

The Lord's Supper is practiced more frequently in ECM churches than in most upstart evangelical churches. And the ECM churches that claim a mainline heritage, like Church of the Apostles and House of Mercy, have renegotiated the practice to suit their contexts. The bricolage communion at Solomon's Porch may border on expressive individualism, but it is also resonant with the lives of the members in their twenties and thirties who populate that congregation. As McLaren's emerging church manifesto, *Generous Orthodoxy* asserts, a Christian should not have to choose just one confessional stance, so Solomon's Porch seems to communicate that a Christian should not be limited to one version of the sacrament of communion.[40]

Worship

When Journey opens worship with an audio recording of an atheistic rant by comedian Julia Sweeney, it's clear that this is not a run-of-the-mill worship setting. Journey is also home to "Bad Blazer Night" and to a chips-and-salsa bowl made from the plaster cast of a pregnant woman's torso.

---

[40] Pagitt has also been known to baptize members of Solomon's Porch multiple times, clearly out of step with historic Christian orthodoxy. But again, he and the members of Solomon's Porch assert that the sacrament of baptism has been open to change and negotiation down through the years.

At Church of the Apostles in Seattle, the "U2charist," featuring the music of U2, is on the calendar, as is the "Dr. Seuss Liturgy," based on the book, *Oh, The Places You'll Go!*,[41] and the regular "Goth" service—"Sanctorum: a dark and lovely mass"—using the 1642 version of the Book of Common Prayer.

In all eight of the churches I visited, parishioners were dressed casually for worship, often in shorts and t-shirts. Karen Ward, at Church of the Apostles, was the only clergyperson to wear any traditional vestment at all, and that was merely a small stole draped over her sweater while she administered the Eucharist.

And at House of Mercy, the trio of preachers is openly ironic—even occasionally sarcastic—in their sermons and announcements. As mentioned in chapter two, even the "blood hymns" played in bluegrass style at House of Mercy are led with a sense of irony.

At first blush this informality is reminiscent of many evangelical churches. But the informal nature of worship in ECM churches goes beyond the casual attire of evangelicalism. The informality of the ECM extends to virtually every aspect of the worship experience: most of the services I attended began ten to fifteen minutes later than advertised; the bands, though excellent musicians, spurned the smooth transitions between worship elements often found at other churches; prayers are read by laypersons with no particular polish; and children freely roam the sanctuary in a couple of the churches. This is not the staged informality of an evangelical megachurch or the solemn informality of a Quaker Friends meeting. This is an ironic, almost reactionary informality, in the same way that blogs and Jon Stewart's *Daily Show* are less formal, more reactionary and ironic versions of newspapers and television newscasts.

The irreverence common in ECM worship services is surely a reflection of the era in which they were born and what they are reacting against, much as the guitar-led music and colloquial preaching of Vineyard and Calvary Chapel churches are reflective of the hippy movement of the late 1960s and early 1970s from which they emerged. *Saturday Night Live* premiered on television in 1975, right at the center point of the birthdates of Generation X. Whereas comedians had been targeting public figures for years, *SNL* took to

---

[41] Seuss, *Oh, the Places You'll Go!* (New York: Random House, 1990).

skewering the president and the pope in a way not before seen. It was in this atmosphere—in the wake of Vietnam and Watergate—that the GenXers who started the ECM came of age, and that atmosphere bred a cynicism that is generally acknowledged by sociologists.[42] Here, then, is another ambiguity being negotiated by ECM churches: reflecting the general cynicism of GenXers without giving themselves and their churches wholly over to cynicism and thereby losing the hope of the gospel. Intriguingly, many emerging church leaders have been attracted to the hope-filled theology of Jürgen Moltmann, which will be explored in the next chapter. This may well be an unconscious choice that nevertheless betrays how ECM leaders are attempting to negotiate this ambiguity.

Preaching

In American Protestantism, the sermon—delivered monologically and by an authority figure—often stands as the centerpiece of the worship experience. Yet we live in an era in which Wikipedia, a collaborative, open-source encyclopedia, has become the largest treasury of human knowledge ever assembled. And it is no longer considered a radical innovation.[43] In 2008, ECM blogger Adam Walker-Cleaveland announced that he would make the sermon that he was preparing "open-source," and he solicited the aid of his blog readers thusly,

> I know there are some different ways of going about writing an "open-source" sermon, but this week I'm just going to be writing it online. I'll be drafting, editing and revising the sermon within this blog post. So, if you want to follow along and leave comments, that would be great! You can Subscribe to the Comments of this post to keep up with the conversation. I have no idea if this will work – or if this is

[42] See Charles H. Lippy, *Faith in America: Changes, Challenges, New Directions*, 3 vols., Praeger Perspectives (Westport, Conn.: Praeger, 2006), 68.

[43] In 2001, the Massachusetts Institute of Technology launched OpenCourseWare, and by 2007 MIT had put almost all of its educational materials online, making them free and available to anyone with Internet access. Hal Ableson, "Reflections on a Decade of Open Sharing: Opening up Opencourseware," in MIT News Blog. Boston: Massachussetts Institute of Technology, 2010. Accessed December 14, 2010.

even a good idea – but I thought I'd try it out for this sermon. Join the conversation & sermon-writing below.[44]

A year prior to that, Walker-Cleaveland had experimented with
developing a collaborative sermon on a "wiki," a type of website that
allows communal editing.[45] It is in this context that preachers in the
ECM are experimenting with the form of the sermon.

When Tim Keel looks across a sea of faces at Jacob's Well and
asks a question as a part of his sermon, it is not simply a rhetorical
device. Instead, congregants immediately begin speaking up, answering the question he has asked. And he calls on them by name.
At Solomon's Porch, a dozen or so people show up on a Tuesday
night for the Bible Discussion Group. There, over a couple hours,
the group dissects the biblical passage to be presented the following
Sunday as the preacher takes notes. By the end of the group discussion, the sermon has pretty well taken shape. And when the sermon
is presented on Sunday evening, the entire congregation joins in the
conversation for the last ten or fifteen minutes of the sermon. And at
Journey, Shroyer facilitates a conversation right in the middle of her
sermon that takes up over half of the time allotted to the sermon and
diverges widely from her topic.

In emerging church congregations, the sermon remains central to
the worship service and to the life of the community, but its potency
has been mitigated somewhat by other elements. For one, the weakening of the role of clergy in the movement undermines the pastor's
traditional hermeneutical authority in the congregation, opening the
interpretation of scripture to all community members. Second, the
high value placed on the Lord's Supper has moved many ECM
churches toward Catholic, Orthodox, and Anglican sensibilities regarding the relative importance of the weekly sacrament over against
the preaching event. Third, the postmodern conception of "language

---

[44] Adam Walker-Cleaveland, "An Open-Source Sermon: Joseph: Unwavering
Faith?," in Pomomusings.com. 2008. Accessed December 14, 2010.

[45] Adam Walker-Cleaveland, "An Experiment in Collaborative Preaching," in
Ibid.2007. Accessed

games"[46] has led many ECM leaders to be suspicious of communities that vaunt an authoritative hermeneut over the rest of the voices in the community.

And fourth, ECM leaders bristle at the monological style in most churches because it feels out-of-step with the participatory, Wikipedia world in which their parishioners live. Pagitt, in his book, *Preaching Re-Imagined*, coined the neologism "speaching" to criticize the way that most sermons are delivered: "Speaching is not defined by the style of the presentation, but by the relationship of the presenter to both the listeners and the content: the pastor uses a lecture-like format, often standing while listeners are sitting. The speacher decides the content ahead of time, usually in a removed setting, and then offers it in such a way that the speacher is in control of the content, speed, and conclusion of the presentation."[47]   Instead, Pagitt suggests that churches convert to using *"progressional dialogue, where the content of the presentation is established in the context of a healthy relationship between the presenter and the listeners, and substantive changes in the content are then created as the result of this relationship."*[48]

While Pagitt, Keel, and Shroyer are surely not the first preachers to converse with their congregations, having parishioners with laptop computers adding to the exegesis of the biblical text with real-time research that they're undertaking online during the worship service is a new challenge and a new opportunity for preachers. At Solomon's Porch, the worship services are streamed live on the Internet,

---

[46] See, for example, J. L. Austin, *How to Do Things with Words* (Oxford: Clarendon Press, 1962). Following Wittgenstein, Austin argues that most sentences do not simply have or not have "truth value," but are instead "performative utterances." That is, most sentences do not simply describe an external referent, as previously thought, but, in a real sense, *do* things. His "speech-act" theory was very influential upon Nancey Murphy of Fuller Theological Seminary, who, in turn, was very influential on early ECM leaders. See Nancey C. Murphy, *Anglo-American Postmodernity: Philosophical Perspectives on Science, Religion, and Ethics* (Boulder, Colo.: Westview Press, 1997).

[47] Doug Pagitt, *Preaching Re-Imagined : The Role of the Sermon in Communities of Faith* (Grand Rapids, Mich.: Zondervan, 2005), 22.

[48] Pagitt, *Preaching Re-Imagined : The Role of the Sermon in Communities of Faith*, 23.

and there has been experimentation with parishioners both in the church building and watching it online sending in their comments on the sermon via Twitter. At The Great Emergence National Event, to launch Phyllis Tickle's eponymous book, a live Twitter feed was shown on a large screen throughout the conference with online input coming from as far away as Kuala Lumpur, Malaysia.

If ECM congregations are on the avant garde of social media, it is not only reflective of the first decade of the twenty-first century, but also in keeping with their theological convictions. The communal hermeneutic with which they are experimenting—crowd-sourced sermons, dialogical preaching, and global conversation partners brought into the sanctuary by technology— is yet another way that these churches and leaders are negotiating the ambiguities at the intersection of an ancient practice and a postmodern culture.

Community

Gathering together for fellowship (*koinonia*) has been central to Christians since the earliest days of the church. The ways and forms of fellowship, however, have evolved significantly from the *domus ecclesiae* of the persecuted Christians in the Roman Empire to the cathedrals of the Middle Ages to the denominational parish churches of nineteenth and twentieth century America to the suburban mega-churches of the past several decades. It cannot be denied that we are currently undergoing a shift of epic proportions regarding the ways that human beings communicate with and relate to one another, and, as might be suspected, based on the demographics of the ECM congregations[49] these are churches that have readily embraced the social media revolution. Of the eight pastors, only Ron Johnson does not have a blog. And all of the churches boast attractive, interactive websites and Facebook pages.

Cedar Ridge Community Church has a standard website full of information about the church including directions, sermon podcasts, and biographies of the leaders. But another area stores much more information and allows those with a log-in name and password to interact with one another and leave comments. The website states, "There are many new features that make the new website a great place for us as a community to share with one another and connect

---

[49] See Appendix A.

on a regular basis even though we might be spread out around the DC/Baltimore area."[50]

At Solomon's Porch, the Sunday evening worship gatherings are often broadcasted live on Ustream, a free video-streaming service. The peripatetic nature of young adulthood means that many men and women have come through Minneapolis—and Solomon's Porch—for a time, and then moved on to another locale for a job, a school, or a romance. Those former parishioners are considered the Solomon's Porch "diaspora," and they are actively encouraged to tune in to the Ustream broadcast on Sunday evenings. On occasion, members of the diaspora have even texted and "tweeted" in questions during the sermon discussion.

House of Mercy boasts a large following on its sermon podcasts, doubling the number of listeners at Sunday evening worship. And they have parlayed those online listeners into a successful online fundraising campaign, receiving donations from individuals who have never attended a House of Mercy service.

The "teaching team" at Journey is the equivalent to Solomon's Porch's "Bible discussion group." It is a small group of theologically-minded staff members and laypersons who meet weekly to discuss the biblical texts of the week and shape the sermon. Recently, the teaching team has forsaken their weekly face-to-face meetings at a pub and instead used Google Wave, a new online collaboration tool. Shroyer says,

> Well we've always collaborated on Sunday night planning. In the beginning, it was a few leaders who met at Starbucks. Over the years, it has become more and more open; that is, anyone in the community can come and be a part of Teaching Team, not just people in a leadership role. Usually we meet on Wednesday nights at Journey...
>
> We had comments from a number of people who wanted to come on Wednesdays but for one reason or another simply couldn't make it — they had kids at home and couldn't get/justify a sitter, they had another meeting or class beforehand and couldn't logistically get from point A to point

---

[50] "What Can I Do with This New Site?," Cedar Ridge Community Church, http://crcc.org/node/1115.

B in a timely manner. Other weeks we just noticed that people were tired and yet another night out seemed too difficult to swing.

We thought Google Wave might address all of these issues, as well as possibly bring in a broader spectrum of voices. If being part of TT (Teaching Team) simply means logging into your computer from home for an hour, maybe more people might be willing to give it a shot.[51]

ECM churches have generally been early adopters of every wave of technological innovation in the past decade—mobile phones, church websites, smart phones, and now social media sites like Facebook and Twitter. They use these services, as the aforequoted webpage from Cedar Ridge Community Church makes clear, to connect churchgoers who live otherwise disparate and disconnected lives. Indeed, there is also much intra-church connection that takes place by these technologies, as sites like Emergent Village[52] and The Ooze[53] function as hubs of conversation, resources, and information as denominations sometimes do for more conventional churches.

Dialogical sermons, online interaction, connection, and collaboration are not simply a reflection of the era in which the emerging church movement was born—though it is surely that—but also a reflection of the very core convictions of the emerging church. Whereas more conventional church leaders may struggle with the idea that anyone can write a comment, be it nice or nasty, on their blog or their church's Facebook page, ECM church leaders seem almost totally unconcerned about this. The leaders of the movement clearly have a high level of trust in the mores of social media. Instead, the belief is often articulated that a plurality of voices is welcome in these congregations, and that the identity of the church is constantly being shaped by this plurality.

---

[51] Tony Jones, "Google Wave as a Sermon Preparation Tool," in WorkingPreacher.com. St. Paul: Luther Theological Seminary, 2010. Accessed July 1, 2010.

[52] http://emergentvillage.org.

[53] http://theooze.com.

Practices of Virtue

Hospitality

In her book, *Hospitality—The Sacred Art*, emerging church Presbyterian pastor Nanette Sawyer writes about her church's attempts to form its congregational life around an ethic of hospitality. But she is also honest about the congregation's struggles with hospitality, and thus proposes that "transformative spiritual hospitality" become the center of the life both of the individual Christian and of the ecclesial community.[54] Sawyer's sentiments are shared by many emerging church congregations, and were reflected in the comments in interviews and focus groups in all eight ECM congregations studied. One example is this comment by David, a college student who attends Cedar Ridge Community Church: "The first thing that kept me there I think was just the warmth of people at Cedar Ridge. I think that church does a fantastic job of connecting people, of helping people to feel engaged and valued. And making their presence there important." A mid-twenties woman at Church of the Apostles echoed that sentiment,

> I mean the number one thing is just the sense of community I've never experienced anywhere else. The ability to enter a room where you just feel like everybody there wants to know you as much as you want to know them. There's this deep wanting to really know and be known and find out about you and why you're here and you know that you want to hear about why I'm here, too. It's just a very authentic sense of connection and something really—that continually reminds me of how important that is when we get visitors from out of town, which happens a lot around here—when they go to leave, they feel—I mean, they almost always say something about just the sense of community here is unlike anything they've experienced anywhere else and they become sort of like part of our family and all of the sudden the world seems smaller because even that far away it's

---

[54] Nanette Sawyer, *Hospitality, the Sacred Art : Discovering the Hidden Spiritual Power of Invitation and Welcome*, Art of Spiritual Living (Woodstock, Vt.: SkyLight Paths Pub., 2008).

connected with them. So, there's something about that. I think that's really unique.

But the hospitality of these churches is not experienced unequivocally. Luke Miller, part-time associate pastor at Journey, worries that their community has become too inwardly focused,

> There's a group of thirty-five or forty of us that—we just feel extremely closely knit and very well connected. So, one of the problems that we've talked about before is the assimilation issue, and I'm not sure how well we care about inviting others in. I think we want to provide the space for others to come in—I'm just not sure that we provide that well. But, one of my hopes is that we would begin to do that—we would begin to think about people outside of our walls and begin to have grace and love for people who share, or who don't share our particular world view or different ideology. I'm not sure we do that very well, either.

In interviews, it is clear that many emerging church congregants are well aware of the public perception of Christians, detailed in David Kinnaman and Gabe Lyons's 2007 book, *UnChristian: What a New Generation Really Thinks about Christianity—and Why It Matters*.[55] Kinnaman and Lyons report that Christians are perceived by non-churchgoers as 1) hypocritical, 2) too focused on getting converts, 3) anti-homosexual, 4) sheltered, 5) too political, and 6) judgmental.[56] Kinnaman and Lyons go on to challenge their fellow evangelicals to change their public posture, if not their theological stances. But their report articulated a growing discomfort within evangelicalism that the evangelical message of Christ's love is getting drowned out by the brashness of their politics.

It can be argued that those who had formed the emerging church movement a decade before *UnChristian* was published were feeling this discomfort acutely enough to abandon their evangelical churches. And the ECM reaction to evangelicalism's public rela-

---

[55] David Kinnaman and Gabe Lyons, *Unchristian: What a New Generation Really Thinks About Christianity—and Why It Matters* (Grand Rapids, Mich.: Baker Books, 2007).

[56] Kinnaman and Lyons, *Unchristian: What a New Generation Really Thinks About Christianity—and Why It Matters*, 29-30.

tions problems has been, in part, to emphasize hospitality as a Christian virtue. Rachel Swan and Karen Mattison spoke in the summer of 2010 about being a lesbian couple at Solomon's Porch, and then Swan posted this reflection on her blog:

> We both feel really grateful to be a part of this community. For a very long time I have looked for a church that would just take me as I am... I have been to a lot of places, worked with a lot of people and been a part of many church/community conversations. There are a lot churches who have stickers, flags and belief statements that explicitly affirm how much they love and fully welcome LGBT people. I am glad that they are a part of our God family. For some who have been told they are going to hell, or worse, these places are a refuge for lesbian, gay, bisexual and transgender people. These churches are places that they can know when they can walk in, worship and participate, that they will not have to face one more fire and brimstone, love the sinner/hate the sin sermon. They won't be barred from participating in communion. The signs and flags mean "we like you gays and you will be safe here."
>
> But for me, I feel safe *here*. When I say I want a church that will take me just as I am, I don't want to belong to the "gay church" or the church for women, or church for cat owners, or churches that gather around the commonality of their members. I like being amongst a diversity of people who share a common purpose and dream for what God is doing, not necessarily focused on what I am doing. Personally speaking, I do not need a flag or sign, though some people may want that. What I have longed for all along is to break bread, to shake hands, to help out, and to serve and participate in what God is doing in the world—just like you. Thank you for your part in making this place feel like home to us.[57]

Swan is not only articulating her experience of hospitality in an ECM congregation, but she is doing that over against her previous

---

[57] Rachel Swan, "Our Soapbox," in The Sweet Bi and Bi: Musings on bisexuality and a "new" old time faith. Minneapolis: 2010. Accessed December 18, 2010.

experiences at more conventional churches. Whereas denominational Protestant churches usually show their hospitality to GLBT
persons by joining the denomination's organized effort in that regard, and then post statements to that effect on websites and in the
Sunday bulletin, Solomon's Porch has never taken a stand on GLBT
issues. Instead, Swan and Mattison testified to a hospitality that is
more ingrained into the very heart of Solomon's Porch. The practice
of hospitality, as they see it, is not a particular campaign on their behalf, but a way of being that made them feel welcome.

Theology

Luke Miller's comments above presage another practice of virtue
in the ECM, that is an openness to many theological and confes-
sional perspectives. Cedar Ridge Community Church founder Brian
McLaren's book *A Generous Orthodoxy* is the premier statement of
that posture, as evidenced by his subtitle: *Why I Am a Missional, Evangelical, Post/Protestant, Liberal/Conservative, Mystical/Poetic,
Biblical, Charismatic/Contemplative, Fundamentalist/Calvinist,
Anabaptist/Anglican, Methodist, Catholic, Green, Incarnational,
Depressed-Yet-Hopeful, Emergent, Unfinished Christian.*[58] Therein,
McLaren meanders through most of the major segments of modern
Christianity, pointing out the aspects of each that he likes and dis-
likes. His bestselling book has been both descriptive of and pre-
scriptive for many in the ECM.

David, at McLaren's own church, seems to have picked up on
that: "At Cedar Ridge, I'm encouraged to think about doctrine and
I'm allowed to think freely about doctrine. Which is actually the
way it's supposed to be rather than me blindly signing the Creed or
the Confession or something like that, you know. So I'm allowed to
think about doctrine rather than having it preached at me." And Allison, at Journey, feels similarly about her church experience,

> I think in terms of theology, I'm not sure that it changed a
> lot because I think that I've always had questions and

---

[58] McLaren, *A Generous Orthodoxy: Why I Am a Missional, Evangelical,
Post/Protestant, Liberal/Conservative, Mystical/Poetic, Biblical,
Charismatic/Contemplative, Fundamentalist/Calvinist, Anabaptist/Anglican,
Methodist, Catholic, Green, Incarnational, Depressed-yet-Hopeful, Emergent,
Unfinished Christian.*

been—I think I've grown more certain in the fact that I cannot ever find all the answers and that I've gained a confidence that questioning isn't going to necessarily result in hell, or the fact that I'm not going with the party line doesn't have this direct consequence. So, I think the confidence that I've gained through my theology has been something that is invaluable to me and I think in practice, especially in the last year, I've gotten a lot more active about how I live out my faith: living a more simplistic life, I think.

But, like her fellow Journey member Luke Miller, Allison is ambivalent about the generous orthodoxy of her church, "My fear for Journey is that we are going to become so open that we don't have any boundaries, that we don't have any stance, and we're so afraid to insult someone or to say something wrong, that we don't say anything at all."

Emerging church congregaations are not only open to various theological influences, but also to the ecclesial practices that spring from various traditions. Kimball's Vintage Faith made waves in evangelical circles in the mid-1990s for encouraging the singing of old church hymns and taking time in worship to explain the origin of each hymn. Cedar Ridge has taught classes on centering prayer (Catholic) and the Jesus prayer (Orthodox). And Jacob's Well hosts the traditionally Catholic practice of the Stations of the Cross during Lent.

Since the Reformation, Protestant Christianity has developed via divorce, with new branches sprouting up often. By the beginning of the twentieth century, Protestantism boasted myriad discrete denominations, each claiming to represent a true and accurate representation of the gospel. During that century, even while new Pentecostal and Charismatic denominations were forming, America saw many of the larger denominations merge, forming large bodies like the Evangelical Lutheran Church in America, the United Church of Christ, the United Methodist Church, and the Presbyterian Church (USA). But by the turn of the twenty-first century, it was generally acknowledged that these mega-denominations, which had been very powerful forces in American society and politics just decades earlier, had lost much of their potency. As of this writing, every one of those denominations is struggling financially, losing members, and closing churches.

Meanwhile, the world became more pluralistic and, thanks to electronic communication, smaller. So Christians who in past times would have been familiar primarily or solely with the theology and practices of their own traditions are now able to learn about the wide variety of beliefs available in Protestantism, and even in Catholicism and Orthodoxy. Plus, the stigma of changing denominations, and even intermarrying between denominations, is virtually non-existent in mainline American Protestantism.

All of these factors have contributed to a growing disenfranchisement among younger Protestants with the denominational identities that were so important to their forebears. The generous orthodoxy of the emerging church movement is a reflection of that. Thus, it is not uncommon to witness practices of various traditions in an ECM worship service, like the hybrid form of communion practiced at Solomon's Porch or the recitation of Orthodox prayers at Jacob's Well.

But even the generous orthodoxy of the ECM is not without its detractors. Dan Kimball of Vintage Faith declared in print that he is a "fundamentalist,"[59] and he has since distanced himself from the ECM.[60] Others have decried McLaren's book as "neither generous nor orthodox."[61] In the end, it seems that the generous orthodoxy McLaren endorses is being held, if tenuously, in fragile equilibrium by most ECM churches.

Creating Art

In a documentary that aired on ABC stations in 2003, a profile of Ecclesia Church in Houston shows a husband-and-wife team painting with oils on a large canvas as Pastor Chris Seay preaches in the background.[62] The building in which the Ecclesia congregation

---

[59] Robert Webber et al., *Listening to the Beliefs of Emerging Churches* (Grand Rapids, Mich.: Zondervan, 2007), 97.

[60] Dan Kimball, "The Emerging Church: 5 Years Later - the Definition Has Changed," in VintageFaith.com. Santa Cruz: 2008. Accessed July 1, 2010.

[61] Albert Mohler, "A Generous Orthodoxy - Is It Orthodox?," in AlbertMohler.com. Louisville: 2005. Accessed July 1, 2010.

[62] Bernie Hargis, "The Changing Face of Worship: The Church in a Postmodern World," (USA: FamilyNet, Inc., 2002).

meets doubles as a coffee shop and art gallery. Jeremy Wells, who paints during Ecclesia's services, says, "A lot of times people ask us if having people paint during the worship service is distracting or confusing to people, and I would just ask them if they think that singing during worship is confusing or distracting."[63]

The emerging churches I visited noticeably and consistently vaunted and encouraged the creation of art as a holy practice. When I visited Vintage Faith Church, they were constructing a similar space in what had been the Fellowship Hall of the former Presbyterian church. And in Kimball's book on designing worship, he repeatedly advocates using art in the worship experience.[64]   At Journey, the art of church member and professional photographer Courtney Perry adorns the walls. At Church of the Apostles and Cedar Ridge, congregants are encouraged to visit art stations before and after they take communion and to create art that is reflective of their experience at the Lord's Supper.

At Solomon's Porch, the walls of the worship area are covered with visual art, all original pieces by members of the community. Luke Hillestad, the artist-in-residence at Solomon's Porch, is an accomplished painter who regularly shows his work at galleries in the Twin Cities. As well as curating exhibitions at Solomon's Porch of Advent and Lent each year, he often stations himself in the balcony during worship gatherings and paints as the community worships. Occasionally, his live painting is projected overhead on the ceiling of the sanctuary during the worship. In the Artisans' Co-op at Solomon's Porch, Hillestad's art is for sale, as well as pieces by other painters, photographers, fabric artists, and jewelry makers.

Emerging church leaders have been keen to note that during vast stretches of Western history, the church served as the primary patron of the arts. They have also been quick to criticize the modern church for forsaking this role. ECM churches have, in turn, proactively recruited artists and have made the display of art essential in their worship environments. This is particularly noteworthy among the ECM pastors who come from evangelicalism, a tradition known for spurning "secular" art. When asked, Seay volunteers that art is the

---

[63] Hargis, "The Changing Face of Worship: The Church in a Postmodern World."

[64] Kimball, *Emerging Worship: Creating New Worship Gatherings for Emerging Generations.*

best way to "tell the beautiful, redemptive story of God" to the young, urban professionals who live in the neighborhood around Ecclesia.[65]

There can be no doubt that, like Seay says, telling the story of God well is a virtue in the overarching practice of Christianity. And, as argued in chapter one, the emerging church movement is particularly attractive to the cultural creative class of younger, American Christians. It is only natural, then, that they would re-introduce the creation of art to the life of their congregations, and this is yet another example of emerging church congregations negotiating the ambiguity of attracting a young cultural creative class with inherited forms of worship.

Priesthood of All Believers

Another cultural ambiguity which the emerging church has to negotiate, as mentioned above, is the increasing suspicion of authority figures—especially clerical ones—while at the same time knowing that communities need leadership. In contrast to traditional mainline ecclesial structures, the ECM churches have a "lower" view of ordination, or a "higher" view of lay involvement. Or both. Although the pastors at seven of the eight churches studied are seminary trained and most were previously ordained in a denominational structure, only at House of Mercy are the pastors demarcated "Rev." in church literature. Only at Church of the Apostles was it clear that an ordained clergyperson was saying the words of institution during the Eucharistic liturgy.

While this is common in certain "low church" versions of evangelicalism, the mitigation of the role of clergy is not the result of a disparagement of seminary training. Just the opposite, in fact. These emerging church pastors—even McLaren, who lacks formal theological training—vaunt theological higher education in their writings and among their congregations. Instead, the discomfort with the appellations acquired by seminary training and ordination seem to be a result of the egalitarian and relational ecclesiology that these leaders are attempting to cultivate.

Throughout history, the church has struggled with the exhortation in 1 Peter 2:9, "You are royal priests, a holy nation, God's very

---

[65] Hargis, "The Changing Face of Worship: The Church in a Postmodern World."

own possession," and articulated succinctly by Martin Luther, who coined the phrase, "the priesthood of all believers." Most recently within Protestantism, there has been an attempt to increase the ministry of laity through many different initiatives at the local and denominational levels. However, these have most often left the two-class system of clergy and laity intact. While laypersons are encouraged to offer counseling to fellow members through a program like the Stephen Ministry, ordained clergy are still the only personnel allowed to perform the pastoral functions of weddings and funerals. Deacons and Eucharistic Ministers are encouraged to pass out the communion elements, but only ordained clergy are permitted to say the "words of institution" that sacralize those elements. And while laypeople give their testimonies in worship, only the pastor gets to preach the sermon.

If the increasing involvement of laypersons has been incremental within modern American Protestantism, the emerging church movement seems to be taking it the next step. As previously mentioned, the majority of the liturgy at Church of the Apostles is administered by laypeople. A different member of the congregation introduces communion each week at Solomon's Porch. Most of these congregations operate a polity that is a kind of hybrid of Congregationalism and a free church evangelical structure. Jacob's Well, Vintage Faith, Journey, and Pathways have boards of elders, and Cedar Ridge has a board of trustees. Solomon's Porch has a "leadership co-op." And House of Mercy and Church of the Apostles have governance that is reflective of their denominational progenitors. Each is loosely democratic in that the board is meant to represent the members of the congregational body, but none is as fiercely democratic as a true Congregational polity would require.

Sacred Space

When the earliest Christians met in one another's homes (*domus ecclesiae*), it was by dint of necessity. However, after the conversion of the Emperor Constantine, Christian worship space took on a dramatically different shape, culminating with the large basilicas and cathedrals still extant in Europe. When Christianity came to North America, it took on yet more spatial forms, from the austerity of New England meetinghouses to the tent meetings of the American South to the theater seating and high tech sanctuaries of evangelical mega-churches. The emerging church movement has continued this tradition of negotiating sacred space. After stops in a retail space and a former sheet metal plant, Solomon's Porch has joined Jacob's Well, Church of the Apostles, House of Mercy, and Vintage Faith in buildings that were built by and formerly home to denominational churches. Journey meets in an office park, Pathways in a former synagogue, and Cedar Ridge built their own physical plant on a former farm, incorporating some of the farm's original elements. The fact that seven of the eight congregations have ultimately settled in an edifice that was originally intended for a worshipping community shows some sense of continuity between the emerging church movement and the iterations of American Christianity that preceded them.

However, these churches have also rearranged the furniture in these settings and have, in some cases, dramatically reshaped the worship environment. Both Vintage Faith and Jacob's Well inhabit formerly Presbyterian buildings; each has changed the staging significantly, including moving (and occasionally removing) the altar in order to make room for a band. Each has large video screens on either side of the stage, and both churches have removed the pulpit, since both Dan Kimball and Tim Keel preach from the floor of the sanctuary.

At Solomon's Porch and Journey, couches, floor lamps, and coffee tables have replaced the pews. Art hangs from the walls at both churches, and each avoids calling its worship space a "sanctuary." Both Doug Pagitt and Danielle Shroyer make use of the living room aesthetic during their sermons, leading discussion and conversation as they preach. It is clear in their cases that the renegotiation of sacred space is reflective of their communication and their theology. When asked, Pagitt says that the in-the-round seating and the comfortable furniture of Solomon's Porch's worship space is meant to encourage reconciliation, in line with Paul's claim in 2 Corinthians 5 that "in Christ God was reconciling the world to himself," and that Christians are consequently made ambassadors of reconciliation. "I don't see how you can live in reconciliation with people when you look at the backs of their heads each week," Pagitt said, referring to the traditional pew seating in many churches.

Every prior arrangement of sacred space in Christian history, be it basilican or auditorium or believers gathered under a tree, has been the result of a combination of cultural forces and theological convictions. The emerging church movement is no different in this regard.

The sacred space in these eight congregations shows a sensitivity to church tradition, but is also clearly a reflection of the informal and relational nature of the people who are drawn to these churches.

Initial Observations

There is a binding characteristic of all the foregoing practices: these are ultimately *practices of relationality*. That is, each of these practices has grown out of the fact that, in the emerging church movement, relationality is placed at a premium. By "relationality," I mean the experience of lived relations between human beings, and between human beings and God. By arranging the seating in the round and on couches, the leaders of Solomon's Porch and Journey are placing relationality at a higher premium than capacity, for each church could seat more people if they opted for a more efficient seating structure. By walking up the center aisle and calling on interlocuters by name, Tim Keel is making clear that voices other than his are also important in the sermon. And by committing to practices of hospitality and a generous view toward other theologies, all of these congregations are vaunting inter-human relationships above doctrinal accuracy or denominational identity.

But even with this commitment to relationality, there is room for theological engagement and even improvement. For example, what is not mentioned at Solomon's Porch, at least overtly, is how the administration of the sacrament of communion— indeed, it is not referred to as a "sacrament"—or how the recitation of a creed and a doxology have shaped the congregation over the last decade. What Solomon's Porch and the rest of the churches in this study have not yet done to any great extent is the second-order discourse of theological reflection. They have, instead, *intuited* their way in to these practices. In the case of communion, for instance, the community of Solomon's Porch, lacking an anchor in any particular, discreet ecclesial tradition, chose nevertheless to incorporate communion as a central mark of its life together. I contend that while this decision was not obviously purposeful in its theological rationale, neither was it entirely accidental. Instead, I assert that the members of Solomon's Porch, and many other churches of the ECM, have a potent, albeit latent, theology that recognizes the authority of the broader church tradition. Even if the "Great Tradition" of the church is not referenced in worship, and even occasionally disparaged, it still exerts a certain level of control over Solomon's Porch. In other words, this is not a congregation which has cut itself off from the historic, orthodox church, and the weekly practice of communion is indicative of the congregation's desire for this connection. What they have yet to do, however, is to overtly claim that theological heritage. If they did, it would both benefit their congregation and other churches that seek to be in relationship with Solomon's Porch.

Further, it is questionable whether cynicism and irony—even revolt—are sustainable attributes of a faith community. It seems unlikely that congregants—and even preachers—can maintain the psychic fortitude needed to engage the world with constant irony. Even the fact that the emerging church movement developed largely in reaction to the mega-churches of the late-twentieth century leaves it open to criticism. What will the movement do when the church against which it protested no longer exists? It may be that as the GenXers age, their ECM churches will mollify their antagonistic stance toward conventional churches, or that the GenXers themselves will gravitate toward more conventional churches.

Another challenge to the emerging church movement was posed by Yale theologian, Miroslav Volf, to the ECM's commitment to innovation in worship. When asked at the 2006 Emergent Village Theological Conversation why he had left the evangelical, Pentecostal tradition of his youth for the Episcopal Church, he argued that it is simply not possible to come up with new worship elements every week that can rival the beauty of the *Book of Common Prayer*.[66] Several of the ECM leaders in attendance took umbrage at his suggestion. Volf's contention seems to be based on an anthropological conviction that quality will suffer over the long haul when human beings are attempting to innovate in worship every week. The anthropological counter to this is that the ECM, as mentioned above, has intentionally catered to the cultural creative class, and these are individuals who might just as well be creating poetry or art or television shows weekly. And further, the theological counter is that a creative God inspires creative worship. But Volf also has a point, because other upstart versions of Christian worship have had similarly creative elements at their genesis but ultimately found constant innovation to be unsustainable and ultimately codified their rubrics in worship books and hymnals.

---

[66] Miroslav Volf, "Conversation with Miroslav Volf" (paper presented at the Emergent Village Theological Conversation, Yale University Divinity School, New Haven, Connecticut, February 6-8 2006).

The emerging church also places a high level of trust in fellow human beings and in the technology that connects people in the twenty-first century. Both the polity that is developing in the ECM, and the embrace of social media as a means for connecting with one another betray a possible naïveté about the nature of human relationships. What is not often heard in these churches is talk about the traditional Western doctrine of original sin, much less the Reformed doctrine of total depravity. Instead, there seems to be a generally optimistic view about humankind. How the movement will deal with the inevitable foibles of its members and leaders remains to be seen. Again, it seems that some cogent theological reflection on this matter would serve the movement well.

Also on the subject of polity, it seems that these congregations are not democratic enough. When asked why Jacob's Well has a board of elders rather than some other structure, be it traditional or innovative, Tim Keel admitted that he simply didn't think much about it when he started the church. What most of these congregations seemed to have defaulted into is a rather traditional, free church evangelical approach to church governance. Whereas they have been highly innovative in other aspects of their ecclesial lives, they have not yet found similar ways to innovate their polity. The danger here lies in the rising prominence of the pastors in these congregations. Without serious deliberation regarding how decisions are made, the board of elders may too easily do the bidding of the pastor. Jürgen Moltmann's ecclesiology, addressed in the next chapter, and the polity of traditional Congregationalism, described in chapter five, both offer the ECM some assistance in this regard.

In the end, the core practices of these eight congregations show that the nascent emerging church movement is deeply committed to a relational ecclesiology, but it is as yet deficient at the robust theological reflection that will enable these practices, and this movement, to be sustainable over the long haul.

Chapter Four: The Relational Ecclesiology of Jürgen Moltmann and the Emerging Church Movement

Among leaders in the emerging church movement, Jürgen Moltmann is possibly the most highly revered twentieth century theologian, and with good reason. Moltmann, in both theology and method, is particularly attuned to the same sensibilities that drive much of the theory and practice of the ECM. Moltmann has called his own work a "theology on the way" and a "theology after Auschwitz." His has been an attempt to write a theology without the foundationalism of his European forbears, a theology that is chastened by the failings of the twentieth century, and a theology that is conversant with many and diverse rationalities—most explicitly, that of science. With these sensibilities, Moltmann is resonant with the transversal methodology of Shrag and van Huyssteen, outlined in chapter one and, I propose, with the general outlook of emerging church congregations.[1] As the ECM has developed, its leaders have looked for theological resources that are both rooted in the tradition of orthodox Christian theology but also seeking a way forward that exemplifies the epistemic humility of postmodern theory. While not necessarily a postmodernist, Moltmann's theology at least sloughs off much of the language of certainty common in post-Enlightenment Protestant theology.

While the emerging church movement has much to learn from Moltmann's entire corpus, his ecclesiology is particularly pertinent to this study. Ecclesiology happens also to be among the least appreciated of Moltmann's theological contributions, so I hope that this book might encourage a broader engagement with his ecclesiology across American Protestantism. Moltmann's ecclesiology offers particular possibilities to the American church in an era in which lay participation is waxing and the potency of mainline denominations is waning.

After an overview of Moltmann's theological project, I will look specifically at Moltmann's radical, if underappreciated and underdeveloped, ecclesiology, and I will investigate both his "early eccle-

---

[1] Richard Osmer has made similar connections between Moltmann, Schrag, and van Huyssteen. See Osmer, *The Teaching Ministry of Congregations*, 308ff.

siology" and "later ecclesiology." Although the ECM has not consciously drawn on Moltmann's ecclesiology, his ecclesiology will serve as both an affirmation and criticism of the burgeoning ecclesiology of the ECM, and will launch us into a proposal of relational ecclesiology in chapter five.

An Overview of Moltmann's Theological Project

Setting the groundwork of Moltmann's overall theological project is necessary, for it gives the context out of which his ecclesiology emerges.   Further, his theological method has been quite influential upon my own, thereby uncovering some important insights into the pragmatic suggestions I proffer in chapter five.

Both at the beginning and end of his career, Jürgen Moltmann has referred to his own theology a *theologia viatorum*: "a theology for us wayfarers."[2] By that, he means that his theological agenda has been ever-shifting, the result of the various contemporary issues that he feels have confronted the church over his career. He has attempted to develop a theology that has a biblical foundation, an eschatological orientation, and a political impetus.[3] Elsewhere, he has written that his theological corpus has three main themes:

a trinitarian thinking about God,

an ecological thinking about the community of creation,

an eschatological thinking about the various indwellings of God (in his people, in Christ, and in creation).[4]

Since Moltmann has truly evolved as a theologian over the years, it makes some sense to thematize his work chronologically, drawing out significant objects of his reflection along the way, particularly those that are relevant to his ecclesiology. His theological career has

---

[2] Jürgen Moltmann, *Sun of Righteousness, Arise! God's Future for Humanity and the Earth* (Minneapolis: Fortress Press, 2010), 181.

[3] Jürgen Moltmann, *History and the Triune God: Contributions to Trinitarian Theology* (New York: Crossroad, 1992), 182.

[4] Jürgen Moltmann, *The Coming of God: Christian Eschatology* (London: SCM, 1996), xii.

basically been comprised of two major phases—the first is his more
famous three-book cycle, and the second, a six-book cycle of "contributions" to systematic theology.

Moltmann's original trilogy is comprised of *Theology of Hope*
(1964), *The Crucified God* (1972), and *The Church in the Power of
the Spirit* (1975).[5] These three books can be seen as reciprocal and
mutually complementary perspectives on his theological vision—Moltmann has described them as leading from Easter to Good
Friday and then to Pentecost. As opposed to a traditional volume of
dogmatic theology in which the author looks extensively at one
theological doctrine or set of doctrines, Moltmann attempts in each
of these books to look at the whole of theology through a single lens:
resurrection hope; the crucifixion; and pneumatological ecclesiology. Therefore, instead of ending up in the final volume of a sys-
tematics, Moltmann's early ecclesial proposals are scattered
throughout these books, coming to culmination most specifically in
the lattermost.

The first two books together develop the first major theme of
Moltmann's work: the dialectical interpretation of the cross and the
resurrection of Jesus Christ. The hope that is represented in the resurrection directly contradicts the suffering and death of the crucifixion, yet in the person of Jesus Christ, this contradiction is
embodied. That is, in the resurrection, God created continuity out of
radical discontinuity—and this continuity-out-of-discontinuity mir-
rors the earthly existence of human beings (and the church) in relationship to our promised eschatological relationship with God. All
of reality, then, in its godlessness, godforsakenness, and transitoriness is identified in Christ as he himself—a member of the community of the Trinity—experiences godlessness, godforsakenness,
and transitoriness.[6] Moltmann's ecclesiology in these volumes is
primarily an exhortation that the church be a community of the god-

---

[5] Jürgen Moltmann, *Theology of Hope: On the Ground and the Implications of a Christian Eschatology*, 1st U.S. ed. (New York: Harper & Row, 1967). Jürgen Moltmann, *The Crucified God: The Cross of Christ as the Foundation and Criticism of Christian Theology*, 1st Fortress Press ed. (Minneapolis: Fortress Press, 1993). Jürgen Moltmann, *The Church in the Power of the Spirit: A Contribution to Messianic Ecclesiology* (Minneapolis: Fortress Press, 1993).

[6] Richard Bauckham, *The Theology of Jürgen Moltmann* (Edinburgh: T&T Clark, 1995), 5.

less and godforsaken, proclaiming gospel hope both within and without its walls.

Significantly for Moltmann's ecclesiology in *The Church in the Power of the Spirit*, and growing out of his reflections on the crucifixion and resurrection in the first two volumes, he develops a social understanding of the Trinity, a theme that overarches all six of his later "contributions" to systematic theology. Moltmann rejects traditional Western trinitarian theories—those held both by the Catholic Church and most Protestants—as "modalism" or "monarchial monotheism" and instead adopts the Eastern conception of God as a *perichoresis*, or an enduring and mutually interpenetrating fellowship of divine love between three persons.[7] For instance, the Holy Spirit is not merely the power between the Father and the Son, but is instead a unique subject (Moltmann strongly rejects the eleventh century creedal addition of the "*filioque* clause"[8]). One characteristic of Moltmann's perichoretic Trinity is that of openness: the fellowship of Father, Son, and Holy Spirit is "other than" creation, but it is open to embrace creation into itself. Thus, Moltmann argues that all of history is actually a part of the "trinitarian history of God."[9]

Moltmann thus proposes a Trinitarian hermeneutic for all of theology. *Contra* Barth, who saw all of history focused in the work of a single subject (Jesus Christ and the crucifixion/resurrection event), Moltmann sees the identification of Jesus Christ as the "Son" defining Christ's identity *relationally*. The history of God is not that of a monolithic and unchanging Lord but the history of the living relationship between the Father, the Son, the Holy Spirit, and all of creation. Moltmann goes on to argue that "monarchial monotheisms"—those doctrines of God that prescribe a hierarchical relationship in the Godhead and throughout creation—result in po-

---

[7] Jürgen Moltmann, *The Trinity and the Kingdom: The Doctrine of God* (Minneapolis, MN: Fortress Press, 1993), 175.

[8] Moltmann, *The Trinity and the Kingdom: The Doctrine of God*, 180-82. See also Jürgen Moltmann, *The Spirit of Life: A Universal Affirmation* (Minneapolis: Fortress Press, 1992), 306ff.

[9] This phrase, which becomes very important in Moltmann's writings, is first introduced in Moltmann, *The Crucified God: The Cross of Christ as the Foundation and Criticism of Christian Theology*, 274ff.

litical and ecclesial dictatorships, with human monarchs and popes ultimately made in the image of a dictatorial Lord.[10] Instead, he argues, the political ramifications of the social Trinity are national democracies and small, communal, egalitarian churches.

Moltmann in Dialogue with Practical Theology

Beginning early in his career, Moltmann was recognized for being a systematician with a particular affinity for practical theology. Editor Theodore Runyan introduces the 1979 volume, *Hope for the Church: Moltmann in Dialogue with Practical Theology*, by writing, "According to Moltmann, good theology must be *practical* theology. He addresses the problems of ministry not just because of his own years of pastoral experience, but because practice is at the heart of his theological method. Theology is the theory of the future of the church, and its purpose is to make a difference in the shape of that future."[11]

Indeed, Moltmann himself came to this conclusion at the very beginning of his career. In 1968, addressing the World Student Christian Federation Conference, he echoed Marx's Theses No. 2 and No. 11 when said, "The new criterion of theology and faith is to be found in praxis...Truth must be practicable. Unless it contains initiative for the transformation of the world, it becomes a myth of the existing world."[12] That commitment to praxis, and to dissolving the traditional remove from the church that systematic theology usu-

---

[10] Moltmann, *The Trinity and the Kingdom: The Doctrine of God*, 200-02.

[11] Jürgen Moltmann, M. Douglas Meeks, and Theodore Runyon, *Hope for the Church: Moltmann in Dialogue with Practical Theology* (Nashville: Abingdon, 1979), 9. On this point, see also Osmer, *The Teaching Ministry of Congregations*, 203ff.

[12] Jürgen Moltmann, *Religion, Revolution, and the Future* (New York: Scribner, 1969), 139. At the other end of his career, Moltmann wrote, "And not least, with the phrase 'systematic contributions to theology' I am acknowledging that theology is more than systematic theology. There is historical, exegetical, and practical theology, and other theological fields still. Systematic theology is only one sector and should no longer be understood as the crown of theological studies, to which all the other forms of theology are ancillary."

Jürgen Moltmann, *A Broad Place: An Autobiography* (Minneapolis: Fortress Press, 2008), 287.

ally inhabits, Moltmann told the audience at Ministers' Week at Candler School of Theology in 1978, "Every change in theory demands a change in practice. Every practice demands a change in theory. Every change in theory and practice must bring a corresponding change in the rituals of life."[13]

To that end, Moltmann echoes the thesis of Paul Tillich that, "Theology, as a function of the Christian church, must serve the needs of the church,"[14] and Moltmann bemoans the chasm between systematic and practical theology,

> This gap between theology and Christian life in the churches is reflected in theology itself in the growing gulf between systematic and practical theology. These disciplines are becoming more and more isolated from each other...As a result, what makes theology *Christian* theology— namely, the vision of God in Christ and concern for the Christian community in the world—is in danger of being lost to both disciplines.[15]

Moltmann's interest in practical theology has always been linked with his affinity for liberation theology—in fact his has more often been called a "political theology." His very first book, *Theology of Hope*, was inspired by the Marxist philosophy of Ernst Bloch,[16] and three decades later he was still writing, "*Liberation* from violence, brutality, and poverty remains the theme of every practical theology and every theological practice."[17]

---

[13] Moltmann, Meeks, and Runyon, *Hope for the Church: Moltmann in Dialogue with Practical Theology*, 18-19.

[14] Paul Tillich, *Systematic Theology / Paul Tillich*, 3 vols. (Chicago: University of Chicago Press, 1951), 3.

[15] Moltmann, Meeks, and Runyon, *Hope for the Church: Moltmann in Dialogue with Practical Theology*, 128-29.

[16] Ernst Bloch, *Das Prinzip Hoffnung*, 3 vols. (Berlin: Aufbau-Verlag, 1954).

[17] Jürgen Moltmann, *God for a Secular Society : The Public Relevance of Theology* (Minneapolis: Fortress Press, 1999), 69. He goes on,

> But we have another theme as well as liberty, a theme which has almost been forgotten and edged out since the

As his career continued, Moltmann's theological method evolved along these same lines, again showing little affinity with his German compatriots who wrote systematized books using traditional theological categories. In 1980, following his initial trilogy, Moltmann wrote that his next cycle of books would not attempt to look at all of theology through a single prism, but would instead be "contributions to theology," an expression which "is intended to avoid the seductions of the theological system and the coercion of the dogmatic thesis." These contributions "presuppose an intensive theological discussion, both past and present. They participate critically in this discussion, offering their own suggestions, their aim being to prepare the way for a theological discussion in the future that will be both broader and more intensive."[18]

From that point of his career on, Moltmann's work became even more dialogical, and he asserted that "truth is to be found in unhindered dialogue."[19] Whereas Moltmann's early writings were in conversation with traditional dialogue partners for systematic theology—process philosophy, Marxism, and linguistic analysis—his later works converse with dialogue partners more common to practical theology: social theory, Freudian analysis, evolutionary psychology, and biomedical ethics. Moltmann's theology, in fact, has much in common with the transversal rationality described in chapter one, for he has pursued an almost *ad hoc* approach, tackling issues that he considers significant for the life of the church. For example, when confronted with the current ecological crisis, Moltmann

---

collapse of the socialist world. This theme is *equality*. Without equality there is no free world. It is in the spirit of early Christianity that we call the truth that all human beings are created *free* and *equal* 'self-evident'. Equality doesn't mean collectivism. It means equal conditions for living, and equal chances of living for everyone. As a social concept, equality means *justice*. As a humanitarian concept, equality means *solidarity*. As a Christian concept, equality means *love*.

[18] Moltmann, *The Trinity and the Kingdom: The Doctrine of God*, xii.

[19] Moltmann, *The Trinity and the Kingdom: The Doctrine of God*, xiii.

developed an "ecological doctrine of creation."[20]   He has also worked extensively to reconcile the chasm between the sciences and religion,[21] and, as we will see below, his ecclesiology is a direct confrontation of the European state-church model, which he considers deeply flawed. Moltmann's transversal approach to theological issues is yet another reason that he is so compatible with a practical theological project like mine.

Moltmann's Early Ecclesiology

Moltmann's third major book—the final book in his first cycle—presents his most fully articulated early ecclesiology. *The Church in the Power of the Spirit: A Contribution to Messianic Ecclesiology* may be his most ignored major book by the theological community, and some have wondered whether this is because it is the closest Moltmann comes to writing a practical theology.[22]   In this

---

[20] Jürgen Moltmann, *God in Creation: A New Theology of Creation and the Spirit of God*, The Gifford Lectures; 1984-1985 (Minneapolis: Fortress Press, 1993).

[21] Jürgen Moltmann, *Science and Wisdom* (London: SCM, 2003). See also Moltmann, *Sun of Righteousness, Arise! God's Future for Humanity and the Earth*, 189-224.

[22] Moltmann himself has written that German church leaders ignored his ecclesiology because his call for the church to be a voluntary community of believers did not comport with their own vision of the church. Moltmann, *History and the Triune God: Contributions to Trinitarian Theology*, 175-76. Richard Baukham agrees, writing,

> The *Church in the Power of the Spirit* seems to have attracted less interest and has certainly provoked far less theological discussion that Moltmann's other major works. This can hardly be because its proposals are less controversial, but it may be because, though rooted in theological argument, they are controversial in their practical thrust towards reforming the life and structure of the church. As such they cross "the growing gulf between systematic and practical theology" and fall outside the central interests of academic theology, which tends to keep its distance from the church, especially from the church as actual "grass-

book, Moltmann descends from the theoretical heights that characterize much German Protestant theology and writes concretely about the implications of his work for actual communities of faith. For instance, his understanding of the Trinity prompts him to argue against large denominations and church bureaucracies and instead propose an ideal of small, local churches that are run by egalitarian groups of believers.

The church, Moltmann argues, lives in the dialectical tension that he laid out in his first two books. That is, the church lives at once remembering the past (crucifixion) and proclaiming the future (resurrection). Just as Jesus Christ embodied this dialectical, eschatological reality, the church as the body of Christ now embodies the same reality. As the primary (but by no means exclusive) conveyer of God's eschatological hope in the world, Moltmann compares the church to a disease's host body, whose job it is to infect the world with a germ—and here the germ is the hope of liberation. The church plays a mediating role in society, reminding the world of the hope in God's eschatological future.

As well as the term "messianic ecclesiology" in the book's subtitle, and his favored appellation for the church, "messianic fellowship," Moltmann occasionally uses the phrase "relational ecclesiology," which truly summarizes the major theme of *The Church in the Power of the Spirit*: "The church cannot understand itself simply from itself alone. It can only comprehend its mission and its meaning, its roles and its functions in relation to others."[23] Those relationships, Moltmann writes, are between the church and believers' experience of belief, between church and the history of the church, and between the church and the present context in which it finds itself. But the most important relationship, and the one which ties Moltmann's ecclesiology with his previous books, is the rela-

---

roots" communities of Christians, which for Moltmann are the real subject of ecclesiology.

Bauckham, *The Theology of Jürgen Moltmann*, 119.

[23] Moltmann, *The Church in the Power of the Spirit: A Contribution to Messianic Ecclesiology*, 19.

tionship between the church and the "trinitarian history of God's dealings with the world:"[24]

> The church can only understand its own position or abode in participation in the movement of the history of God's dealings with the world, and therefore as one element in this movement. Its attempts to understand itself are attempts at understanding the movement of the trinitarian history of God's dealings with the world; and its attempts to understand this movement are attempts at understanding itself.[25]

That is, the church is not the *subject* of Moltmann's ecclesiology, for the church does not have a mission. Instead, the subject is always the *mission of Christ*—carried out by the power of the Holy Spirit, through the Father—for it is in that mission that the church is engaged. The church is but one of the *objects* of Christ's mission in the world, and "it discovers itself as one element in the movements of the divine sending, gathering together and experience."[26] In saying this, Moltmann is contradicting previous theologians who have, since the Council of Florence in 1442, subscribed to *extra ecclesiam nulla salus* and placed the church as the centerpiece of God's mission and God's salvific activity.[27] This is an absolutism that Moltmann cannot abide, and he asks,

> But must the church not rethink its position even more radically? Outside Christ no salvation. Christ has come and was sacrificed for the reconciliation of the whole

---

[24] Moltmann, *The Church in the Power of the Spirit: A Contribution to Messianic Ecclesiology*, 19.

[25] Moltmann, *The Church in the Power of the Spirit: A Contribution to Messianic Ecclesiology*, 53.

[26] Moltmann, *The Church in the Power of the Spirit: A Contribution to Messianic Ecclesiology*, 64.

[27] See, for example, Miroslav Volf, *After Our Likeness: The Church as the Image of the Trinity*, Sacra Doctrina (Grand Rapids, Mich.: William B. Eerdmans, 1998), 174ff. Moltmann rejects *extra ecclesiam nulla salus* as an "eschatological dualism" carried by a "chiliastic church" into the "ambivalences and pluralities of history." Moltmann, *The Coming of God: Christian Eschatology*, 182-83.

world. No one is excluded. Outside the salvation that
Christ brings to all men there is therefore no church. The
visible church is, as Christ's church, the ministry of reconciliation exercised upon the world. This the church is to be
seen, not as an absolute, but in its relationship to the divine
reconciler and to reconciled men and women, of whatever
religion.[28]

Moltmann's emphasis on the relational nature of the church is his
attempt to guide the church between the Scylla of absolutism on the
one hand and the Charybdis of relativism on the other. He is navi-
gating the ambiguities of a Christian theologian working in a pluralistic, postmodern age, and he is attempting to maintain Christian
identity while at the same time respecting other religions.

Moltmann sees many ecclesiologies making the mistake of ab-
solutizing the church by assuming the subjectivity of the church.
The problem here, according to Moltmann, is that those ecclesiologies ignore the fact that the existence of the church is entirely contingent upon God's use of the church in God's mission in the world.
On the other hand, Moltmann sees in his own backyard, in the
national churches of Europe, the danger of relativism in that they
adopted a posture of *"sceptical tolerance"* [sic], by which the en-
lightened upper classes of Europe could discount the myths of the
"three imposters," Moses, Jesus, and Mohammed, while still pre-
tending to be tolerant of those who held religious convictions.[29]

This seemed to be the right choice for the churches of Europe in
the wake of the Holocaust, for it allowed them to reject absolutisms
and therefore any similarity to Nazism or fascism. But it ultimately
gutted the church of any prophetic voice in society because the
church had unconsciously abdicated its own particularity. The
church maintains—or regains—particularity, Moltmann argues, by
understanding its relationships to the many other forces in culture:
"It is only out of the growing web of living relationships that some-

---

[28] Moltmann, *The Church in the Power of the Spirit: A Contribution to Messianic
Ecclesiology*, 153-54.

[29] Moltmann, *The Church in the Power of the Spirit: A Contribution to Messianic
Ecclesiology*, 155.

thing new can come into being for a wider community."[30] Only then can the church act as a "critical catalyst" in society, wherein "Christianity's vocation must be presented as clearly as possible, but it must be a presentation in relationship, and must not precede that relationship."[31] In other words, the church is *relativized*—its role in society is only known in regards to its relationship to other societal forces and institutions and to its subsumption by the mission of God.

Moltmann's early ecclesiology is not without pragmatic suggestions for the life of the church. The church can best be what he is calling it to be, Moltmann argues, if it stays small, mobile, and fluid, avoiding top-heavy bureaucracies and power-hungry individuals. The church can check itself as to whether it is fulfilling this role by always making sure that it is primarily a fellowship of the "godless and godforsaken." When the church becomes the territory of the elite and the powerful, it has *de facto* ceased being the church.[32]

He also writes quite specifically about the sacraments. The practice of infant baptism, Moltmann asserts, has both theological and political problems.[33] Theologically, it is problematic because the infant is necessarily non-resistant to the practice—instead of men and women being called to a vibrant faith, traditions with infant baptism propagate themselves by initiating submissive children into the faith. Politically, infant baptism stands as a central practice of national churches and the "Christian society" seen in many countries, so a continuation of this practice is necessarily a vote in favor of some form of "Christendom." Instead, Moltmann argues, baptism should always be linked to John the Baptist and his prophetic call to

---

[30] Moltmann, *The Church in the Power of the Spirit: A Contribution to Messianic Ecclesiology*, 157.

[31] Moltmann, *The Church in the Power of the Spirit: A Contribution to Messianic Ecclesiology*, 158-59.

[32] These are reflected in Moltmann's "Marks of the Church," which comprise the final chapter of the book: 1) the one, holy, catholic, and apostolic church; 2) unity in freedom; 3) catholicity and partisanship; 4) holiness in poverty; and 5) the apostolate in suffering. Moltmann, *The Church in the Power of the Spirit: A Contribution to Messianic Ecclesiology*, 337-61.

[33] Moltmann, *The Church in the Power of the Spirit: A Contribution to Messianic Ecclesiology*, 226ff.

repentance—thus, a reformation of the practice of baptism will necessarily require a reformation of the social structures of the church,
and Moltmann presumes that the many revival movements that have
practiced adult baptism are exactly that (this reflects Moltmann's
growing experience throughout the 1960s and 1970s with liberation
and other contextual theologies, his visits to "base communities,"
and his participation in ecumenical dialogues). Ultimately, baptism
should be a practice of liberation, a call to decision for adults.

Moltmann has a similar reflection on the Lord's Supper. Proposing that it should always be a practice of unity and unification
among Christians, he reprimands churches that have turned communion into a "controversial theological function."[34]   Christ, Moltmann writes, put no preconditions on the disciples' participation at
the Last Supper, thus he argues for an open table.[35]   Further, everyone who follows the call of Christ as Lord "has the authority to
break the bread and dispense the wine...Hierarchical legalism spoils
the evangelical character of the Lord's Supper just as much as dogmatic and moral legalism."[36]   Immediately the resonance is clear
with the emerging church congregations profiled in chapter three,
particularly their practice of an open table and their use of laypersons to initiate the rite of communion. Moltmann also implicitly af-
firms the dialogical practice of preaching when he suggests that the
Lord's Supper always be complemented by a common meal, at
which the needs of the community and the world are discussed.[37]
Ultimately, Moltmann argues that the Lord's Supper is the primary
eschatological practice of the Christian community, and he writes
that there are six important aspects to its practice. Each of these
characteristics more or less jibes with the typical practice of communion in the emerging church movement:

---

[34] Moltmann, *The Church in the Power of the Spirit: A Contribution to Messianic Ecclesiology*, 245.

[35] Moltmann, *The Church in the Power of the Spirit: A Contribution to Messianic Ecclesiology*, 246.

[36] Moltmann, *The Church in the Power of the Spirit: A Contribution to Messianic Ecclesiology*.

[37] Moltmann, *The Church in the Power of the Spirit: A Contribution to Messianic Ecclesiology*.

1) Communion must be central to the Christian community, must be integrated into the heart of the worship service, and must be celebrated with bread and wine.

2) The table must be open to those of varying theological views.

3) Baptism and confirmation must not be prerequisites for the fellowship of the table.

4) Everyone who follows Christ is qualified to invoke the sacrament, and everyone is called upon to offer and distribute the elements.

5) Not only should the person performing the liturgy face the congregation, but the entire worship space should, if possible, be redesigned to a "'common room' in which the participants can see and talk to one another.'"

6) Communion should always be followed by "a common meal, and the proclamation of the gospel by a common discussion of people's real needs and the specific tasks of Christian mission."[38]

Indeed, Moltmann's list could well serve as a theological description of the practice of communion in some ECM congregations.

From a practical theological perspective, Moltmann is truly writing ecclesiology in a praxis-theory-praxis rhythm. In his section on living the "messianic way of life," he writes of this more explicitly than he does in the sections on liturgical practice; he writes that theology is always a reflection on the lived experience of human beings as they attempt to follow Jesus Christ as the Messiah, and he fleshes out his proposal for a "messianic ecclesiology."[39] In other words, the church is a messianic fellowship that is cooperating with Christ in the progression toward the eschatological future; this is re-

---

[38] Moltmann, *The Church in the Power of the Spirit: A Contribution to Messianic Ecclesiology*, 259-60.

[39] Moltmann, *The Church in the Power of the Spirit: A Contribution to Messianic Ecclesiology*, 275ff.

lational in that the church's identity is based on its relationship with Christ and its involvement with Christ's mission. The church is not primarily a worshipping community, but a missional community—worship is an aspect of the mission of the church. And the church is only missional insofar as it holds itself in relationship to Christ. One way that the church does this is by looking forward, in a temporary and fragmentary way, to the ultimate and eschatological kingdom, and by looking backwards, rehearsing and telling the story of Christ's suffering. The church exists for the sake of the world and works toward the missions of the Father, the Son, and the Holy Spirit, the missions of which, though mutually interpenetrating, are distinct. This final point is key to Moltmann's conception of the Trinity as a social relationship of three divine persons, each with independent (and interdependent) activities. Again, it is *relationship* that is central.

"Friend" as Christological Office

One aspect of Moltmann's early ecclesiology deserves special mention, both because it is a noteworthy break between Moltmann and other dominant christologies, and because it has special resonance with a key motif in the emerging church movement.[40] In *Church in the Power of the Spirit*, Moltmann reflects on the three traditional offices of Christ: prophet, priest, and king. To those, Moltmann adds the office of "transfigured Christ" to emphasize the aesthetic dimension of the resurrection. That is, in the Transfiguration, we are given a vision of the resurrected Christ and of our eschatological resurrection that transcends the traditional, rational categories of prophet, priest, and king.[41]

And then Moltmann adds a fifth office: "But the fellowship which Jesus brings men, and the fellowship of people with one another to which he calls, would be described in one-sided terms if another 'title' were not added, a title to describe the inner relationship

---

[40] Richard Osmer has made similar connections between Moltmann's Christology and the mission of the church. See Osmer, *The Teaching Ministry of Congregations*, 224.

[41] Moltmann, *The Church in the Power of the Spirit: A Contribution to Messianic Ecclesiology*, 108-14.

between the divine and the human fellowship: the name of friend."[42] For Moltmann, the term "friend" signifies a relationship that is voluntary and personal, based on loyalty, not obligation, and so complements the traditional Christological titles. "Friendship unites affection with respect."[43] He particularly likes that friendship is entered into freely: "friendship is a human relationship which springs from freedom, exists in mutual freedom and preserves that freedom."[44]

Moltmann notes that the term "friend" is only used twice of Jesus in the Gospels—in the synoptic tradition, it is used as an insult by the opponents of Jesus and John the Baptist: "For John the Baptist has come eating no bread and drinking no wine, and you say, 'He has a demon'; the Son of Man has come eating and drinking, and you say, 'Look, a glutton and a drunkard, a friend of tax-collectors and sinners!' Nevertheless, wisdom is vindicated by all her children."[45]   And in the Johanine tradition, Jesus refers to himself as a friend of his disciples,

> 'This is my commandment, that you love one another as I have loved you. No one has greater love than this, to lay down one's life for one's friends. You are my friends if you do what I command you. I do not call you servants any longer, because the servant does not know what the master is doing; but I have called you friends, because I have made known to you everything that I have heard from my Father. You did not choose me but I chose you. And I appointed you to go and bear fruit, fruit that will last, so that the Father will give you whatever you ask him in my name. I am

---

[42] Moltmann, *The Church in the Power of the Spirit: A Contribution to Messianic Ecclesiology*, 115.

[43] Moltmann, *The Church in the Power of the Spirit: A Contribution to Messianic Ecclesiology*, 115.

[44] Moltmann, *The Church in the Power of the Spirit: A Contribution to Messianic Ecclesiology*, 115.

[45] Luke 7: 33-35, NRSV.

giving you these commands so that you may love one another.[46]

In the first case, Moltmann writes, "As a friend, Jesus offers the
unlovable the friendship of God," and in the second, "The sacrifice
of a man's own life for his friends is the highest form of love."[47]

The most potent aspect of Jesus' friendship of human beings is
the inherent openness in the friendship relationship. In befriending
sinners and the lovable, Jesus opens the eternal relationship of the
Trinity to all human beings. Moltmann concludes, "Thus, theologically, the many-faceted work of Christ, which in the doctrine of
Christ's threefold office was presented in terms of sovereignty and
function, can be taken to its highest point in his friendship."[48]

Moltmann's Later Ecclesiology

As mentioned above, Moltmann has not dedicated another entire
book to ecclesiology as he did with *Church in the Power of the
Spirit*. During his six-book cycle—his "contributions to theology"—he wrote of the church sporadically, but not in a comprehensive way. Moltmann has felt less constrained by the conventional,
systematic approaches to theology as his career wore on. While he
did write on traditional theological topics, like the doctrine of creation, he also followed other avenues and wrote about less traditional
topics. As he had promised in the preface to *The Trinity and the
Kingdom of God*, he pursued an "intensive theological discussion,"
developing themes that are the traditional purview of systematic theology, but also going further afield to address contemporary issues.
His doctrine of creation, for instance, was written specifically to confront the "progressive industrial exploitation of nature and its irrepa-
rable destruction."[49]   Other works dealt with the intersections
between religion and science, feminist theory, and political theory.

---

[46] John 15: 12-17, NRSV.

[47] Moltmann, *The Church in the Power of the Spirit: A Contribution to Messianic
Ecclesiology*, 117.

[48] Moltmann, *The Church in the Power of the Spirit: A Contribution to Messianic
Ecclesiology*, 119.

[49] Moltmann, *God in Creation: A New Theology of Creation and the Spirit of God*,
xiii.

But Moltmann did not return to ecclesiology in a significant way until his 2010 book, *Sun of Righteousness, Arise! God's Future for Humanity and the Earth*, a compilation of essays and lectures over the past decade, through which Moltmann hopes to shape the Christian perception of God as the "God of Christ's resurrection" and "the righteousness which creates life and puts things to rights."[50] Further, he wants Christians to pay attention to the "traces and signs of God [that] give the world meaning."[51]

In *Sun of Righteousness, Arise!*, Moltmann posits that the future of the Christian faith hinges on nothing less than the future of the church:

> "My theses in this essay can be reduced to simple formulas:
>
> 1) The future of Christianity is the church;
>
> 2) The future of the church is the kingdom of God."[52]

This seems to contradict Moltmann's early ecclesiology, in which he refused to equate the mission of God with the church. Now, three decades later, he claims nothing less than that the future of faith rests in the church. It is possible that Moltmann's confidence in the institution of the church has grown in the past thirty years has increased, or maybe his definition of "the church" in these theses is broader than in his previous writings. What is at stake in this change is whether the church is still, in Moltmann's opinion, to be understood relationally, or whether the church is in fact the primary avenue of God's mission in the world.

He begins his chapter, "The Rebirth of the Church," with this premise: "The great event of the twentieth century was the end of Christendom, the Christian era and the Christian nations, and the beginning of the church's rebirth as an independent and resisting community, a community with a universal mission and an all-embracing

---

[50] Moltmann, *Sun of Righteousness, Arise! God's Future for Humanity and the Earth*, 1.

[51] Moltmann, *Sun of Righteousness, Arise! God's Future for Humanity and the Earth*, 1.

[52] Moltmann, *Sun of Righteousness, Arise! God's Future for Humanity and the Earth*, 7.

hope for the kingdom of God as the future of the world."[53] Moltmann then walks through the changes wrought upon the church by
the twentieth century with special emphasis on the issues he knows
best: the theologies of Karl Barth and Adolf von Harnack and the
national church of Germany. For example, Barth's "churchification"
of theology unintentionally led to the church's retreat from public
theology, thus further denuding the church of prophetic status after
the national church's sins in Nazi Germany.

But Moltmann sees these changes as positive, making way for:

1) The rebirth of an independent church in the contexts of
its ecumenical breadth;

2) A new theology of the church;

3) The rediscovery of the Old Testament as a living force,
and the search for new community with the synagogue;

4) A new turn to the future.[54]

The result, Moltmann writes, is that the twenty-first century will
be a "millennium of the Holy Spirit," ushering in a "transformation
in the fundamental paradigm of the church."[55] That paradigm, he
goes on, will be the third major paradigm in the history of the
church. The first is the *hierarchical paradigm*, inherited from the
Graeco-Roman world and institutionalized as early as Ignatius of
Antioch (*c.* 35–*c.* 107). Moltmann has long been critical of this
model, which he sees as *"one God—one bishop—one community or
church."*[56] Calling it "monarchial monotheism," Moltmann argued
as early as 1980 that subverting the Son to the Father and the Spirit

---

[53] Moltmann, *Sun of Righteousness, Arise! God's Future for Humanity and the Earth*, 17.

[54] Moltmann, *Sun of Righteousness, Arise! God's Future for Humanity and the Earth*, 19-20.

[55] Moltmann, *Sun of Righteousness, Arise! God's Future for Humanity and the Earth*, 20.

[56] Moltmann, *Sun of Righteousness, Arise! God's Future for Humanity and the Earth*.

to the Father and the Son "justifies the church as hierarchy, as sacred dominion."[57] While Moltmann admits that, for example, the Catholic church has made strides in mitigating the authority of the ecclesiastical hierarchy since the Second Vatican Council, he still sees problem areas in the relationships between laity and clergy and between men and women. Moltmann seems to believe that the "congregationalization" of the Catholic church is inevitable as parishes claim more autonomy and become subjects rather than objects in their own history.[58]

The *christocentric paradigm* is the second, and it came into fashion with the Protestant Reformation. Therein, Christ alone is head of the church, and "fellowship with Christ makes the church a brotherly and sisterly community of equals...All are priests and kings equally."[59] But while the christocentric paradigm should serve to equalize everyone in the congregation, Moltmann admits that "practically speaking the distinction between trained theologians and people without any theological training has taken the place of the priestly hierarchy."[60] Even so, the Reformation paradigm, at least in theory, holds that,

> The people of God is a general community of theologians. The unity of the church is established through the brotherhood of Christ, not through a patriarchal hierarchy. Consequently the church is a community of free and equal men and women, joined with each other in an open, inviting friendship. All are joint heirs of God's coming kingdom, and are therefore a community of hope for the future of the world.[61]

---

[57] Moltmann, *The Trinity and the Kingdom: The Doctrine of God*, 202.

[58] Moltmann, *Sun of Righteousness, Arise! God's Future for Humanity and the Earth*, 21-22.

[59] Moltmann, *Sun of Righteousness, Arise! God's Future for Humanity and the Earth*, 22.

[60] Moltmann, *Sun of Righteousness, Arise! God's Future for Humanity and the Earth*, 23.

[61] Moltmann, *Sun of Righteousness, Arise! God's Future for Humanity and the Earth*, 23.

"Covenant" is the theological motif associated with this paradigm, and democracy is the contemporaneous political parallel. While Moltmann admits that christocentrism did not entirely overwhelm the hierarchical church, he fails to acknowledge, at least in *Sun of Righteousness, Arise!*, that hierarchy has been just as prevalent in his own Reformed tradition, from its inception with John Calvin to the present day, as it was in the ancient or medieval church. He can be faulted for not admitting that a church system has to do a lot more than remove the titular head of the papacy in order to achieve the egalitarian, revolution community that he envisions the church to be. What is needed is a more thoroughgoing reevaluation of the practices of ecclesial leadership if Moltmann's vision of a christocentric, egalitarian church is to be realized.

Third is the *charismatic paradigm*, of which Moltmann writes, "In a congregation which perceives its diverse gifts and tasks—its 'charismata'—all are accepted just as they are, and their individual talents and powers are used to build up the congregation and spread God's kingdom. No one has a higher or lower position than anyone else with what he or she can contribute to the community."[62] While Moltmann does distinguish between the charismatic paradigm and the charismatic movement as a denominational identity, he also acknowledges that this is the fastest growing version of Christianity in the world. In the charismatic paradigm, Moltmann writes, "Christians at last 'come of age.' They leave behind their self-imposed immaturity and have the courage to love their own faith for themselves."[63] Moltmann insists that this is not merely ecclesiological idealism, arguing that "communities of this kind are possible," and pointing up the example of the Moravian Brethren in the eighteenth century.[64] What Moltmann fails to acknowledge, however, is that contemporary congregations in the charismatic paradigm are often the most rife with abuses of power, reified hierarchies, and clear delineations between clergy and laity.

---

[62] Moltmann, *Sun of Righteousness, Arise! God's Future for Humanity and the Earth*, 24.

[63] Moltmann, *Sun of Righteousness, Arise! God's Future for Humanity and the Earth*, 25.

[64] Moltmann, *Sun of Righteousness, Arise! God's Future for Humanity and the Earth*, 25.

Surely, emerging church congregations—especially those that are unhinged from denominational structures—run a similar risk of allowing charismatic personalities to take advantage of an egalitarian polity. When it comes to the charismata, it is particularly difficult for a congregation to discern when a leader is leading in the Spirit, and when that person is instead taking advantage of the nebulous nature of the Spirit. Whereas the Reformation paradigm was founded on doctrinal understandings, which are articulable, the charismata afford no such clarity. Thus, congregations in the charismatic paradigm will have to develop practices that aid in the communal discernment of the movements of the Spirit.

Be that as it may, Moltmann concludes by equating each of the ages of the church with one of the persons of the Trinity: "After the *hierarchical church* of God the Father, Christianity came to know the *brotherly church* of God the Son. Today we are experiencing the *charismatic church* of God the Spirit."[65] While Moltmann's taxonomy is too tidy—and quite possibly too anthropologically naïve—it does have heuristic value for understanding the age in which the emerging church movement was born, at least from a theological perspective. The inception of the ECM did, indeed, correspond with a global awakening to the power of the Holy Spirit. Whether this means that the "christological age" is really over, or whether emphases on the Son and Spirit can coexist in the ECM and contemporaneous movements remains to be seen.

Social Trinity as the Basis for a Relational Ecclesiology

Moltmann's recent hopefulness about the future of the church, and his parallels between the church and the Trinity are not without precedent in his work. In 1980, to counteract the "monarchial monotheism" that he considered the root of ecclesial hierarchies, Moltmann counterproposed a "social" Trinity, in which he argued that the three mutually-indwelling persons of the Godhead live in an egalitarian communion with one another. The Western theological tradition, Moltmann argues, has always begun with the unity of God and, having established that, moved on to reflections about the Trinity. That has led to the "trinity of substance" and the "trinity of

---

[65] Moltmann, *Sun of Righteousness, Arise! God's Future for Humanity and the Earth*, 25.

subject."[66] The social Trinity, in contrast, emphasizes the three persons of the Godhead and their eternal, perichoretic relationship: "The unity of the triunity lies in the eternal perichoresis of the trinitarian persons. Interpreted perichoretically, the trinitarian persons form their own unity by themselves in the circulation of the divine life."[67] On this basis, Moltmann rejects the traditional Western notion of *filioque*, arguing that each of the three persons of the Trinity is sent by the other two, thus equalizing the three and affirming the Trinity as an egalitarian communion.[68]

Creation itself, Moltmann writes, is the "overflowing rapture" of God's "trinitarian perfection and completeness."[69] Interestingly, Moltmann subscribes to the Jewish concept of *Shekinah*, by which God is understood to have practiced self-limitation in order to make room for a creation that is other than God.[70] However, God reabsorbs all of creation back into Godself by making the eternal love-relationship that is the Trinity available to all creation, and the perichoretic relationship of the Trinity is then the archetype for all relations:

> Our starting point here is that all relationships which are analogous to God reflect the primal, reciprocal indwelling and mutual interpenetration of the trinitarian perichoresis: God *in* the world and the world *in* God; heaven and earth *in* the kingdom of God, pervaded by his glory; soul and body united *in* the life-giving Spirit to a human whole; woman and man *in* the kingdom of unconditional and uncondi-

---

[66] Moltmann, *The Trinity and the Kingdom: The Doctrine of God*, 19.

[67] Moltmann, *The Trinity and the Kingdom: The Doctrine of God*, 175.

[68] Moltmann, *The Trinity and the Kingdom: The Doctrine of God*, 74-75.

[69] Moltmann, *God in Creation: A New Theology of Creation and the Spirit of God*, 84.

[70] Moltmann, *God in Creation: A New Theology of Creation and the Spirit of God*, 15.

tioned love, freed to be true and complete human beings. There is no such thing as solitary life.[71]

This, of course, has enormous implications for a relational ecclesiology. Moltmann consistently rails against ecclesial hierarchies, as noted above. And though he does not return to the phrase from *The Church in the Power of the Spirit*, "relational ecclesiology," he continues to emphasize that the perichoretic life of the Trinity is the basis for his ecclesiology:

> The doctrine of the Trinity constitutes the church as a "community free of dominion." The trinitarian principle replaces the principle of power by the principle of concord. Authority and obedience are replaced by dialogue, consensus, and harmony. What stands at the center is not faith in God's revelation on the basis of ecclesiastical authority, but faith on the basis of individual insight into the truth of revelation. The hierarchy which preserves and enforces unity is replaced by the brotherhood and sisterhood of the community of Christ.[72]

In other words, Moltmann believes that the church should be an egalitarian community of mutual love, both formed by and exhibiting the perichoretic love of the three persons of the Trinity.

Weaknesses in Moltmann's Ecclesiology

Moltmann's ecclesiology in general, and *The Church in the Power of the Spirit* in particular, are not without critics. Geiko Müller-Farenholz accuses Moltmann of "theological and...sociological inconsistencies" that stem from Moltmann's commitment to developing a messianic ecclesiology without duly addressing ecclesiological, sociological, and historical questions. For example, Müller-Farenholz believes that Moltmann should have conversed with homileticians in order to more fully develop his

---

[71] Moltmann, *God in Creation: A New Theology of Creation and the Spirit of God*, 17. Moltmann writes this *contra* Barth, who maintained a "theological doctrine of sovereignty" which resulted in a doctrine of God that was "one-sided," reifying antithetical relationships of "superiority and subordination, command and obedience, master and servant."

[72] Moltmann, *The Trinity and the Kingdom: The Doctrine of God*, 202.

thoughts on "economic" and "cultural" preaching, introduced in *Theology of Hope*, but never revisited in his later ecclesiological writings.[73] Müller-Farenholz wonders if Moltmann, at least at this early point in his career, felt that these issues were better addressed by practical theologians than systematic theologians.

Ton van Prooijen takes issue with Moltmann's rejection of *extra ecclesiam nulla salus*, at least insofar as Moltmann does not seem to offer a viable third way between classical absolutism and the relativism of the Enlightenment.[74] Instead of hewing to the middle ground, van Prooijen thinks that Moltmann falls into the ditch of universalism and, therefore, relativism. For instance, Moltmann is reluctant to acknowledge what happens when, say, a Buddhist is challenged to accept the "messianization" that Christ offers. Instead of using traditional theological language to talk about conversion, Moltmann demurs, writing that Christ will open that person up to "real human identity" or "real future." This is a problem common to the "contextual theologians," Prooijen writes, and he expounds with an example from Moltmann's own corpus: Moltmann's attempt to use Christian theology to undergird a theory of universal human rights in the 1970s.[75] Prooijen concludes that, try as he might, Moltmann cannot quite overcome the charge of universality, and therefore Molttmann fails to maintain the particularity of Christ.

And Arne Rasmusson, in defending Stanley Hauerwas's ecclesiology, rejects Moltmann's ecclesiology as little more than a bastion of left-wing activism. Moltmann, he argues, is out of step with the average churchgoer, who does not go to church in search of an activist community. Further, Rasmusson, with Hauerwas, rejects secular resources for the church and argues that the church should stand in prophetic counter-resistance to secular culture, using its own distinct language and practices. According to Rasmusson, Moltmann's

---

[73] Geiko Müller-Fahrenholz, *The Kingdom and the Power: The Theology of Jürgen Moltmann* (London: SCM, 2000), 101.

[74] Ton van Prooijen, *Limping but Blessed: Jürgen Moltmann's Search for a Liberating Anthropology*, Currents of Encounter (Amsterdam ; New York: Rodopi, 2004), 168-69.

[75] Jürgen Moltmann, "Theological Basis of Human Rights and the Liberation of Man," *Reformed World* 31 (1971). Jürgen Moltmann, "A Christian Declaration on Human Rights," *Reformed World* 34 (1976).

ecclesial vision denudes the church of any particularity, and therefore of any reason to exist.[76] Rasmusson (and Hauerwas) are proponents of the Aristotelian vision of *polis* and practice detailed above, leading Rasmusson to reject Moltmann's political theology and resultant ecclesiology and argue instead for a church that has its own language and practices, much like an Aristotelian *polis*:

> A church with a strong sense of community, living with a tradition and practices that partly stand apart from the dominating stories, traditions, and practices of modernity (as a contrast society), might have a larger ability (because of a different "grid") and the social space to see modern society from other perspectives, and to form and sustain different ways of thinking and living.[77]

Rasmusson is correct that Moltmann is not friendly to Hauerwas's ecclesiology, an idea that will be explored in the next chapter. This is a significant difference because the very different visions of the church put forth by Hauerwas and Moltmann are competing for primacy in the emerging church movement, and in the related missional church conversation.

My primary criticism of Moltmann's ecclesiology is that it is too idealistic, rooted in an anthropological naiveté.[78] In his latest book, for instance, Moltmann glosses over the many theological and ethical problems with churches in the Pentecostal and Charismatic traditions. In other words, many autonomous and even some denominational churches today are quick to use the language of the charismatic paradigm to cover abuses of authoritarian leadership structures. Moltmann too easily gives them his imprimatur without sufficiently criticizing them for co-opting the language of the charismatic paradigm that he is extolling. Moltmann has made this mistake before, lifting up the "base communities" of the Catholic

---

[76] Arne Rasmusson, *The Church as Polis: From Political Theology to Theological Politics as Exemplified by Jürgen Moltmann and Stanley Hauerwas*, Studia Theologica Lundensia (Bromley, Kent, England: Lund University Press, 1994), 150.

[77] Rasmusson, *The Church as Polis: From Political Theology to Theological Politics as Exemplified by Jürgen Moltmann and Stanley Hauerwas*, 373.

[78] As it so happens, I also think that Hauerwas's ecclesiology is too idealistic.

liberation movement without paying heed to the weaknesses of that movement. Indeed, Moltmann seems almost oblivious to the failure, in a practical sense, of Catholic liberation theology in the global south and the victory of a version of Pentecostalism that promotes the "prosperity gospel," most often enriching the preachers at the expense of the poor.[79] The "prosperity gospel," of course, flies directly in the face of the very core of Moltmann's theology, and it deserves a written rebuke from Moltmann, a theologian who has consistently sided with the poor, the oppressed, and the godforsaken.

By anthropological naïveté, I mean that Moltmann has never taken human fallibility fully into account when developing his ecclesiology. In his early ecclesiology, Moltmann pushes for a rather radical version of Congregationalism in which all members of the church have the authority to administer communion. In proposing this, he is quick to point out the abuses inherent in hierarchical systems. However, he neglects to address the abuses possible in total egalitarianism, the very abuses that led the early church to institute a bishop-led hierarchy. Similarly, in his later ecclesiology, Moltmann does not adequately address the shortcomings of the present "charismatic age," nor the real danger to global Christianity if the "prosperity gospel" is allowed, in the name of the Holy Spirit, to develop unchecked.

Even with those weaknesses, Moltmann's relational ecclesiology, based on a social doctrine of the Trinity, and his suggestions for a polity that is reflective of that Trinity, provide an excellent basis for the twenty-first century church. In fact, Moltmann's vision of churches that are small, autonomous, and voluntarily connected with one another surely have more potential in this century when he introduced it last century. That is, the technological and social changes that have transformed Western society since Moltmann penned *The Church in the Power of the Spirit* may well provide just the catalyst needed for the church he envisioned in the 1970s.

Many congregations in the emerging church movement are instinctively using the very relational ecclesiology that Moltmann proposes. Some of these intersections will be outlined in chapter five, but first, Moltmann's ecclesiology the nascent practices of the emer-

---

[79] Philip Jenkins, *The New Faces of Christianity: Believing the Bible in the Global South* (Oxford ; New York: Oxford University Press, 2006), 90ff.

ging church movement will be put in dialogue, exhibiting strengths and weaknesses in each.

Moltmann and the ECM in Mutual Critique

If theology does, indeed, lie in "unhindered dialogue," as Moltmann asserts, then we will do well to put his ecclesiology in robust conversation with the ecclesial practices of the ECM. When that is done, the strengths of each come into clearer profile, as do their weaknesses. While those will be developed in further detail below, there are also meta-level critiques that become evident when the two are placed in dialogue.

Regarding Moltmann's ecclesiology, the ECM points up several weaknesses. The first is the uncritical idealism of Moltmann's ecclesiology. As noted above, Moltmann seems unaware of the failures of some of the ecclesial examples that he has championed. For instance Moltmann seems oblivious to the widespread belief that the base communities of Central and South America, meant to be primary example of liberation theology, have "withered, and failed to become the nuclei of a radical Catholic reformation."[80] Even in his most recent book, though all evidence is to the contrary, Moltmann asserts, "In Latin America, in the new base communities, people are experiencing the trinitarian fellowship with God."[81] The other example that Moltmann points to throughout his writings, and again is his latest book, are sects within Anabaptism, including Hutterites, Moravians, and Old-Order Mennonites.

Arne Rasmusson criticizes Moltmann's ecclesiology for envisioning a church that no one would actually want to belong to, and he contends that a Moltmannian church is nothing more than a left-

---

[80] Philip Jenkins, *The Next Christendom: The Coming of Global Christianity* (Oxford; New York: Oxford University Press, 2002), 147. Jenkins continues, "Much of the impulse that originally inspired the communities has been diverted into Pentecostalism, which appeals to similar constituencies among the urban poor. In part, Pentecostal growth can be seen as a response to the failed revolutionary expectations of earlier years."

[81] Moltmann, *Sun of Righteousness, Arise! God's Future for Humanity and the Earth*, 143. See also p. 23, where Moltmann writes, "Today we find exactly these [democratic, christocentric] forms of life forms of life in the base communities of the Roman Catholic Church in Latin America."

wing, social union.[82]   While this criticism is off the mark—the ecclesial exemplars to which Moltmann points in his writings are basically the opposite of what Rasmusson is suggesting—Moltmann has
nevertheless failed to find communities of Christians that have
championed his ecclesiology. And, more disappointing still, he has
failed to find exemplary communities that have actually practiced his
ecclesiology (though the ECM may be the first). I suspect that is
because Moltmann's ecclesiology is so idealistic that he does not
adequately recognize the realities facing developing church communities in the postmodern world. The two examples provided above
show just how difficult it can be. Moltmann encourages ecclesial
communities that are both christocentric and political. The Catholic
base communities were the latter, and the Anabaptist sects are the
former. But being both, particularly in as radical a fashion as Moltmann suggests, is a very difficult task. The emerging church movement may have a chance at being both robustly christocentric and
robustly political, as Moltmann advises, while also avoiding the de-
nominationalism that he warns against, but it will do so only by
making pragmatic choices that circumvent Moltmann's idealisms.

Secondly, Moltmann's ecclesiology is contingent upon his experience as a German, which does not necessarily translate into the
postmodern context facing the emerging church in the twenty-first
century. Moltmann, especially early in his career, made many of his
ecclesial suggestions in reaction to the state-church model, prevalent
in Europe and particularly in Germany. For instance, his argument
for forsaking infant baptism is rooted in its use as an initiation into
the "Christian society" of Europe.[83]   In cultures like the United
States, lacking a history of an official state-church, Moltmann's ecclesiology can seem less applicable. While I appreciate the rootedness of Moltmann's theological proposals, his ecclesiology now
needs to be expanded to apply to the free-church history of North
America and other areas of the world. In fact, the church-state relationship in the United States, which might be called an "implicit
Christendom," has come under withering scrutiny by Hauerwas,

---

[82] Rasmusson, The Church as Polis: From Political Theology to Theological
Politics as Exemplified by Jürgen Moltmann and Stanley Hauerwas, 150.

[83] Moltmann, The Church in the Power of the Spirit: A Contribution to Messianic
Ecclesiology, 229.

Douglas John Hall, and others.[84] Yet Moltmann has failed to develop such a critique, and as such, his criticism of the now-failed European church-state model seems archaic and overly Teutonic. The ECM stands as a critique of Moltmann in this regard, for the ECM has, since its inception, joined the Hauerwasians and others in struggling against the legacy of implicit Christendom in America. Whereas Moltmann is rooted in his twentieth century European context, the emerging church—like Hauerwas—is a product of Christianity in late twentieth century America. As such, the ECM will like be subject to a similar critique a generation or two hence.

Conversely, Moltmann's ecclesiology stands in critique of the emerging church movement in one particular sense: the emerging church has not yet practiced a relational ecclesiology in nearly as radical a way as Moltmann would contend it should be. For example, the particular aspects of the practice of the Lord's Supper that Moltmann commends—a radically open table, the liturgy led by laypersons, the reorganization of the sanctuary, and a regular communal meal—have been instituted only sporadically and only by a couple of ECM congregations. Across most of the emerging church movement, communion is still practiced very conventionally: at the end of the service and administered by clergypersons. While it is clearly difficult to dramatically change one of the core practices of the Christian church, this is exactly what Moltmann says is necessary for the church to become a community that truly embodies the eschatological promise of God. In this and other ways, the emerging church movement stands challenged by the radically relational ecclesiology of Jürgen Moltmann. In order to instantiate a relational ecclesiology, more ECM congregations will need to embrace more radical practices, like a truly open table at the Lord's Supper, or a completely egalitarian form of church government.

Political Ecclesiology and Practices of Social Engagement

Now we move to several areas in which the ecclesiology of Jürgen Moltmann and the practices of the emerging church movement have considerable transversal intersection, which will show the

---

[84] Douglas John Hall, *The End of Christendom and the Future of Christianity*, Christian Mission and Modern Culture (Valley Forge, PA: Trinity Press International, 1997).

resonances between the two and provide the context for an ever-increasing engagement. For each, the theological underpinnings will be explored, as will the extant practices in the ECM, and both theological and practical suggestions will be offered. The first intersection to be explored stems from Moltmann's overtly political theology.

Arne Rasmusson is in league with Stanley Hauerwas, a theologian who has been very influential in groups related to the ECM.[85] Hauerwas's ecclesiology and ethics have been described by Jeffrey Stout as "sectarian," much to Hauerwas's chagrin.[86] Stout says that for Hauerwas, the church's only goal is *to be the church*," which "is a matter of maintaining a pacifist community of virtue in the midst of a violent world, thus providing a foretaste of the peaceable kingdom in which God reigns absolutely and eternally."[87]   John B. Thomson, sympathetic to Hauerwas, puts it similarly, writing that Hauerwas "seeks to transcend the pathology of post-Enlightenment attempts to articulate human liberation and…he locates true freedom in the politics and practices of the church."[88] What Hauerwas does, according to Stout, is embrace John Howard Yoder's radical distinction between church and world and combine that with MacIntyre's antiliberalism.[89] In so doing, Hauerwas conceives of a church that is a "city on a hill"—a sectarian vision of a church that operates by its own rules, assumptions, language, and practices. It is a *polis* of sorts; it is "in but not of the world."

---

[85] The Ecclesia Network, for example, is a group of pastors and seminary professors sympathetic to Hauerwas's project. A "relational network of churches, leaders and movements that seek [sic] to equip, partner, and multiply missional churches and movements," the Ecclesia Network has significant overlap with the ECM, and it uses some of the same language. "Ecclesia," http://www.ecclesianet.org.

[86] "Hauerwas does not like being called a 'sectarian.'" Stout, *Democracy and Tradition*, 147.

[87] Stout, *Democracy and Tradition*, 146.

[88] John B. Thomson, *The Ecclesiology of Stanley Hauerwas: A Christian Theology of Liberation* (Burlington, VT: Ashgate, 2003).

[89] Stout, *Democracy and Tradition*, 148.

Moltmann is not particularly friendly to the Hauerwasian eccle-sial project insofar as Hauerwas seems to assume that church should be in some sense atemporal—that is, its character should be unaf-fected by the vicissitudes of society over time. For Moltmann, the church is, and should be, as deeply ensconced in the messiness of society as any institution. Even Moltmann's own theological method is telling in its difference with Hauerwas. Moltmann does not hesitate to draw upon cultural resources to implicate his theol-ogy, nor does he warn the church against using extra-ecclesial re-sources.[90] While Hauerwas (and Yoder before him) wants the church to develop a distinct internal language that bespeaks a par-ticular, theological ethic, Moltmann is constantly seeking dialogue. Moltmann desires the church to be conversant in the language of many rationalities, which is why he has delved deeply into the vari-ous fields of feminist theory, ecology, social theory, science, and psychology over his career. Moltmann is looking for transversal connections between theology and other rationalities, and he is ex-hibiting the three moves of transversal rationality introduced in chapter one: praxial critique, articulation, and disclosure.

Foundational to this transversal method, according to van Huyssteen and exemplified in Moltmann's work, is epistemic hu-mility.[91] One cannot enter into full dialogue with other rationalities without maintaining epistemic humility, for lack of this humility will foreclose true dialogue before it even begins. Further, van Huyssteen argues, "Because our epistemic communities never exist in complete isolation from one another, it [is] important to realize that an adequately contextualized notion of rationality is necessary to facilitate intersubjective, cross-disciplinary conversation."[92] This sentiment stands in contradistinction to the Aristotelian notion held by MacIntyre and Hauerwas that the language and practices of the church instantiate a discrete rationality that has little or no resonance with non-ecclesial rationalities.

---

[90] In this way, Moltmann subscribes to the revised correlational method of interdisciplinarity, introduced in chapter one. For more on the various modes of interdisciplinary thinking in theology, see Appendix D.

[91] van Huyssteen, *The Shaping of Rationality: Toward Interdisciplinarity in Theology and Science*, 131.

[92] van Huyssteen, *The Shaping of Rationality: Toward Interdisciplinarity in Theology and Science*, 153.

While Hauerwas's ecclesiology seems to be lacking the characteristics of transversal rationality, Moltmann's ecclesiology exemplifies them. This important for a movement that looks to engage the extra-ecclesial resources of culture in a robust fashion. Moltmann relies on various rationalities in an effort to catalyze the "unhindered dialogue" that he takes to be central to the theological enterprise. Likewise, the ECM's nascent ecclesial practices exhibit these same characteristics, showing forth yet another connection between the movement and Moltmann's relational ecclesiology. The practices described in chapter three all betoken pastoral leadership that is premised on a significant amount of epistemic humility, whether that be regularly opening the sermon to communal dialogue or engaging various modes of communion during the weekly practice of the Lord's Supper.

Emerging church movement congregations engage practices of relational ecclesiology, though not necessarily in the ways that Moltmann has imagined. Critics of the emerging church movement often mention that the leaders of the movement are at fault for allowing culture to dictate the discourse in which the movement engages.[93] They argue that neither culture nor one's experience should set the agenda for the church; only the gospel should have that role. But this position is not only naïve to the realities of cultural hermeneutics, but also ignores the three moments of transversal rationality: evaluative critique, engaged articulation, and incursive disclosure. While granting priority to theological rationality is a valid posture to take—be it marginal priority, like the Barthians and Hauerwasians, or totalizing priority, like the conservative evangelicals—that is not the stance of either Moltmann or the ECM. Instead, theirs is the posture of epistemic humility, of openness to other rationalities, of self-reflexive critique, and of a quest for transversal connections, in hope that those connections will ultimately strengthen Christian theology and ecclesial practice.

Engaging public, ecclesial practices, however, is an area in which the emerging church movement has a mixed record. With the notable exception of Brian McLaren's arrest in 2005 for protesting

---

[93] See Carson, *Becoming Conversant with the Emerging Church: Understanding a Movement and Its Implications*, 131ff.

the federal budget,[94] ECM leaders have not chosen the path of civil disobedience, common among other proponents of political theology. Moltmann would likely be disappointed with this, as he has often upheld the civil disobedience of Catholic priest in Latin America as exemplars of political theology. The public acts that have been undertaken by ECM congregations are often local in nature, like "Operation Turkey Sandwich," during which members of House for All Sinners and Saints in Denver hand out bag lunches to Denverites who have to work on Thanksgiving Day.[95] At Solomon's Porch, instead of a children's Christmas service, congregants sing carols at a local hospital on Christmas Eve afternoon. Acts of this sort are not, of course, unique to the ECM; churches everywhere and of every stripe engage in just this type of public act. While public acts of this sort do not make the ECM unique, they do accord with Moltmann's vision of a political ecclesiology: "He calls for the church to understand itself as two fellowships combined: the fellowship of the apostles and the fellowship of the poor."[96]

Emerging church leaders have more closely fulfilled Moltmann's desire for a political theology from a political church in another way: electronically. Among the first to adopt various electronic media like blogs, Facebook, and Twitter, ECM leaders often have online followings that far outnumber the membership of their churches. Nadia Bolz-Weber of House for All Sinners and Saints is an example. A Lutheran church planter in Denver, she has developed a significant audience on her blog, *Sarcastic Lutheran*, that far outstrips the 40-60 members of her church, and she has used that platform to advocate for the full inclusion of GLBT persons in the broader church. Her writings have become particularly influential among Lutheran leaders.

Other ECM leaders are similarly outspoken on this and other issues, with Brian McLaren leading the way in his most recent

---

[94] Jonathan Weisman and Alan Cooperman, "A Religious Protest Largely from the Left," *Washington Post*, December 14 2005.

[95] Nadia Bolz-Weber, "Operation: Turkey Sandwich," in Sarcastic Lutheran Blog. Denver: 2010. Accessed December 23, 2010.

[96] Peter Scott and William T. Cavanaugh, *The Blackwell Companion to Political Theology*, Blackwell Companions to Religion (Malden, MA: Blackwell Publishing House, 2004), 239.

books.[97]   But they still seem to be lacking the truly robust political theology for which Moltmann advocates, possibly because they have not yet reflected on the connection between their ecclesiology and the church's public engagement, or possibly because emerging church leaders consider this kind of public engagement to be the purview of liberal Protestantism.   For the ECM to more fully realize a political ecclesiology, some concrete practices of social engagement must be developed.   One of these can be to advance an extant strength of the movement by linking politically engaged ECM members in disparate congregations through some kind of electronic means.   Another would be for ECM leaders to take a leading role on an issue for which they share a passion.   An example of this is planned for the Wild Goose Festival, scheduled for June, 2011.   There, at the first major gathering of the ECM since the Emergent Convention in 2005, leaders will be attempting to garner public support for prison reform in the U.S.   Time will tell if this gathering and this cause will gain the needed traction to make it a significant political cause for the ECM.

The ecclesiology of Jurgen Moltmann and the ecclesial practices of the emerging church movement clearly have much in common, and they also stand as a challenge to one another.   Moltmann proposes an ecclesiology that is radically egalitarian.   The eight congregations introduced in chapter two have initiated some practices that embody this ecclesiology, but they have not embraced a relational ecclesiology to the extent that they could.   In chapter five, I will propose some practices for emerging church congregations that would move them further in the direction of a truly relational ecclesiology.

---

[97] See, for example, Brian D. McLaren, *Everything Must Change: Jesus, Global Crises, and a Revolution of Hope* (Nashville: Thomas Nelson, 2007).

Chapter Five: Pragmatic Suggestions for a Relational Ecclesiology in the Emerging Church Movement

Defining "Relational Ecclesiology"

Jürgen Moltmann introduces the phrase "relational ecclesiology" early in *The Church in the Power of the Spirit*. He writes that "no ecclesiology can stand on its own feet. The doctrine of the church must, as it were, evolve of itself from christology and eschatology, that is, from insight into the trinitarian history of God's dealings with the world."[1] "The church cannot understand itself simply from itself alone," he writes, "It can only truly comprehend its mission and its meaning, its roles and its functions in relation to others."[2] By "relational ecclesiology," Moltmann means that the church is defined by its relationships: to God's trinitarian history, to other doctrines, and to other institutions and movements in the world. While the strength of this position is that "it leads to an understanding of the living nature of the church," Moltmann admits this weakness: it does not allow for a ready-made definition of just what the church is.[3] Although Moltmann never again uses the term, "relational ecclesiology," he is faithful to the concept when he describes the church as a "messianic fellowship," which is his favored ecclesiological appellation throughout the rest of his writings.[4] And the inherent relation-

---

[1] Moltmann, *The Church in the Power of the Spirit: A Contribution to Messianic Ecclesiology*, 20.

[2] Moltmann, *The Church in the Power of the Spirit: A Contribution to Messianic Ecclesiology*, 19.

[3] Moltmann, *The Church in the Power of the Spirit: A Contribution to Messianic Ecclesiology*, 20.

[4] Others, however, have picked up on the term and used it to describe Moltmann's ecclesiology: Veli-Matti Kärkkäinen, *An Introduction to Ecclesiology: Ecumenical, Historical & Global Perspectives* (Downers Grove, Ill.: InterVarsity Press, 2002), 129-30. Bauckham, *The Theology of Jürgen Moltmann*, 122ff. David Ford and Rachel Muers, *The Modern Theologians: An Introduction to Christian Theology since 1918*, 3rd ed., Great Theologians (Malden, MA: Blackwell Publishing House, 2005), 154.

ality of the social Trinity imbues all of Moltmann's writing about the church with thoroughgoing relationality, from the beginning of his career to the present.

While Moltmann does not use the phrase "relational ecclesiology" again, this idea pervades all of his ecclesiological proposals, both in the *Church in the Power of the Spirit* and the rest of his writings. Building on his introduction of this phrase, I propose the following definition as a way to frame the suggestions of this concluding chapter:

> A *relational* ecclesiology understands the church to be constituted by its existence-in-relationship:
>
> The relationship of the church to Christ and Christ to the church;
>
> The relationships of the human beings who belong to the church, especially as they are bound to one another by the Holy Spirit;
>
> The relationship of the Christian church to the other religions and belief systems of the world;
>
> The relationship of the church of the present to the church of the past;
>
> The relationship of the church of the present to the eschatological church of the future.

In other words, under a *relational ecclesiology* the church is understood as a network of relationships, primarily the relationship of people who constitute the church have to God through Christ, and the relationship that they have to one another in Christ.

This has significant implications for Christian practice. With this definition as a guide, the practices of the church must primarily be concerned with nurturing those relationships. Be they practices for those within the church, evangelistic practices, or practices by which the church corporately deals with other institutions and religions, the standard against which the efficacy of these practices is measured is that of the eternal relationality of the Trinity. And the ideal toward which these practices must point is the eschaton: "The future of the church in God's new creation is the mutual personal indwelling of the triune God and of his glorified people."[5] This is, of course, an impossible standard to achieve. But, just as the "imitation of Christ" is the (impossible) goal of individual Christian discipleship, so is the community of the Trinity the ideal for Christian community. Just how the doctrine of the social Trinity affects ecclesial practice will be explored below.

Biblically, a relational ecclesiology can be understood in light of the doctrine of reconciliation, articulated by Paul in 2 Corinthians:

> All this is from God, who reconciled us to himself through Christ, and has given us the ministry of reconciliation; that is, in Christ God was reconciling the world to himself, not counting their trespasses against them, and entrusting the message of reconciliation to us. So we are ambassadors for Christ, since God is making his appeal through us; we entreat you on behalf of Christ, be reconciled to God.[6]

The work of Christ was to facilitate reconciliation between God and humankind, a rapprochement out of which the church was born. Subsequently, Paul states, the work of the human beings who constitute that church is to foster further reconciliation between God and humankind and between fellow human beings. Thus, our ecclesial practices must be judged on that basis. I will now attempt just that, examining the extant practices of the emerging church in light of a robust relational ecclesiology and offering suggestions for a way forward.

Practices of a New Social Movement

As established in chapter one, the emerging church movement fits the classification that sociologists have used to describe "new social movements," that is, movements that do not conform to the traditional Marxian conception of movements but nevertheless bring about significant societal change. The ECM, however, is not primarily comprised of people who transcend traditional class lines, though it does reflect several other characteristics of new social movements. Whereas in traditional movements, the working class

---

[5] Volf, *After Our Likeness: The Church as the Image of the Trinity*, 128.

[6] 2 Corinthians 5:18-20, NRSV.

rises up in an attempt to claim wealth and property from the elite class, new social movements are instead a struggle for cultural capital. Using Bourdieu, American Protestantism can be seen as a "field of power," with many players vying for a finite amount of cultural capital.[7] The emerging church movement can be seen as a young, upstart group of leaders who have very quickly made a play for some of the cultural capital that is afforded to Protestantism in America. In fact, some of the criticism of the ECM by established church leaders can be attributed to this struggle for power. According to my findings, those in the emerging church movement are younger, more white, better educated, and wealthier than the average American churchgoer. According to Bourdieu, this means that they have the upper hand in the struggle for cultural capital. This is where Bourdieu offers us a grammar to understand new social movements in general and the emerging church movement in particular, and using Bourdieuian language, we can understand some of what is at stake with the birth and growth of the ECM.

Bourdieu writes that there is a "structural homology" between social class and the lifestyle to which members of that social class will aspire.[8] If members of the emerging church movement are, indeed, among the educated, upper-middle class in America, Bourdieu posits that their *habitus* has already been deeply internalized and will compel them to a lifestyle of consumerism built on predetermined tastes. This can serve as a warning to the emerging church movement: while the participants in the movement often pride themselves on their countercultural challenge to the conventional church, they are already predisposed to the consumeristic tendencies that are well-known attributes of upper-middle class America. These characteristics of the social class from which the ECM sprang may indeed preclude them making some of the ecclesial reforms that they are attempting.

In order to mitigate against this, the emerging church movement must inculcate practices that guard against the danger that it becomes yet another brand name within the meta-brand of American Christianity. The movement has already struggled with this: leaders in the movement have written many books, spoken at conferences, and

---

[7] Swartz, *Culture & Power: The Sociology of Pierre Bourdieu*, 117ff.

[8] Swartz, *Culture & Power: The Sociology of Pierre Bourdieu*, 163.

even started consulting firms that leverage the "emerging church" brand. While this has surely been borne out of a true concern for the future of American Christianity, it nevertheless has soured some of the movement's potential admirers. While there has been talk in the movement about establishing platforms for various and diverse voices to be heard on the issues that matter to the proponents of the movement, most of those attempts have stalled out. It is incumbent upon the leaders of the movement to instantiate practices that allow a wide range of voices, and primacy should be given to voices that come from other social classes. This will help insure that the emerging church movement does not become co-opted by the consumerism that is prevalent in the social class from which it is predominantly drawn.

The ECM also has something to learn from the fate of another new social movement. The Jesus Movement of the 1960s and 1970s was a Christian parallel to the hippie movement, among the first of the new social movements. Like the emerging church, the Jesus Movement's growth was consonant with its time: members of that movement shunned the traditional church and embraced the music, clothing, and even the drug use of the larger hippie movement. But the Jesus Movement was ephemeral, swallowed up in less than a decade by larger, more (culturally and theologically) conservative forces and absorbed into churches like the Calvary Chapel and Vineyard Church associations.[9]

This is yet another danger for the emerging church movement: if it remains merely a protest movement against the evangelical megachurches and the mainline denominational churches of the late-twentieth century and does not establish its own theological identity, then it has the potential to be absorbed, *in toto* or in fragments, by the forces of American Protestantism. The participants in the emerging church movement can avoid this potential pitfall by developing practices that are reflective of distinctive and overt theological commitments, theological commitments that the movement has thus far left unarticulated. Below are three theological predispositions in the ECM that I clearly recognize. But each could be more clearly expressed by the movement, and each can provide the impetus for particular practices in the movement. For each, I will develop the

---

[9] Shawn David Young, "From Hippies to Jesus Freaks: Christian Radicalism in Chicago's Inner-City," *Journal of Religion and Popular Culture* 22, no. 1 (2010).

theological commitment in conversation with Jürgen Moltmann and the other theorists already introduced and then suggest resonant practices.

Theological Commitments and Related Ecclesial Practices

In the following sections, I will reference a particular theological doctrine that is central to the theology of Jürgen Moltmann, describe how the emerging church movement has intuitively embraced this theology, and then offer suggestions for the ECM and the broader Protestant church as to how they can more deliberately embody a relational ecclesiology. It is my contention that Moltmann has not adequately developed actual practices that embody his ecclesiology and the emerging church has not adequately reflected on the practices that have emerged over the past decade. The following will be an attempt ameliorate both of those weaknesses.

Table 2: Moltmannian Doctrine and Corresponding ECM Practice and Characteristics

Theological Doctrine	Overarching Practice	Characteristics
Panentheism	Sacraments of Life	Sacralize the world and desacralize the church
Social Trinity	Relationality	Egalitarian and democratic approaches to church governance
Christological Office of Friend	Public Friendship	Interreligious and intra-church relations built on the language of trust
Communal Hermeneutic	Corporate Interpretation	Dialogical patterns of preaching and teaching

Panentheism and Sacraments of Life

John Howard Yoder's deep bifurcation between church and world stems from a particular view of God and plays itself out in particular practices. And the same goes for Moltmann. Moltmann is, as noted above, a panentheist. As such, his ecclesiology does not jibe with Yoder's church-world distinction. For Moltmann, God is not exclusively, or even primarily active in the church, since God inhabits all of creation equally. Moltmann's panentheism serves to tear down the sacred-secular divide evident in the ecclesiologies that demarcate the church as unique because it is indwelt by God's Spirit in a special way.[10]   Because of Moltmann's panentheism, his ecclesiology does not afford more accessibility to God's Spirit from within the church than from without: "It is...possible to experience God *in, with, and beneath* each everyday experience of the world, if God is in all things, and if all things are in God."[11]   The Spirit of God is available equally everywhere and to all because God is in all things, and all things are in God.[12]

This panentheism is not overtly mentioned—or realized—in Moltmann's ecclesiology.   But it is evident in the practices of the emerging church movement.   As with Moltmann, leaders and parishioners in the ECM tend to reject the traditional divide between sacred and secular.   The Sunday-Monday gap that many clergypersons bemoan is virtually unknown, or at least not mentioned, in the ECM.   The members of Journey spend an inordinate amount of time with one another throughout the week, at bars and work as well as in church on Sunday.   As Doug Pagitt sometimes reminds the worshipping congregation on Sunday evening, there are members of Solomon's Porch who rarely or never come to worship; they belong to the community in other ways.   Even Pagitt's dethroning of the sermon, relativizing of the role of the Sunday worship gathering in the life of the community, and renaming of the worship space from a "sanctuary" to a "living room" can be seen as rejections of the sacred-secular divide.   If God speaks through all means, why is the sermon more important than your incoming phone call?   And if God

---

[10] Moltmann repeatedly makes it clear that the church is special—but it is special because of its role in the mission of God and its responsibility to the poor, not because God's grants the church special sacredness.

[11] Moltmann, *The Spirit of Life: A Universal Affirmation*, 34.

[12] To be fair, Moltmann does not consider the term "panentheism" to fully represent his position: "For Moltmann the key concept is reciprocal indwelling, most simply and commonly expressed as: 'God *in* the world, and the world *in* God'...The concept is an integrating, holistic one, which does not divide reality but finds the presence of God in all things and sees all things being taken up into the new creation which God will indwell in glory." Bauckham, *The Theology of Jürgen Moltmann*, 243. In other words, Moltmann's panentheism has a particularly eschatological focus; he repeatedly emphasizes 1 Corinthians 15:28 ("God will be all in all"), quoting it in at least nine of his books, most often to make the point that panentheism will be fully realized only in the eschaton.

166 The Church Is Flat

is everywhere, why is the church sanctuary more important that your cubicle at work?[13]

The ecclesial practices that stem from panentheism have a dual effect. Firstly, they sacralize the world. By believing that God's presence is in all things, congregation members are encouraged to recognize that presence as they go about their daily lives. Life becomes a sacrament, and all endeavors become holy. Although Moltmann fails to explore this aspect of ecclesiology, it is embodied in the ECM. Secondly, these practices desacralize the church. That is, they relativize the church's standing among the many institutions in which their members are involved; the church is thus no more or less important than these many other institutions. This tendency to desacralize the church is admittedly not shared across the emerging church movement, and it comes as a threat first and foremost to those who earn a living from working in the church. But the ECM's practices of mitigating and dispersing the activities traditionally afforded to clergy is yet another move in the direction of desacralizing the church and sacralizing the world.

Finally, the emerging church movement has underrealized the extent to which panentheism plays a role in its practices, and here Moltmann offers a corrective. While the leaders of the ECM have made many ecclesial choices that accord with Moltmann's theology, rarely have those been clearly articulated, or even reflected on. To embrace panentheism, and to reflect on it in a thoroughgoing manner, will only serve to strengthen the practices that embody panentheism and that will, in turn, strengthen the theological identity of the ECM. Further practice that (re-)sacralize the world will be the result—practices that can surely be incorporated by churches across American Protestantism.

---

[13] There is some resonance between the ECM, Moltmann's ecclesiology, and the American Congregationalist tradition. For example, the early Congregationalists refused to call their worship spaces "sanctuaries," but opted instead for "meetinghouses," connoting both the public nature of the building and the belief that God was no more or less present in a church building than anywhere else. See Arthur A Rouner, *The Congregational Way of Life* (Englewood Cliffs, N.J.: Prentice-Hall, 1960), 84ff.

Social Trinity and Practices of Relationality

If Moltmann's panentheism is underrealized in his ecclesiology, the same cannot be said of his view of the social Trinity, to which we now turn our attention. As noted in chapter four, the social doctrine of the Trinity is a central tenet to Moltmann's overall project. In several books, Moltmann makes is clear that he considers the traditional Western doctrine of the Trinity to be deeply flawed in that the *filioque*-clause established a Father-Son-Spirit hierarchy. Once established, this "monarchial monotheism" lent theological backing to titular hierarchies in government and the church. The result, according to Moltmann, has been nothing short of disastrous, evidenced by popes, kings, bishops, and dictators, all of whom premise their power on being a reflection of the Godhead, and all of whom consequently take power away from the people under their authority.

Instead, Moltmann holds to a social doctrine of the Trinity, in which the three divine persons of the Godhead dwell in eternal, mutually interpenetrating, and co-equal relationship. Being that this is the very nature of God, Moltmann asserts that human institutions—both governmental and ecclesial—should similarly be based on egalitarian, relational principles. Thus, Moltmann considers democracy to be the best—albeit not perfect—form of human government, and he advocates for small, autonomous congregations in which every member has an equal voice.

The emerging church movement has already taken the opportunity to partially realize Moltmann's vision for a relational ecclesiology based on a social doctrine of the Trinity by instantiating certain practices in that regard, though they have not done this with any overt acknowledgement of Moltmann. For example, six of the eight congregations profiled in chapter two have opted to forego membership in a denomination, thus implicitly rejecting the hierarchies thereof. It is possible that these emerging church congregations have concluded that as American Protestant denominations struggle to survive, they will inevitably provide less and less support for innovative church plants. As with any bureaucracy, these denominations will turn resources inward, toward the maintenance of the existing system.[14]   Updating the criticisms first put forth by Karl Marx and Max Weber, Michael Crozier writes of modern bureaucracies,

> *A bureaucratic organization is an organization that cannot correct its behavior by learning from its errors.*   Bureaucratic patterns of action such as the impersonality of the rules and the centralization of decision-making, have been so stabilized that they have become part of the organization's self-reinforcing equilibria.   Finally, when one rule prevents adequate dealing with one case, its failure will not generate pressure to abandon the rule, but, on the contrary, will engender pressure to make it more complete, more precise, and more binding.[15]

In other words, bureaucratic systems are, by their very nature, incapable of adjusting themselves to make room for innovative ecclesial experiments like those emerging in the ECM.   Denominations, inherently bureaucratic because of their size and scope, may attempt to co-opt those innovative congregations in their midst, forcing them to live by the already established rules.

The bureaucracies of American Protestantism are just as antithetical to Moltmann's relational ecclesiology as the Catholic hierarchy that he frequently criticizes.   Indeed, a significant shortcoming of Moltmann's ecclesiology is that he is quite critical of the Catholic church for its hierarchy, but he fails to see that the denominations of Protestantism fall prey to the very same patterns.   And further, Moltmann neglects to turn his criticism on ecclesial bureaucracies, which often exhibit similar non-relational traits.   The emerging church movement can posit alternative practices by first forging a

---

[14] Karl Marx was quick to point the finger at religious leaders for developing the first bureaucracies in order to maintain their control of the masses in primitive societies. Bureaucracy, he wrote, is "a web of *practical* illusions." And of governmental bureaucracy, "The spirit of bureaucracy is thoroughly Jesuitical and theological. The bureaucrats are the state's Jesuits and theologians. Bureaucracy is the priest's republic." Karl Marx, Loyd David Easton, and Kurt H. Guddat, *Writings of the Young Marx on Philosophy and Society* (Indianapolis: Hackett Publishing Company, 1997), 185.

[15] Michel Crozier, *The Bureaucratic Phenomenon* (Chicago: University of Chicago Press, 1964), 187.

more robust network of autonomous congregations. The advent of social media technology affords ECM congregations the ability to connect with one another in ways that were not possible in earlier eras. Churches today do not require a centralized bureaucracy to connect with one another. However, deliberate practices of inter-congregational connection are required to overcome the allure of se-curity that denominations offer to church planters. Among these practices, organizations like Emergent Village might offer a network of support that includes mentoring from experienced church planters and pastors, and should facilitate regular gatherings locally, region-ally, and nationally. To date, these organizations have not under-taken the more traditional denominational functions of providing job security, health insurance, and the imprimatur of ordination. If they were to do so, it would be a fatal flaw, for the very hierarchies and bureaucracies that the emerging church movement has protested would be an inevitable consequence of such institutional moves. As long as the organizations that support ECM congregations and min-istries stay small and nimble, they will be able to continue to advo-cate for congregations to stay autonomous and avoid reliance on larger, denominational and denomination-like bodies.

While the forgoing suggestions are practices at the inter-congregational level, there are also practices of relational ecclesiol-ogy that can be engaged within congregations. For one, ECM con-gregations might consider embracing a traditional Congregationalist polity in which each member is afforded one vote, clergy included. ECM congregations might need to remain small enough that a democratic or a consensus model of decision making is practical; when it is not practical, a small representative body may be charged with making decisions on behalf of the larger community. And, in-asmuch as possible, ECM congregations will likely continue to miti-gate the role and functions of clergy, thereby catalyzing a more egalitarian community.

There is a direct connection between these ecclesial practices and the culture in which these emerging church congregations are being formed, and the work of Jeffrey Stout, introduced in chapter two, is helpful at understanding that context. Stout's vision for liberal de-mocracy is an outgrowth of what he sees as the best of American democracy, and the traits of democratic thinking are clearly seen in the origins of the ECM. Using Stout's three characteristics of a ro-bust, liberal democracy as a guide, we can propose some practices that will enhance the burgeoning polity in the emerging church movement and, consequently, serve as an example in American Protestantism. First, practices of *hermeneutical enrichment* are those that catalyze conversation in a congregation. This shifts the role of the clergyperson from that of the community's primary hermeneut to one of a facilitator of conversations. Whether it be the community's act of interpreting the Bible or the more mundane aspects of congregational life like electing leadership or deciding on a budget, conversation is encouraged, and the conviction is repeatedly articulated that everyone's interpretive skills are enriched when more people are invited into the process of conversation and decision making.

Second, practices of *ad hoc immanent critique* mean that members of the congregation are allowed to ask anyone else for the reasons that compel their belief. In this context, requesting the warrants for another's beliefs and articulating a critique of those beliefs is not seen as an affront to a fellow congregation member, but is seen as part and parcel of the democratic process of church governance. Further, the *ad hoc* nature of the ongoing conversation in a congregation mitigates against the committees and bureaucracy in which so many congregations get bogged down. Instead of multiple checks and balances on the decision making process, the ongoing communal conversation itself is what keeps the potential abuses of power in check. Indeed, congregations that have embraced the *ad hoc* nature of decision making will be much better situated to respond to crises, both within the congregation and around the world.

Thirdly, a *dialectical relationship between reflection and action* means that the congregation develops practices that facilitate the question, "Is it working?" In other words, the congregation must constantly look at its worship, its programs, even its beliefs, and ask very pragmatic questions about their efficacy. In this scenario, no aspect of ecclesial life is off limits from critique, no practice is repeated simply because "we've always done it this way." Instead, the very dialectic of the hermeneutical circle is built into the practice of the church. Any member, since all are equal, may bring up a criticism or a question about a practice or belief of the congregation. And since dialectical conversation is woven into the very fabric of what the church is, this is not seen as a threat but instead embraced as central to congregational life together.

The Christological Office of "Friend" and Practices of Public Friendship

In adding the relational title, "friend," to the honorific titles, "prophet, priest, and king," Moltmann proposes that "there is no human hope" for a world free of class struggles and domination without "a classless society free of domination, without repression and without privileges."[16] And that comes only by friendship, characterized by "affection, loyalty, reliability, constancy in disaster, openness, freedom, sympathy, and noncompetitiveness."[17] Moltmann also issues a corrective to the modern conception of friendship by insisting that the friendship for which he is calling not be private but public: "The friendship of Jesus cannot be lived and its friendliness cannot be disseminated when friendship is limited to people who are like ourselves and when it is narrowed down to private life."[18]

"Friend" has been a core theological rubric in the emerging church movement since its inception. The leaders of Emergent Village, arguably the most significant organization in the ECM between 2001 and 2008, identify the organization as a "growing, generative friendship among missional Christian leaders."[19] Supporters and funders of the organization go by the appellation, "Friend of Emergent Village," and the organization distributes iconographic web badges with that phrase that are common in the Christian blogosphere. In my book *The New Christians: Dispatches from the Emergent Frontier*, I proposed that, "Emergents believe that an envelope of friendship and reconciliation must surround all debates about doctrine and dogma."[20] Moltmann proposed "Friend" as a fifth christological office in 1975; Emergent Village's introduction

---

[16] Moltmann, *The Church in the Power of the Spirit: A Contribution to Messianic Ecclesiology*, 116.

[17] Scott and Cavanaugh, *The Blackwell Companion to Political Theology*, 237.

[18] Moltmann, *The Church in the Power of the Spirit: A Contribution to Messianic Ecclesiology*.

[19] Jones, *The New Christians: Dispatches from the Emergent Frontier*, xi.

[20] Jones, *The New Christians: Dispatches from the Emergent Frontier*, 77.

of that term as the hallmark of their network in 2001 did not rely on Moltmann, but the connection is more than coincidental.

To some extent, the emerging church movement has exemplified the public friendship for which Moltmann advocates in his ecclesiology. The next step in the ECM's process of theological friendship will be to develop practices that explicitly encourage public friendship. One of these will be to engage in inter-religious dialogue, an area with which the ECM has little experience. Other than a meeting in 2005 with the leaders of Synagogue 3000, a Jewish think tank, the movement has done little to pursue public friendship with non-Christians. Some consider the inter-religious dialogues of the twentieth century disappointing in their results, but the ECM's emphasis on practices of public friendship may model an alternative of inter-religious conversation. The ECM has an opportunity to forge a type of inter-religious relation that, like Moltmann's theology, maintains a robust Christian identity while remaining truly open to the life of the other. These practices of public friendship with adherents of other religions—and no religion—should be pursued aggressively.[21]

The concept of friendship can also be more fully operationalized within the movement itself. As J.L. Austin and other philosophers of language have conclusively shown, words do things.[22] Thus, the words that are used to describe the adherents to the movement will necessarily shape the self-perception of those adherents and will shape the perception of the movement by those who observe it.

The adoption and use of the language of friendship will aid emerging church congregations in becoming the egalitarian fellowships that they long to be. These congregations have largely abdicated the traditional titles taken by clergy (Reverend, Pastor, Father), titles which sometimes serve to prop up traditional hierarchical structures and the attitudes of domination and submission that so often accompany them. Now, at a time when public distrust of clergy is on the rise due to the many public scandals of the past several decades, clergypersons may do well to relinquish antiquated and honorific titles in favor of a single designator, like "friend," that clearly com-

---

[21] This is not unique to the emerging church movement. It is the very model being used by Interfaith Youth Core. But the ECM is uniquely poised within American Protestantism to catalyze a similar dialogue.

[22] Austin, *How to Do Things with Words*.

municates an equivalency between all members of a faith community. Practices that relocate ecclesial authority in language of trust—like the office of friend—communicate the equivalency of all members of the faith community before God and downplay the traditional power differential between clergy and laypeople.

A Communal Hermeneutic and Practices of Interpretation

Central to a relational ecclesiology, and related to the ideal of egalitarian friendship, is the theological conviction that the Bible is better understood by a Christian community when the interpretation thereof is engaged by the entire community. While Moltmann does not deal specifically with biblical hermeneutics, it is implied throughout his work in his insistence on the church as a community of equals. Plus, others do help in this regard. Mentioned in chapter two, under the auspices of phenomenological research, is the work of Hans-Georg Gadamer. In his magnum opus, *Truth and Method*, Gadamer develops the argument that the hermeneutical problem is the universal human problem.[23] That is, "Gadamer supported the idea that 'all understanding *is* interpretation'; this claim constitutes *the universal claim of hermeneutics* in the sense that any understanding we can achieve exhibits its hermeneutical dimensions as a linguistic interpretation."[24] Gadamer contends that "truth" comes to human beings in a phenomenological sense, as much through art and text as through the social sciences or "hard" sciences. Therefore, according to Gadamer, no scientific method is ever epistemically sufficient. The ideal of "total enlightenment," he writes, is a "fatal confusion," and he continues, "To me it seems just as mistaken as the ideal of fully rational self-clarity, of an individual who would live in full consciousness and control of his impulses and motives."[25]

---

[23] Gadamer, *Truth and Method*.

[24] Demetrius Teigas, *Knowledge and Hermeneutic Understanding: A Study of the Habermas-Gadamer Debate* (Cranbury, NJ: Associated University Presses, 1995), 144-45. Gadamer's universalizing claims are one of the main points of unease for Jürgen Habermas in their famous debates, and Habermas entitled one of his retorts to Gadamer, "The Hermeneutic Claim to Universality," in Josef Bleicher, *Contemporary Hermeneutics: Hermeneutics as Method, Philosophy, and Critique* (London: Routledge, 1980).

[25] Gadamer, *Truth and Method*, 571-72.

In other words, total enlightenment and fully rational self-clarity have never existed except in the minds of philosophers. Instead, we *know* something only insofar as we are able to *understand* that thing, and we understand only insofar as we are able to *interpret* its meaning.[26] And, according to Gadamer, "the noblest task of the citizen [is] decision-making according to one's own responsibility."[27]

Gadamer famously adopts Husserl's concept of "horizon" as a metaphor for the "flow of experience" that constitutes the human "temporality of consciousness."[28] The "universal hermeneutic process," then, is the formation and fusion of horizons.[29] Every human being is constantly developing and amending a horizon of meaning, and each horizon is inevitably and forever changed when it comes into "fusion" with another horizon. This, for Gadamer, is the key to understand understanding:

> In the process of understanding, a real fusing of horizons occurs – which means that as the historical horizon is projected, it is simultaneously superseded. To bring about this fusion in a regulated way is the task of what we call histori-

---

[26] This does not, for Gadamer, mean that we slide into a pool of relativism; instead, he believes that there are practical steps we can take (he calls his endeavor a "practical philosophy") that can lead to *better* – though not perfect – interpretation. "Application" is the interpretive moment, "the mediation between the past and the present." Gadamer, *Truth and Method*, xxxiii.

[27] The entire quote, from Teigas, *Knowledge and Hermeneutic Understanding: A Study of the Habermas-Gadamer Debate*, 166.

> The chief task of philosophy is to justify this way of reason and to defend practical and political reason against the domination of technology based on science. That is the point of philosophical hermeneutic. It corrected the peculiar falsehood of modern consciousness: the idolatry of scientific method and of the anonymous authority of the sciences and it vindicates again the noblest task of the citizen – decision-making according to one's own responsibility – instead of conceding the task to an expert.

[28] Gadamer, *Truth and Method*, 245.

[29] Gadamer, *Truth and Method*, 576.

cally effected consciousness. Although this task was obscured by aesthetic-historical positivism following on the heels of romantic hermeneutics, it is, in fact, the central problem of hermeneutics. It is the problem of *application*, which is to be found in all understanding.[30]

Even in its early days, the leaders of the emerging church movement have already shown an intuitive understanding of the importance of hermeneutics in a Gadamerian sense. They have opened the sermon up for discussion, and at Journey and Solomon's Porch, they have opened the process of exegeting the scripture texts and constructing the sermon to the community. This is in line with Stanley Fish, who builds on the work of Gadamer by arguing that interpretive authority always resides in "authoritative communities." That is, communication always takes place within situations, and "to be in a situation is already to be in possession of (or to be possessed by) a structure of assumptions, of practices understood to be relevant in relation to purposes and goals that are already in place."[31]   In other words, communities have structured predispositions that necessarily affect their interpretations of texts. The point, according to Fish, is not to be naïve to this fact. Too often, churches are. And rather than embracing the interpretation of sacred text as the noblest task of the citizen, congregants often abdicate their hermeneutical authority to a clergyperson. Many practices of conventional churches exacerbate this problem: the internal design of most churches sets the preacher in an elevated pulpit, thereby granting him the visual accoutrements of hermeneutical authority; the vestments worn by a clergyperson often communicate her level of theological education and are yet another way that clergy are set apart from the congregation; even the use of electronic amplification and lighting in many sanctuaries is used to highlight the presence of the preacher. Churches that do use these traditional modes of worship have reasons that are rooted in theological convictions, too. The Geneva gown of the Reformed tradition is worn so that the preacher's clothes will not be a distraction to the congregation, and the monk's garments are part of his

---

[30] Gadamer, *Truth and Method*, 307.

[31] Stanley Fish, *Is There a Text in This Class? The Authority of Interpretive Communities* (Cambridge: Harvard University Press, 1980), 318.

vow of poverty. Microphones, of course, are meant to enable every-one in a large congregation to hear the scripture and the sermon.

That emerging church congregations have opted out of some of these conventions is an indication that they are attempting to con-sciously acknowledge the hermeneutical authority of every member of the congregation. At Solomon's Porch, microphones are not used, so as not to give the impression that one person's voice is deserving of amplification at the expense of other voices. Other congregations have rearranged the seating in the worship space to enhance egali-tarian patterns of communication.

But even so, these ECM congregations are battling long-standing patterns in the lives of many community members. Despite our national premise that all men are created equal, there nevertheless seems to be something in human nature that leads some people to claim ultimate hermeneutical authority, and others to quickly abdi-cate their own hermeneutical authority. Most people who were reared with Christian church involvement assume that the clergyper-son is the expert on the sacred text and the one member of the com-munity with the authority to interpret it—or at least to preach about it in a public setting. Counteracting these patterns of belief and be-havior takes a deliberate and considered set of practices. Emerging church congregations do this best in worship, sharing the preaching and songwriting duties across the congregation. Among these prac-tices are dialogical sermons, communal sermon preparation, and classes in which congregants are taught the exegetical methods most often taught in seminaries. Whether the ECM can take these prac-tices to a broader audience remains to be seen. That is, some of the practice—like not using amplification—necessarily precludes the numeric growth of a congregation beyond a certain size, as does the commitment to dialogical sermons. And how these faith communi-ties will deal with the inevitable situation of a person who abuses the hermeneutical openness will also be telling.

Gleanings for the Enterprise of Practical Theology

It is my hope that this book contributes in some way to the field of practical theology. Specifically, I think there are four questions raised in this project that might provoke some interesting conversa-tion in the field.

Why does it matter that the emerging church movement—or any Christian movement—is a new social movement? Practical theologians have long been conversant in the traditional Marxian categories of social movement theory. But the advent of new social movements has significantly changed social theorists' understanding of what a social movement is and how it works. In some ways, it has lowered the bar as to what can be considered a "movement," because massive societal upheaval is no longer necessarily the result. However, and recent global events have shown, the very technologies that enable new social movements to foment have also been pivotal in the development of the ECM. Practical theologians will do well to understand the characteristics of new social movements and to consider the nexus of the movement of God and the movements of humans in this regard.

This leads to the second question: *How can the work of Pierre Bourdieu and Jürgen Moltmann complexify our understanding of practice?* Investigating and understanding practice and practices have been among the most pressing issues for practical theologians for years now, with many embracing the Neo-Aristotelian trajectory that practices are constitutive of a faith community's identity. But Bourdieu and Moltmann bring a hearty critique to this perspective. Bourdieu problematizes the Neo-Aristotelian view that human beings are rational actors who consciously choose their practices. Without going all the way to post-structuralism, he convincingly posits a thick theory of practice that acknowledges pre-reflective *habitus* that individuals bring to practices. And Moltmann reminds us that practices don't actually tell us about God—they tell us about individuals' and communities' experiences of God. This is a challenge to practical theologians to think more explicitly about how practices are a nexus of divine and human action, and about how practices fall short of fully explaining both human action and divine action.

Thirdly, *what are the merits of transversal rationality for practical theology?* As I wrote in chapter one, practical theologians have, more often than not, afforded theological rationale trump value in interdisciplinary conversations.[32] In this, they are not much different from their systematic colleagues. But as practical theologians work to expand our field—possibly even to once again find a place on university faculties—it will only happen inasmuch as we are able to

---

[32] See also Appendix A.

converse with other rationalities as peers. The transversal rationality of Schrag and van Huyssteen is worthy of consideration in this regard because, while it allows for peer-to-peer conversations with other disciplines, it does not give up any of the uniqueness, conviction, or truth claims of the theological enterprise.

Finally, *how can we expand upon Moltmann's ecclesiology?* Practical theologians have an untapped resource of great value in Jürgen Moltmann's ecclesiology. From one of the greatest theologians of the twentieth century, we have a doctrine of the church that lends itself to practical theological reflection, and yet has hardly been touched by subsequent theologians. Moltmann's ecclesiology is ripe for consideration among practical theologians who want a more robust ecclesiology that is grounded in Christology, pneumatology, and a social doctrine of the Trinity.

Conclusion

The emerging church movement has risen from the American Protestant church of the late twentieth century. In both its mainline denominational and evangelical mega-church form, that church had become monolithic and, in the perspective of emerging church leaders, overly bureaucratic. More distressingly, that late twentieth century church had lost sight of its role in the eschatological mission of God. In an effort to reclaim that role, a small band of GenXers began new faith communities, and they began meeting with each other under various auspices, including the "Young Leaders Network" and, ultimately, the "emerging church movement."

The ECM can be understood not only by its history and what it emerged from, but also by the ecclesial practices in which its congregations have engaged over the last decade. In looking at those practices, we find a movement that both renews traditional Christian practices, and also innovates new practices. Examples of the former category include a commitment to weekly communion—although that practice has been renegotiated as a pastiche of many confessional versions of the Lord's Supper—and a dedication to the Christian virtue of hospitality. In the latter category, we find congregations that are actively pursuing online connections for their parishioners, and churches that have opened the traditionally monological sermon up to include everyone in the community.

Implicit in the emerging church movement's use of a relational ecclesiology are several questions that are important to the church as a whole. Among them is the ever-changing relationship between clergy and laity, especially in a time when new media are flattening hierarchies across our culture. The use of a pastiche of worship practices from across confessional boundaries is another area with unknown long-term results. And the future of polity as mainline denominations attempt to redefine themselves is yet another area of inquiry. The practices of the ECM are emerging out of these congregations' understandings of God, and out of their attempts to make meaning. Thus, their practices also raise questions about God—both about how they understand God in both traditional and new ways, and about how God is moving and revealing Godself to these congregations.

Sometimes, the ecclesial practices of the emerging church movement are not backed by sufficient theological reflection. And so we turned to Jürgen Moltmann's ecclesiology as a resource. Most of Moltmann's ecclesiological suggestions are directly traceable to his core theological conviction of a social doctrine of the Trinity. Moltmann introduces the term "relational ecclesiology," which I have picked up as a descriptor with much merit for the emerging church movement. As indicated in chapter three, most of the practices of the ECM detailed therein were *intuited* by ECM leaders. To their credit, they recognized that something was missing in the conventional churches of their rearing, and they went looking for inventive resources to combat these inadequacies. In their disaffection with church-as-usual, they did not walk away from the institution, as so many in their generation have, but instead have spent the last decade attempting to reform American Christianity by starting new churches and innovating new practices. However, they have done so without the deliberate theological reflection that has been part of many reformations of the past. Be it the monastic reformation led by Benedict or Nursia, or the Great Reformation of Luther, Calvin, and Zwingli, most of the reformations of Christianity that have had staying power have been backed by thorough and robust theological reflection. To avoid the fate of the Jesus Movement of the 1960s and 1970s, the emerging church movement needs to undertake serious theological reflection on the practices described above, as well as other practices with which their communities are engaged. Again, this is the responsibility of entire communities, not simply of those with seminary training.

This is not to take anything away from Pagitt, Keel, or Shroyer, or the other leaders in the ECM. With the exception of McLaren, each of them has a seminary degree. In many ways, they fall into what Antonio Gramsci calls "organic intellectuals," those thought-leaders who rise from the lower social class and foment revolution from within. "Traditional intellectuals," on the other hand, are those who, unbeknownst to themselves, support the existing systems. According to Gramsci, while revolution begins with the work of organic intellectuals, it can only be completed when enough traditional intellectuals are recruited to the cause to upset the current order of things.[33] Gramscian analysis is helpful to understand the ECM insofar as the originators of the movement are primarily organic intellectuals, not co-opted by the conventional forms of ecclesial life in America. Thus they have had the intellectual freedom to reimagine ecclesial forms and practices in a way not available to traditional intellectuals in the ecclesial sphere. However, the progress of the ECM will be limited unless those organic intellectuals can recruit a critical mass of traditional intellectuals to join the movement. Only then will the ECM begin to develop the intellectual backing needed to sustain it as it ages and, most likely, institutionalizes.

There is a danger here as well. As Max Weber prophesied, religious movements seem inevitably to routinize the charisma that precipitated their founding. It is highly unlikely that the emerging church movement can avoid institutionalization. The question is how the movement will navigate the ambiguities of routinization as it ages. It is my belief that if the movement commits to a relational ecclesiology and embraces egalitarian practices, it will stave off the pitfalls of bureaucracy and hierarchy that have so vexed the modern church. This means that clergy will have to dramatically rethink their role in communities of faith, and members of those communities will need to reclaim their authority as hermeneuts of scripture, tradition, and experience.

The emerging church movement holds the promise of renewal within American Protestantism, and key to that is an embrace of a relational ecclesiology.

---

[33] Antonio Gramsci, *Prison Notebooks*, ed. Joseph Buttigieg, vol. 2 (New York: Columbia University Press, 1996), 202-07.

Appendix A: Focus Group and Interview Lines of Questioning

Focus Group Line of Questioning

Welcome: Introduction of myself and of the project.

Let's go around and briefly tell our names and interesting fact about ourselves.

What it is that particularly attracted you to _____ Church?

What is it that has kept you here? (Follow up: Is it surprising that it's different/the same?)

If you would be so bold to tell us, how has your life of faith changed as a result of being involved in _____ Church? I'm not so much interested in how you *believe* differently but how you *live* differently as a result of being a part of this church.

What, specifically, has the church done that has fostered this change in you? I'm not so interested in what the church *teaches* as in what it does—*how* it does things like teaching, small groups, worship, outreach, etc. (Follow up: How is this church's way of fostering your faith different than other churches that you've been involved with?)

What else do you think I should know about how _____ Church encourages the everyday practice of the Christian faith.

If time permits: What do you think about the future direction of the church? Do you feel excited about it? Anxious? Indifferent?

Line of Questioning: Founding Pastor Interview

Tell me the story of starting this church.

Was there any particular theological school or emphasis that guided you in starting the church?

Have you, from the beginning, emphasized any particular practices of faith or of communal life that you think are particularly important

How successful do you think the church has been at fostering these faith practices?

Are there other faith practices—maybe ones that you didn't expect—that have emerged as particularly important in the congregation?

How have you deliberately nurtured/fostered these communal and individual faith practices?

Are there yet other practices or themes of the Christian life that you hope to emphasize in the future?

Finally, is there anything else about the life of the congregation as it bears on the practice of the Christian faith that you think I should know?

Line of Questioning: Layperson Interview

Tell me the story of your faith journey.

If they haven't answered already: What brought you to _____ Church?

Tell me what you consider to be the most important part of the Christian faith. That is, if you had the chance to write a *Time* magazine cover article on Christianity, what would you put on the cover? What would be the thrust of the article?

If they emphasized a point of doctrinal belief over an aspect of practice: Now if you had to write the same article, but it had to be on an aspect of *living the faith*, what would it be on?

Why do you consider _____ to be the most important aspect of living the Christian faith?

How does your church foster this aspect of living the faith? (Follow up: How could the church do better at fostering this?)

What other aspects of *living the Christian faith* do you think that the church emphasizes? How do they do this? How is this different from other churches that you've been a part of?

Finally, is there anything else about how your church nurtures the Christian life that I should know about?

Appendix B: Church Census Survey

Church Survey Form

    1) What is your gender? Female   Male

    2) What is your age? _____

    3) What is your marital status? *(circle one)*

Single   Single/Divorced   Single/Widowed

    Married   Live with Partner

    4) Do you have any children?

I have no children

I have children (or step-children) who live with me

I have children (or step-children) who are grown

I have children (or step-children) who live with another adult

    5) What is your race? Indicate one or more races that you consider yourself to be:

White

Black

Hispanic

American Indian

Asian Indian

Chinese

Filipino

Japanese

Korean

Vietnamese

Other Asian

Samoan

Other Pacific Islander

Some Other Race not listed here

Don't Know

    6) What is your highest level of education? *(circle one)*

Some high school

High school degree completed

Some college/university/vocational training

College/university/vocational degree completed

Some post-college

Master degree completed

Ph.D. or equivalent—in process or completed

    7) What best describes what you currently do? *(circle one)*

Work full-time

Work part-time and/or attend school part-time

Attend school full-time

Unemployed

Retired

None of the above

8) Rounded up the nearest year, how many years have you been attending Cedar Ridge? _____

9) Which of the following best describes your attendance at Cedar Ridge? *(circle one)*

This is my first time at Cedar Ridge

I attend worship once per month or less

I attend worship 1-3 times per month

I attend worship 1-3 times per month and some other activities

Attend worship almost every week

Attend worship almost every week and some other activities

10) How would you characterize your involvement at Cedar Ridge? *(circle one)*

I worship occasionally, and that's all

I worship regularly, and that's all

I am involved in a ministry or group outside of worship (small group, Sunday school, etc.)

I am a very involved lay leader

I am on paid staff

11) Do you attend another church as well as Cedar Ridge?

Yes   No

12) Which best describes your church involvement in the *two years* before you came to Cedar Ridge? *(circle one)*

I was a member at another church

I was attending another church, but not a member

I used to go to another church, but I hadn't been there in over two years

I've never been a part of a church before this one

13) What attracted you to Cedar Ridge? *(circle as many as are applicable)*

The preaching

The music

The ministry to children and youth

The social justice ministries

The adult education, small groups, and Bible studies for adults

The pastoral care for people in times of need
The social activities
Other: _____

14) Does Cedar Ridge have a clear vision, goals, or direction for its ministry and mission?

I am not aware of such a vision, goals, or direction
There are ideas but no clear vision, goals, or direction
Yes, and I am strongly committed to them
Yes, and I am partly committed to them
Yes, but I am not committed to them

15) Of the following, which *one* best describes your opinion of the future direction of Cedar Ridge:

We need to get back to the way we did thing in the past
We are faithfully maintaining past directions
We are currently deciding on new directions
We are currently moving in new directions
We need to rethink where we are heading
Our future is unclear or doubtful
I don't know

16) How would you describe Cedar Ridge? *(circle one)*

Evangelical
Mainline
Independent
Pentecostal
None of the Above

17) In what ZIP Code do you live? _____

Please make any other comments here:

Appendix C: Empirical Findings

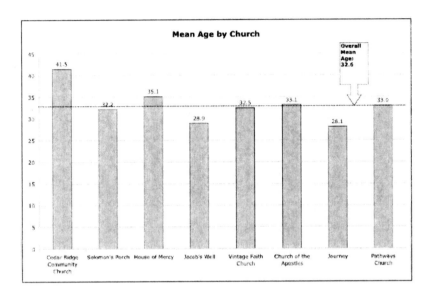

	Responses	Male	Female	% Male	% Female	Mean Age
Cedar Ridge	243	111	132	45.7%	54.3%	41.5
Solomon's Porch	113	56	57	49.6%	50.4%	32.2
House of Mercy	99	48	51	48.5%	51.5%	35.1
Jacob's Well	647	286	358	44.2%	55.8%	28.9
Vintage Faith	277	118	158	42.6%	57.4%	32.5
COTA	44	17	27	38.6%	61.4%	33.1
Journey	34	17	17	50.0%	50.0%	28.1
Pathways	565	244	320	43.2%	56.8%	33.0
TOTALS	2022	897	1120	44.4%	55.6%	32.6

Percent Male Respondents

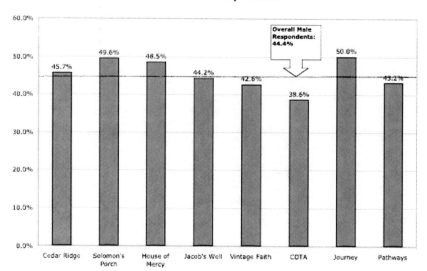

What Attracted You to this Church?

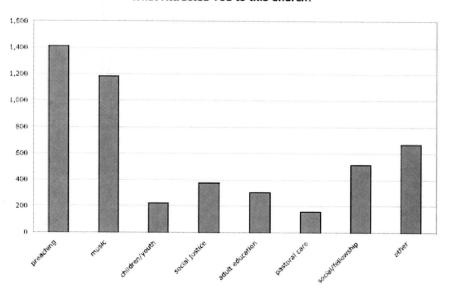

	Some High School	Completed High School	Completed Some College/Vocational	Completed College/Vocational	Some Post-College	Completed Masters	Completed PhD
Cedar Ridge	1.7%	7.0%	15.3%	31.4%	10.7%	26.9%	7.0%
Solomon's Porch	2.7%	3.6%	20.5%	40.2%	12.5%	14.3%	6.3%
House of Mercy	2.0%	2.0%	12.2%	36.7%	16.3%	27.6%	3.1%
Jacob's Well	3.9%	3.6%	24.5%	38.9%	9.6%	13.6%	6.0%
Vintage Faith	7.2%	8.3%	36.2%	29.0%	10.1%	7.2%	1.8%
Church of the Apostles	2.4%	0.0%	9.5%	52.4%	9.5%	16.7%	9.5%
Journey	0.0%	0.0%	23.5%	47.1%	17.6%	11.8%	0.0%
Pathways Church	1.8%	2.3%	11.6%	44.1%	14.1%	20.5%	5.7%
TOTALS	3.2%	4.1%	20.2%	38.5%	11.7%	17.0%	5.3%

Completed Level of Education of All Respondents

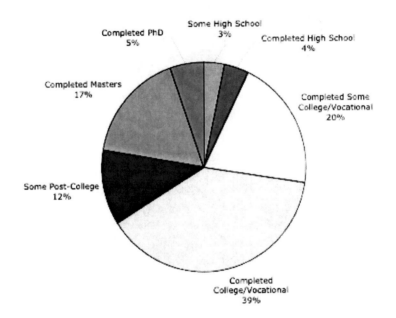

Appendix D: An Excursus on Modes of Cross-Disciplinary Thinking in Practical Theology

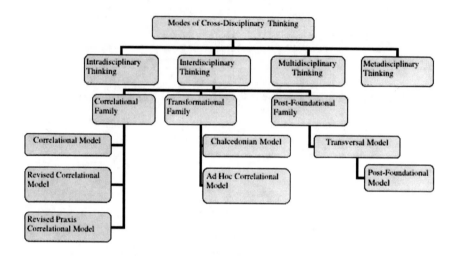

Those who employ *multidisciplinary* modes of thought often have an altogether different view of how theology relates to other disciplines. The assumption here is that each field of thought has a distinct role to play in the quest for knowledge. The theologian, then, may draw upon many disciplines in her development of a doctrinal position; however, it is noteworthy that the multidisciplinary theologian does not then think that theology is ultimately reliant upon any of these findings—theology stands alone. The converse, however, can be true; for instance, Johannes van der Ven is critical of Karl Rahner for being indiscriminate in his multidisciplinarity and ultimately allowing theology to subsume its dialogue partners.[1] Instead, multidisciplinary practical theology attempts to use *many* other disciplines as complementary (whereas interdisciplinarity usually confines itself to one or two). In this way, multidisciplinarity is more of mapping of the entirety of human knowledge and finding theology's place on the map.[2]

---

[1] Cf. Midali, *Practical Theology: Historical Development of Its Foundational and Scientific Character*, 237-38.

[2] Cf. Osmer, "Johannes Van Der Ven's Contribution to the New Consensus in Practical Theology."

One example of this is Nancey Murphy and George F. R. Ellis's book, *On the Moral Nature of the Universe: Theology, Cosmology, and Ethics.*[3] Here a Christian theologian/philosopher (Murphy) and a mathematician/astronomer (Ellis) make it clear that theology and the natural sciences, while each playing a role in the ultimate quest for knowledge, have different starting points, different methodologies, and different goals. Theology employs a top-down methodology, beginning with theory and moving toward life experience; the natural or 'hard' sciences have empirical evidence as their starting point, and they make a practice of working toward theory to explain said evidence. After dividing the sciences into two complementary hierarchies (the natural sciences and the human sciences), Murphy and Ellis argue that these sciences have "boundary questions," limiting their ability to answer questions that are better left to theology and metaphysics.[4] Much of their multidisciplinary work, then, is discerning the boundaries between disciplines and doing what work one can without answering questions that are better left to other fields.

Finally, *metadisciplinarity* takes five steps back and attempts to see the networks and connections between all fields of knowledge. The first goal here is to define exactly what is a discipline, a task that has become more difficult in the face of the postmodern challenge. Then the metadisciplinarian attempts to articulate the *"problems whose solution demands that all possible cognitive tools come together and help."*[5] Finally, the theologian who employs metadisciplinarity faces the formidable task of designing a global solution to a theological quandary, "reaching a global understanding of a particu-

---

[3] Nancey C. Murphy and George Francis Rayner Ellis, *On the Moral Nature of the Universe: Theology, Cosmology, and Ethics*, Theology and the Sciences (Minneapolis, Minn.: Fortress Press, 1996).

[4] For instance, they write, "Science itself cannot resolve the metaphysical issues raised by questioning the reason for (a) existence of the universe, (b) the existence of any physical laws at all, or (c) the nature of the physical laws that actually hold," Murphy and Ellis, *On the Moral Nature of the Universe: Theology, Cosmology, and Ethics*, 5.

[5] Midali, *Practical Theology: Historical Development of Its Foundational and Scientific Character*, 245.

lar range of either religious or ecclesial problems and developing unitary and operative projects."[6]

Metadisciplinarity, then, aids all other forms of multidisciplinary thinking in defining disciplines, articulating assumptions among disciplines, elucidating intersections between them, and pointing out conflicts.[7] This last critical role may be the most important.

While all of the above will certainly be helpful to the practical theologian, the most common method of work will be, and has been, *inter*disciplinary. In working on a problematic issue in Christian education, homiletics, or pastoral care, the practical theologian will look to psychology, sociology, cultural anthropology, or a number of other disciplines and sub-disciplines for help and resources. In this section, we will look at two dominant models and one promising model for work between and among disciplines.

The word "correlation" refers to the causal, reciprocal, or parallel relationship that one thing has to another. In this case, the correlation between theology and the non-theological resources of culture was developed as a part of the liberal theological project of modernism. After the Enlightenment, many of the traditional structures of society were questioned, especially the authority of the church, and theological liberalism "was deeply aware of the changes modernization was unleashing in contemporary life and the challenges they posed to the inherited beliefs and practices of Christianity."[8] The response of theological liberals was to change their stance towards these societal, scientific, and philosophical movements. Instead of standing over against them, or attempting to guide them, theologians began to allow these modes of thought influence and shape their theology. In a mutually influential way, theology would shape culture and culture would shape theology. The impact of this shift can hardly be overstated, and theological conservatives in the 20th century reacted strongly against this move. Indeed, as the 20th century

---

[6] Midali, *Practical Theology: Historical Development of Its Foundational and Scientific Character*, 245.

[7] Cf. Osmer, "Johannes Van Der Ven's Contribution to the New Consensus in Practical Theology."

[8] Osmer, "Johannes Van Der Ven's Contribution to the New Consensus in Practical Theology."

wore on, even liberals became less idealistic about the contributions of culture in the shadow of two world wars and the Holocaust, which greatly affected the evolution of this school of thought.

One of the first theologians to argue that "Christian theology necessarily engages the non-theological resources of a particular culture"[9] was Paul Tillich (1886-1965). In *Systematic Theology*, Tillich used psychoanalysis, modern art, and existentialism to show how these resources of culture pointed to a "depth dimension" in modern life;[10] that is, investigations into these disciplines showed how modern life was causing people to ask questions for which theology holds the answers. Tillich's message was that for theology to maintain its relevance in the modern world, it must set its agenda to answer the questions that culture is asking. Only by doing this, he argued, will theology avoid the dangers of traditionalism.

University of Chicago theologian David Tracy (b. 1939) has revised Tillich's thesis, stating, "*Theology* is the discipline that articulates mutually critical correlations between the meaning and truth of an interpretation of the Christian fact and the meaning and truth of an interpretation of the contemporary situation."[11] Tracy sets theology and non-theological resources as equals, each asking questions and each providing answers. To understand Tracy's position, it is important to note his emphasis on the word "interpretation" and his emphasis on situational rootedness; following philosopher Hans-Georg Gadamer, Tracy reminds us that everyone comes to her or his understanding of contemporary problematics via selective and subjective interpretation and as a historically embedded person.

Tracy has been critical of practical theology's myopic focus on technical pastoral skills (a mistake that has largely been corrected in the past two decades); he has instead argued for a public practical

---

[9] Osmer, "Johannes Van Der Ven's Contribution to the New Consensus in Practical Theology."

[10] Osmer, "Johannes Van Der Ven's Contribution to the New Consensus in Practical Theology."

[11] David Tracy, "The Foundations of Practical Theology," in Don S. Browning, *Practical Theology*, 1st ed. (San Francisco: Harper & Row, 1983), 62. Cf. also David Tracy, *Blessed Rage for Order: The New Pluralism in Theology* (San Francisco: Harper & Row, 1988).

theology with an emphasis on eschatological praxis.[12] Both theology
and social theories, he argues, are concerned with human transformation. Practical theology, then, should facilitate a conversation including "all those seeking a true consensus based on a
comprehensive notion of reason and guided by various future ideals
for the actualization of a shared emancipatory thrust of reason itself
toward freedom."[13]

Another proponent of the revised correlational approach (and another emeritus faculty member of the University of Chicago Divinity
School) is Don Browning. While a fan of Tracy's work, Browning
wants practical theology to be more critical in nature, thus moving
closer to Rebecca Chopp and others who are more rooted in emancipatory praxis. Whereas Tracy makes room for Christian faith claims
and praxis to be critically tested at the theoretical/metaphysical level,
Browning adds that they should be tested philosophically as well.[14]
Thus Christian validity claims are opened to another level of secular
critique.

Browning also builds on Tracy by emphasizing the importance
of contemporary praxis. For instance, he proposes that the first

---

[12] Defining praxis with an Aristotelian slant, Tracy writes, "What we can affirm
with Aristotle and the classical tradition is that praxis is the action of moral agents
guided by some goal of the good and virtuous life and directed to the development
of a character possessing *phronesis* or practical wisdom. What we can also affirm
in our period is, first, that praxis is mediated through a historical and social
consciousness that needs explicit study; second, that praxis must be explicitly
related to the techniques of modern technology in order to prove effective; and,
third, that the goal of the good and virtuous life is itself a projected possibility for
any agent," Browning, *Practical Theology*, 75-76.

[13] Browning, *Practical Theology*, 76. Tracy then proposes four steps in seeking
this consensus: 1) a collection of non-theological models of human transformation,
the adequacy of which would be tested by practical theologians; 2) a collection
and analysis of public claims of human transformation, also tested for adequacy,
particularly in their visions for the future; 3) a critical theoretical explication of the
hermeneutical assumptions of the models analyzed in steps 1) and 2); and 4)
reflection on mutually critical correlations between the non-theological models
and Christian faith praxis (which Tracy defines as "faith working through justice
and love and guided by the hope of a genuinely eschatological ideal," Browning,
Practical Theology, 76-78.

[14] Don S. Browning, *A Fundamental Practical Theology: Descriptive and
Strategic Proposals* (Minneapolis: Fortress Press, 1991), 52.

movement of theology should be the description theory-laden religious and cultural practices: "this first movement is horizon analysis; it attempts to analyze the horizon of cultural and religious meanings that surround our religious and secular practices."[15] We do this in order to discern points of connection and conflict at these horizons.

Finally, Browning utilizes the philosophy of Jurgen Habermas (b. 1929) in emphasizing the importance of communicative action in the revised correlational approach to practical theology:

> The revised correlational approach is an apologetic approach to practical theology that enhances the non-coercive communication of the Christian faith. It should help communicate the Christian faith to the wider world. It should help communicate its wisdom as a crucial element in the reconstruction of the wider civil order. It should help guide the communication process in the churches' work of education and care both within their institutional boundaries and beyond...

Specific communicative messages come out of particular narrative traditions. Understanding these communications is a mutually transformative dialogue. It is a dialogue with many levels of meaning that are tested by several different kids of rationality.[16]

While in many ways indebted to the (revised) correlational approaches of Tillich, Tracy, and Browning, Rebecca Chopp is also sharply critical of them.[17] The correlational approach, she argues, is inextricably tied to the modern liberal project, a project that has caused churches and seminaries to focus almost exclusively on the theoretical aspects of theology at the expense of the true message of the gospel: emancipatory praxis. The most condemning indictment of this model is the passivity and ideological captivity that this stance has bred in mainline liberal congregations. Chopp criticizes

---

[15] Browning, *A Fundamental Practical Theology: Descriptive and Strategic Proposals*, 47.

[16] Browning, *A Fundamental Practical Theology: Descriptive and Strategic Proposals*, 291-92.

[17] Cf. also Matthew L. Lamb, *Solidarity with Victims: Toward a Theology of Social Transformation* (New York: Crossroad, 1982).

both the hierarchy of theologies (fundamental-systematic-practical) taught by most practical theologians and the "subtle romanticization of the congregation" whereby many practical theologians desire the local church to set the agenda for theology.[18]

Chopp proposes instead that practical theology must relate "a new theological substance to a new theological method that speaks to a new experience and role of Christianity in history."[19] This "newness" is found in social movements that struggle against oppression and for liberation. And correlation takes place at the nexus of this social emancipatory praxis and the praxis of communities of faith struggling toward the same goals. The church is found not in seminary classrooms or suburban congregations, but in the midst of this massive struggle.

As one might expect, the enormous influence of Karl Barth (1886-1968) in 20th century theology has been felt in practical theology, too. Barth's reemphasis on the uniqueness of Christ, the singularity of the Christ event, and the significance of revelation stands in stark contrast to the liberal theology of cultural correlation that we have just examined. Ultimately, Barth argued that there is no way from humanity to God, but that we are only able to speak of God because of the Christ event.[20] Similarly, all history is seen through the lens of Jesus Christ, who fulfilled and transformed the history of Israel and set the course for the future. From this vantage point, theologians can look to history and culture for "parables" or "analogies," but these are always contingent upon and relative to the revelation of Christ.[21] It is by this standard that all social theories, psychologies, etc. are judged. The practical theological schools of thought that follow Barth are the "transformational" model of James Loder and the "ad hoc correlational" model of Hans Frei.

---

[18] Rebecca Chopp, "Practical Theology and Liberation" in Lewis Seymour Mudge and James N. Poling, *Formation and Reflection : The Promise of Practical Theology* (Philadelphia: Fortress Press, 1987), 124.

[19] Mudge and Poling, *Formation and Reflection : The Promise of Practical Theology*, 125-26.

[20] Osmer, "Johannes Van Der Ven's Contribution to the New Consensus in Practical Theology."

[21] Osmer, "Johannes Van Der Ven's Contribution to the New Consensus in Practical Theology."

James Loder (1932-2001) taught Christian education at Princeton Theological Seminary and did significant thinking on the relationship between theological knowledge and other forms of human knowledge. Like Barth, Loder took the debate over the person of Jesus Christ at the Council of Chalcedon as his metaphor.[22]   At Chalcedon, it was decided that Jesus Christ was both fully human and fully divine, and these two essences stand in an inseparable, albeit asymmetrical, unity. In interdisciplinary work in practical theology, theology has logical and ontological priority over all other disciplines, much like Christ's divinity was ultimately over and above his humanity. And yet theology does not subsume the other disciplines but allows them to interact in bipolar unity, even as theology retains "marginal control" over other forms of reasoning.[23]   So Loder develops his methodology to always preserve the *theological* center of practical theology: "This relationality is characterized in Barthian terms as 'indissoluble differentiation', 'inseparable unity', 'indestructible (asymmetrical) order', and may be translated into an analytical and critical model through the logic of complementarity. This constellation of factors is succinctly designated as an asymmetrical, bi-polar, relational unity."[24]

---

[22] Cf. Karl Barth, Geoffrey William Bromiley, and Thomas F. Torrance, *Church Dogmatics, I/1* (Edinburgh: T. & T. Clark, 1936), 181ff. and Karl Barth, *Church Dogmatics, I/2* (Edinburgh: T. & T. Clark, 1956), 160ff. Cf. also Barth interpreters Thomas F. Torrance, *The Trinitarian Faith : The Evangelical Theology of the Ancient Catholic Church*, Paperback ed. (Edinburgh: T.& T. Clark, 1997). and George Hunsinger, *How to Read Karl Barth: The Shape of His Theology* (New York: Oxford University Press, 1991), 185-88, 202-18.

[23] Osmer, "Johannes Van Der Ven's Contribution to the New Consensus in Practical Theology."

[24] James Edwin Loder, "Normativity and Context in Practical Theology: 'The Interdisciplinary Issue'" in Friedrich Schweitzer and J. A. van der Ven, *Practical Theology: International Perspectives*, Erfahrung Und Theologie ; Bd. 34 (Frankfurt am Main ; New York: P. Lang, 1999), 359. Another Princeton Theological Seminary proponent of the Chalcedonian model is Deborah van Deusen Hunsinger, who writes of the relationship between theology and psychology that it should be "without separation or division, without confusion or change, and with the conceptual precedence assigned to theology (asymmetrical order)." Deborah van Deusen Hunsinger, *Theology and Pastoral Counseling: A New Interdisciplinary Approach* (Grand Rapids, Mich.: Eerdmans, 1995), 213.

This methodology is in response to what Loder sees as the major problematic in interdisciplinary practical theology: the *tertium quid*. In attempting to have two disciplines in dialogue while preserving the integrity of each, an objective baseline ("third place") is established, and it's at this baseline that the two disciplines meet to talk.[25] The problem, as Loder sees it, is that this *tertium quid* is *not no place—it is a place*, and as such it has standards and rules that, knowingly or unknowingly, guide the conversation. Most importantly, these standards and rules are most likely non-theological, which betrays the theological core of practical theology. To overcome this problem, Loder proposed a transformational model in which theology always has at least marginal priority over its dialogue partners.

Post-liberal theologian Hans Frei (1922-1988) of Yale Divinity School proposed a model of interdisciplinary dialogue that might even be closer to Barth's own model. In general, the post-liberal movement has attempted to correct liberalism's reliance upon universal human spiritual experience by stating that the Christian tradition has within itself all of the resources necessary for explaining its own truth claims.[26] In describing Barth, to whom he is obviously sympathetic, Frei writes, "theology has its own set of rules of what makes it a science—a set of rules that are usually implicit and developed only as the context of theology itself develops...Theology is Christian self-description first."[27] This gives theology an even stronger priority (Frei calls it "absolute priority"[28]) than in Loder, and in some ways obviates the motivation for interdisciplinary work.

---

[25] Schweitzer and Ven, *Practical Theology: International Perspectives*, 362.

[26] Frei "pinches" his own description of the theological task from Barth when he writes, "(1) Theology involves a critical task, 'a scientific' or *wissenschaftlich* test. (2) What is done theologically is done within a religious *community*, the Church; it is the communal self-description of the community, rather than the individual creed of the individual Christian, even if he or she is Christian. (3) Theology constitutes an inquiry into the specific language peculiar to, in fact constitutive of, the specific semiotic community called the Christian Church or churches." Hans W. Frei, George Hunsinger, and William C. Placher, *Types of Christian Theology* (New Haven: Yale University Press, 1992), 78.

[27] Frei, Hunsinger, and Placher, *Types of Christian Theology*, 39.

[28] Frei, Hunsinger, and Placher, *Types of Christian Theology*, 41.

The model, then, for interdisciplinary work is "unsystematic" and "asymptomatic"—"how it is done is a matter of seeing the application in a given context."[29] First-order discourse is using the grammar internal to the church to describe the Christian faith; second-order discourse is engaging non-Christian, non-theological dialogue partners in a case-by-case or *ad hoc* way. Osmer notes that this method places three limits on interdisciplinary dialogue:

First, theology must be clear of the differences between its task, based on God's revelation in Jesus Christ, and the task of other fields...Second, when theology does make use of concepts or methods from other fields, it must not appropriate them at the level of a system...Third, such concepts and methods must be reworked as they are placed in the service of this or that particular task in theology.[30]

[29] Frei, Hunsinger, and Placher, *Types of Christian Theology*, 41.

[30] Osmer, "Johannes Van Der Ven's Contribution to the New Consensus in Practical Theology."

Bibliography

Ableson, Hal. "Reflections on a Decade of Open Sharing: Opening up Opencourseware." In *MIT News Blog*. Boston: Massachussetts Institute of Technology, 2010.

Anderson, Ray Sherman. *An Emergent Theology for Emerging Churches*. Downers Grove, Ill.: IVP Press, 2006.

Austin, J. L. *How to Do Things with Words*. Oxford: Clarendon Press, 1962.

Baker, Jonny, Doug Gay, and Jenny Brown. *Alternative Worship: Resources from and for the Emerging Church*. Grand Rapids: Baker Books, 2004.

Barth, Karl. *Church Dogmatics, I/2*. Edinburgh: T. & T. Clark, 1956.

Barth, Karl, Geoffrey William Bromiley, and Thomas F. Torrance. *Church Dogmatics, I/1*. Edinburgh: T. & T. Clark, 1936.

Bass, Diana Butler. *The Practicing Congregation: Imagining a New Old Church*. Herndon, Va.: Alban Institute, 2004.

Bauckham, Richard. *The Theology of Jürgen Moltmann*. Edinburgh: T&T Clark, 1995.

Bird, Warren. "Emerging Church Movement." In *Encyclopedia of Religion in America*, edited by C.H. Lippy and P.W. Williams, 682-87. Washington, D.C.: CQ Press | A Division of SAGE Publications, 2010.

Bleicher, Josef. *Contemporary Hermeneutics: Hermeneutics as Method, Philosophy, and Critique*. London: Routledge, 1980.

Bloch, Ernst. *Das Prinzip Hoffnung*. 3 vols. Berlin: Aufbau-Verlag, 1954.

Blue, Debbie. *Sensual Orthodoxy*. St. Paul: Cathedral Hill Press, 2004.

Bohannon, John S. *Preaching and the Emerging Church: An Examination of Four Founding Leaders: Mark Driscoll, Dan Kimball, Brian Mclaren, and Doug Pagitt*. Clarksville, Virginia: CreateSpace 2010.

Bolz-Weber, Nadia. "Operation: Turkey Sandwich." In *Sarcastic Lutheran Blog*. Denver, 2010.

Bourdieu, Pierre. *Distinction: A Social Critique of the Judgement of Taste*. Cambridge, Mass.: Harvard University Press, 1984.

————. *The Logic of Practice*. Stanford, Calif.: Stanford University Press, 1990.

————. *The Rules of Art: Genesis and Structure of the Literary Field*. Cambridge: Polity Press, 1996.

Bourdieu, Pierre, and Randal Johnson. *The Field of Cultural Production: Essays on Art and Literature*, European Perspectives. New York: Columbia University Press, 1993.

Browning, Don S. *A Fundamental Practical Theology: Descriptive and Strategic Proposals*. Minneapolis: Fortress Press, 1991.

————. *Practical Theology*. 1st ed. San Francisco: Harper & Row, 1983.

Bruce, Reginald A. "Leadership in High Performing Congregations: Uncovering the Secrets of Success." In *Society for the Scientific Study of Religion*, 10. Rochester, New York, 2005.

Buechler, Steven M., and F. Kurt Cylke. *Social Movements: Perspectives and Issues*. Mountain View, Calif.: Mayfield Pub., 1997.

Byassee, Jason. "Emerging Model: A Visit to Jacob's Well." *Christian Century*, September 19 2006, 20-24.

————. "New Kind of Christian: An Emergent Voice." *Christian Century*, November 30 2004, 28-31.

Carson, D. A. *Becoming Conversant with the Emerging Church: Understanding a Movement and Its Implications*. Grand Rapids, Mich.: Zondervan, 2005.

Certeau, Michel de. *The Practice of Everyday Life*. Berkeley: University of California Press, 1988.

Chalke, Steve, and Alan Mann. *The Lost Message of Jesus*. Grand Rapids, Mich.: Zondervan, 2003.

"Church Champions Update: Ideas, Impact and Innovation." Dallas: Leadership Network, 2000.

"Church of the Apostles: Story."
http://www.apostleschurch.org/about/story/.

Clark, Peter J. Walker with Tyler. "Missing the Point? The Absolute Truth Behind Postmodernism, Emergent, and the Emerging Church." *Relevant* July/August 2006, no. 21 (2006): 70-74.

Connor, Steven. *Postmodernist Culture: An Introduction to Theories of the Contemporary.* Oxford: Basil Blackwell, 1989.

Cooperman, Jonathan Weisman and Alan. "A Religious Protest Largely from the Left." *Washington Post,* December 14 2005, 2.

Crozier, Michel. *The Bureaucratic Phenomenon.* Chicago: University of Chicago Press, 1964.

Dean, Andrew Root and Kenda. *The Theological Turn in Youth Ministry.* Downers Grove, IL: InterVarsity Press, 2011.

Dean, Kenda Creasy. *Almost Christian : What the Faith of Our Teenagers Is Telling the American Church.* Oxford ; New York: Oxford University Press, 2010.

———. *Practicing Passion: Youth and the Quest for a Passionate Church.* Grand Rapids, MI: W.B. Eerdmans Pub., 2004.

DeWaay, Bob. *The Emergent Church: Undefining Christianity.* St. Louis Park, MN: Bethany Press International, 2009.

DeYoung, Kevin, and Ted Kluck. *Why We're Not Emergent: By Two Guys Who Should Be.* Chicago: Moody Publishers, 2008.

"Ecclesia." http://www.ecclesianet.org.

Fish, Stanley. *Is There a Text in This Class? The Authority of Interpretive Communities.* Cambridge: Harvard University Press, 1980.

Florida, Richard L. *The Great Reset : How New Ways of Living and Working Drive Post-Crash Prosperity.* New York: Harper, 2010.

———. *The Rise of the Creative Class: And How It's Transforming Work, Leisure, Community and Everyday Life.* New York, NY: Basic Books, 2002.

Flory, Richard W., and Donald E. Miller. *Finding Faith: The Spiritual Quest of the Post-Boomer Generation*. New Brunswick, N.J.: Rutgers University Press, 2008.

———. *Gen X Religion*. New York: Routledge, 2000.

Ford, David, and Rachel Muers. *The Modern Theologians: An Introduction to Christian Theology since 1918*. 3rd ed, Great Theologians. Malden, MA: Blackwell Publishing House, 2005.

Frei, Hans W., George Hunsinger, and William C. Placher. *Types of Christian Theology*. New Haven: Yale University Press, 1992.

Gadamer, Hans Georg. *Truth and Method*. 2nd, rev. ed. New York: Crossroad, 1989.

Galli, Mark. "The Long View: The Virtue of Unoriginality." *Christianity Today*, April 1 2002, 62.

Garrison, Becky. *Rising from the Ashes: Rethinking Church*. New York: Seabury Books, 2007.

Gibbs, Eddie. *Churchmorph: How Megatrends Are Reshaping Christian Communities*. Grand Rapids, Mich.: Baker Academic, 2009.

Gibbs, Eddie, and Ryan K. Bolger. *Emerging Churches: Creating Christian Community in Postmodern Cultures*. Grand Rapids, Mich.: Baker Academic, 2005.

Gorski, Eric. "Evangelical Church Opens Doors Fully to Gays." *Aurora Centinal*, December 20, 2009, 2.

Graf, Kurt J. Bauman and Nikki. "Educational Attainment: 2000." *Census 2000 Brief* (2003).

Gramsci, Antonio. *Prison Notebooks*. Edited by Joseph Buttigieg. Vol. 2. New York: Columbia University Press, 1996.

Guder, Darrell L., and Lois Barrett. *Missional Church: A Vision for the Sending of the Church in North America*. Grand Rapids, Mich.: W.B. Eerdmans Pub., 1998.

Hall, Douglas John. *The End of Christendom and the Future of Christianity*, Christian Mission and Modern Culture. Valley Forge, PA: Trinity Press International, 1997.

Hargis, Bernie. "The Changing Face of Worship: The Church in a Postmodern World." USA: FamilyNet, Inc., 2002.

Healy, Nicholas M. "Practices and the New Ecclesiology: Misplaced Concreteness?" *International Journal of Systematic Theology* 5, no. 3 (2003): 22.

Hunsinger, Deborah van Deusen. *Theology and Pastoral Counseling: A New Interdisciplinary Approach*. Grand Rapids, Mich.: Eerdmans, 1995.

Hunsinger, George. *How to Read Karl Barth: The Shape of His Theology*. New York: Oxford University Press, 1991.

Hunter, James Davison. *Evangelicalism: The Coming Generation*. Chicago: University of Chicago Press, 1987.

Jenkins, Philip. *The New Faces of Christianity: Believing the Bible in the Global South*. Oxford ; New York: Oxford University Press, 2006.

———. *The Next Christendom: The Coming of Global Christianity*. Oxford; New York: Oxford University Press, 2002.

Jones, Andrew. "Emerging Church Movement (1989 - 2009)?" In *TallSkinnyKiwi.com*, 2009.

Jones, Tony. "Google Wave as a Sermon Preparation Tool." In *WorkingPreacher.com*. St. Paul: Luther Theological Seminary, 2010.

———. *Postmodern Youth Ministry: Exploring Cultural Shift, Creating Holistic Connections, Cultivating Authentic Community*. Grand Rapids, Mich.: Youth Specialties/Zondervan, 2001.

———. *The New Christians: Dispatches from the Emergent Frontier*. San Francisco, CA: Jossey-Bass, 2008.

Kärkkäinen, Veli-Matti. *An Introduction to Ecclesiology: Ecumenical, Historical & Global Perspectives*. Downers Grove, Ill.: InterVarsity Press, 2002.

Keel, Tim. *Intuitive Leadership: Embracing a Paradigm of Narrative, Metaphor, and Chaos.* Grand Rapids, Mich.: Baker Books, 2007.

Kimball, Dan. *Emerging Worship: Creating New Worship Gatherings for Emerging Generations.* Grand Rapids, MI: Zondervan, 2004.

———. "The Emerging Church: 5 Years Later - the Definition Has Changed." In *VintageFaith.com.* Santa Cruz, 2008.

———. *The Emerging Church: Vintage Christianity for New Generations.* Grand Rapids, Mich.: Zondervan, 2003.

Kinnaman, David, and Gabe Lyons. *Unchristian: What a New Generation Really Thinks About Christianity—and Why It Matters.* Grand Rapids, Mich.: Baker Books, 2007.

Knox, Paul L. *Metroburbia, USA.* New Brunswick, NJ: Rutgers University Press, 2008.

Kolb, Robert, Timothy J. Wengert, and Charles P. Arand. *The Book of Concord: The Confessions of the Evangelical Lutheran Church.* Minneapolis: Fortress Press, 2000.

Lamb, Matthew L. *Solidarity with Victims: Toward a Theology of Social Transformation.* New York: Crossroad, 1982.

Laraña, Enrique, Hank Johnston, and Joseph R. Gusfield. *New Social Movements: From Ideology to Identity.* Philadelphia: Temple University Press, 1994.

Lawton, Kim. "The Emerging Church, Part One." In *Religion and Ethics Newsweekly.* USA: PBS, 2005.

Lee, Shayne, and Phillip Luke Sinitiere. *Holy Mavericks: Evangelical Innovators and the Spiritual Marketplace.* New York: New York University Press, 2009.

Leland, John. "Hip New Churches Sway to a Different Drummer." *New York Times*, February 18 2004.

Lippy, Charles H. *Faith in America: Changes, Challenges, New Directions.* 3 vols, Praeger Perspectives. Westport, Conn.: Praeger, 2006.

Long, Jimmy. *Generating Hope: A Strategy for Reaching the Post-modern Generation*. Downers Grove, Ill.: InterVarsity Press, 1997.

Lyotard, Jean François. *The Postmodern Condition: A Report on Knowledge*, Theory and History of Literature; V. 10. Minneapolis: University of Minnesota Press, 1984.

Lytch, Carol E. *Choosing Church: What Makes a Difference for Teens*. 1st ed. Louisville, Ky.: Westminster John Knox Press, 2004.

MacIntyre, Alasdair C. *After Virtue: A Study in Moral Theory*. 2nd ed. Notre Dame, Ind.: University of Notre Dame Press, 1984.

———. *Whose Justice? Which Rationality?* Notre Dame, Ind.: University of Notre Dame Press, 1988.

Marx, Karl, Loyd David Easton, and Kurt H. Guddat. *Writings of the Young Marx on Philosophy and Society*. Indianapolis: Hackett Publishing Company, 1997.

McKnight, Scot. "Blogossary." In *JesusCreed.org*. New York: Beliefnet, 2006.

McLaren, Brian. *A New Kind of Christianity: Ten Questions That Are Transforming the Faith*. San Francisco: HarperOne, 2010.

McLaren, Brian D. *A Generous Orthodoxy: Why I Am a Missional, Evangelical, Post/Protestant, Liberal/Conservative, Mystical/Poetic, Biblical, Charismatic/Contemplative, Fundamentalist/Calvinist, Anabaptist/Anglican, Methodist, Catholic, Green, Incarnational, Depressed-yet-Hopeful, Emergent, Unfinished Christian*. Grand Rapids, MI: Zondervan/Youth Specialties, 2004.

———. *A New Kind of Christian: A Tale of Two Friends on a Spiritual Journey*. San Francisco: Jossey-Bass, 2001.

———. *Everything Must Change: Jesus, Global Crises, and a Revolution of Hope*. Nashville: Thomas Nelson, 2007.

"Mclaren Talk Canceled by Kentucky Baptists." *Christian Century*, March 22 2005.

Midali, Mario. *Practical Theology: Historical Development of Its Foundational and Scientific Character*. Roma: LAS, 2000.

Mohler, Albert. "A Generous Orthodoxy - Is It Orthodox?" In *AlbertMohler.com*. Louisville, 2005.

Moltmann, Jürgen. *A Broad Place: An Autobiography*. Minneapolis: Fortress Press, 2008.

———. "A Christian Declaration on Human Rights." *Reformed World* 34, (1976): 14.

———. *God for a Secular Society : The Public Relevance of Theology*. Minneapolis: Fortress Press, 1999.

———. *God in Creation: A New Theology of Creation and the Spirit of God*, The Gifford Lectures; 1984-1985. Minneapolis: Fortress Press, 1993.

———. *History and the Triune God: Contributions to Trinitarian Theology*. New York: Crossroad, 1992.

———. *Religion, Revolution, and the Future*. New York: Scribner, 1969.

———. *Science and Wisdom*. London: SCM, 2003.

———. *Sun of Righteousness, Arise! God's Future for Humanity and the Earth*. Minneapolis: Fortress Press, 2010.

———. *The Church in the Power of the Spirit: A Contribution to Messianic Ecclesiology*. Minneapolis: Fortress Press, 1993.

———. *The Coming of God: Christian Eschatology*. London: SCM, 1996.

———. *The Crucified God: The Cross of Christ as the Foundation and Criticism of Christian Theology*. 1st Fortress Press ed. Minneapolis: Fortress Press, 1993.

———. *The Spirit of Life: A Universal Affirmation*. Minneapolis: Fortress Press, 1992.

———. *The Trinity and the Kingdom: The Doctrine of God*. Minneapolis, MN: Fortress Press, 1993.

———. "Theological Basis of Human Rights and the Liberation of Man." *Reformed World* 31, (1971): 9.

————. *Theology of Hope: On the Ground and the Implications of a Christian Eschatology.* 1st U.S. ed. New York: Harper & Row, 1967.

Moltmann, Jürgen, M. Douglas Meeks, and Theodore Runyon. *Hope for the Church: Moltmann in Dialogue with Practical Theology.* Nashville: Abingdon, 1979.

Moltmann, Jürgen, Robert E. Neale, Sam Keen, and David LeRoy Miller. *Theology of Play.* New York: Harper & Row, 1972.

Morris, Aldon D., and Carol McClurg Mueller. *Frontiers in Social Movement Theory.* New Haven, Conn.: Yale University Press, 1992.

Moustakas, Clark E. *Phenomenological Research Methods.* Thousand Oaks, Calif.: Sage, 1994.

Mudge, Lewis Seymour, and James N. Poling. *Formation and Reflection : The Promise of Practical Theology.* Philadelphia: Fortress Press, 1987.

Müller-Fahrenholz, Geiko. *The Kingdom and the Power: The Theology of Jürgen Moltmann.* London: SCM, 2000.

Murphy, Nancey C. *Anglo-American Postmodernity: Philosophical Perspectives on Science, Religion, and Ethics.* Boulder, Colo.: Westview Press, 1997.

Murphy, Nancey C., and George Francis Rayner Ellis. *On the Moral Nature of the Universe: Theology, Cosmology, and Ethics,* Theology and the Sciences. Minneapolis, Minn.: Fortress Press, 1996.

Norris, Pippa. *Democratic Phoenix : Reinventing Political Activism.* Cambridge, UK ; New York, NY: Cambridge University Press, 2002.

Notes from the Second Year: Women's Liberation; Major Writings of the Radical Feminists. Edited by Shulie Firestone and Anne Koedt. New York: Radical Feminism, 1970.

O'Brian, Brandon. "Emergent's Divergence: Leaders Hope Decentralizing Power Will Revitalize the Movement." *Christianity Today,* January, 2009.

Osmer, Richard R. "Johannes Van Der Ven's Contribution to the New Consensus in Practical Theology." In *Essays in Honor of Johannes Van Der Ven*. Leiden: Brill, forthcoming.

Osmer, Richard Robert. *The Teaching Ministry of Congregations*. Louisville, Ky.: Westminster John Knox Press, 2005.

Osmer, Richard Robert, and Friedrich Schweitzer. *Religious Education between Modernization and Globalization: New Perspectives on the United States and Germany*, Studies in Practical Theology. Grand Rapids, Mich.: W.B. Eerdmans, 2003.

Pagitt, Doug. *Preaching Re-Imagined : The Role of the Sermon in Communities of Faith*. Grand Rapids, Mich.: Zondervan, 2005.

———. *Preaching Re-Imagined: The Role of the Sermon in Communities of Faith*. Grand Rapids, Mich.: Zondervan, 2005.

Pichardo, Nelson A. "New Social Movements: A Critical Review." *Annual Review of Sociology* no. 23 (1997): 411-30.

Prooijen, Ton van. *Limping but Blessed: Jürgen Moltmann's Search for a Liberating Anthropology*, Currents of Encounter. Amsterdam ; New York: Rodopi, 2004.

Putnam, Robert D., David E. Campbell, and Shaylyn Romney Garrett. *American Grace: How Religion Divides and Unites Us*. New York, NY: Simon & Schuster, 2010.

Rah, Soong-Chan. *The Next Evangelicalism : Releasing the Church from Western Cultural Captivity*. Downers Grove, Ill.: IVP Books, 2009.

Rasmusson, Arne. *The Church as Polis: From Political Theology to Theological Politics as Exemplified by Jürgen Moltmann and Stanley Hauerwas*, Studia Theologica Lundensia. Bromley, Kent, England: Lund University Press, 1994.

Rogers, Everett M. *Diffusion of Innovations*. 5th ed. New York ; London: Free Press, 2003.

Rouner, Arthur A. *The Congregational Way of Life*. Englewood Cliffs, N.J.: Prentice-Hall, 1960.

Sargeant, Kimon Howland. *Seeker Churches: Promoting Traditional Religion in a Nontraditional Way*. New Brunswick, N.J.: Rutgers University Press, 2000.

Sawyer, Nanette. *Hospitality, the Sacred Art : Discovering the Hidden Spiritual Power of Invitation and Welcome*, Art of Spiritual Living. Woodstock, Vt.: SkyLight Paths Pub., 2008.

Schrag, Calvin O. *The Resources of Rationality: A Response to the Postmodern Challenge*, Studies in Continental Thought. Bloomington: Indiana University Press, 1992.

Schweitzer, Friedrich, and J. A. van der Ven. *Practical Theology: International Perspectives*, Erfahrung Und Theologie ; Bd. 34. Frankfurt am Main ; New York: P. Lang, 1999.

Scott, Peter, and William T. Cavanaugh. *The Blackwell Companion to Political Theology*, Blackwell Companions to Religion. Malden, MA: Blackwell Publishing House, 2004.

Seuss. *Oh, the Places You'll Go!* New York: Random House, 1990.

Sine, Tom. *The New Conspirators: Creating the Future One Mustard Seed at a Time*. Downers Grove, Ill.: IVP Books, 2008.

Smith, Christian. *American Evangelicalism: Embattled and Thriving*. Chicago, Ill.: University of Chicago Press, 1998.

———. *Soul Searching: The Religious and Spiritual Lives of American Teenagers*. Oxford: Oxford Press, 2005.

Smith, Christian, and Patricia Snell. *Souls in Transition: The Religious and Spiritual Lives of Emerging Adults*. Oxford: Oxford University Press, 2009.

Smith, R. Scott. *Truth and the New Kind of Christian : The Emerging Effects of Postmodernism in the Church*. Wheaton, Ill.: Crossway Books, 2005.

Stout, Jeffrey. *Democracy and Tradition*. Princeton, N.J.: Princeton University Press, 2004.

———. *Ethics after Babel: The Languages of Morals and Their Discontents*. Boston: Beacon Press, 1988.

Swan, Rachel. "Our Soapbox." In *The Sweet Bi and Bi: Musings on bisexuality and a "new" old time faith*. Minneapolis, 2010.

Swartz, David. *Culture & Power: The Sociology of Pierre Bourdieu.* Chicago: University of Chicago Press, 1997.

Swidler, Ann. "Culture in Action: Symbols and Strategies." *American Sociological Review* 51, (1986): 273-86.

Taylor, Verta. "Mobilizing for Change in a Social Movement Society." *Contemporary Sociology* 29, (2000): 219-30.

Teigas, Demetrius. *Knowledge and Hermeneutic Understanding: A Study of the Habermas-Gadamer Debate.* Cranbury, NJ: Associated University Presses, 1995.

"Themes of the Emerging Church." In *YoungLeader.org.* Dallas: Leadership Network, 1998.

Thomson, John B. *The Ecclesiology of Stanley Hauerwas: A Christian Theology of Liberation.* Burlington, VT: Ashgate, 2003.

Tickle, Phyllis. *The Great Emergence: How Christianity Is Changing and Why.* Grand Rapids, Mich.: Baker Books, 2008.

Tillich, Paul. *Systematic Theology / Paul Tillich.* 3 vols. Chicago: University of Chicago Press, 1951.

Torrance, Thomas F. *The Trinitarian Faith : The Evangelical Theology of the Ancient Catholic Church.* Paperback ed. Edinburgh: T.& T. Clark, 1997.

Tracy, David. *Blessed Rage for Order: The New Pluralism in Theology.* San Francisco: Harper & Row, 1988.

van Huyssteen, J. Wentzel. *Alone in the World? Human Uniqueness in Science and Theology.* Grand Rapids, Mich.: Wm. B. Eerdmanns Pub. Co., 2006.

———. *The Shaping of Rationality: Toward Interdisciplinarity in Theology and Science.* Grand Rapids, Mich.: W.B. Eerdmans, 1999.

"Vintage Vibe." http://www.vintagechurch.org/about/vibe.

Volf, Miroslav. *After Our Likeness: The Church as the Image of the Trinity,* Sacra Doctrina. Grand Rapids, Mich.: William B. Eerdmans, 1998.

———. "Conversation with Miroslav Volf." Paper presented at the Emergent Village Theological Conversation, Yale University

Divinity School, New Haven, Connecticut, February 6-8 2006.

———. *The End of Memory: Remembering Rightly in a Violent World.* Grand Rapids, Mich.: W.B. Eerdmans Pub. Co., 2006.

Volf, Miroslav, and Dorothy C. Bass. *Practicing Theology : Beliefs and Practices in Christian Life.* Grand Rapids, Mich.: W.B. Eerdmans, 2002.

———. *Practicing Theology: Beliefs and Practices in Christian Life.* Grand Rapids, Mich.: W.B. Eerdmans, 2002.

Walker-Cleaveland, Adam. "An Experiment in Collaborative Preaching." In *Pomomusings.com*, 2007.

———. "An Open-Source Sermon: Joseph: Unwavering Faith?" In *Pomomusings.com*, 2008.

Webber, Robert, John Burke, Dan Kimball, Doug Pagitt, Karen M. Ward, and Mark Driscoll. *Listening to the Beliefs of Emerging Churches.* Grand Rapids, Mich.: Zondervan, 2007.

———. *Listening to the Beliefs of Emerging Churches: Five Perspectives.* Grand Rapids, Mich.: Zondervan, 2007.

Wenger, Etienne. *Communities of Practice: Learning, Meaning, and Identity*, Learning in Doing. Cambridge, U.K.; New York, N.Y.: Cambridge University Press, 1998.

"What Can I Do with This New Site?". Cedar Ridge Community Church, http://crcc.org/node/1115.

Willimon, Stanley Hauerwas and William. *Resident Aliens: Life in the Christian Colony.* Nashville: Abingdon Press, 1989.

Wuthnow, Robert. *After Heaven: Spirituality in America since the 1950s.* Berkeley: University of California Press, 1998.

Young, Shawn David. "From Hippies to Jesus Freaks: Christian Radicalism in Chicago's Inner-City." *Journal of Religion and Popular Culture* 22, no. 1 (2010).

Zornberg, Avivah Gottlieb. *The Particulars of Rapture: Reflections on Exodus.* New York; London: Doubleday, 2001.

About the Author

Tony Jones, M.Div. (Fuller Theological Seminary), Ph.D. (Princeton Theological Seminary) is the theologian-in-residence at Solomon's Porch in Minneapolis. He has written many books on spirituality, ministry, and the emerging church movement, including *The New Christians: Dispatches from the Emergent Frontier*. Tony has worked at several churches, a mission agency, and served as the national coordinator of Emergent Village for several years. Currently, he is a writer and small business owner, running events and social media training for church leaders. Tony lives in Edina, Minnesota with his wife and three children.

You can find Tony on his website: **http://tonyj.net**

Author photo by Courtney Perry.

CPSIA information can be obtained at www.ICGtesting.com
Printed in the USA
LVOW12s2122040514

384419LV00011B/130/P

9 780615 524313